THIS IS YOUR **PASSBOOK**® FOR ...

REAL ESTATE OFFICER I, II

NATIONAL LEARNING CORPORATION®
passbooks.com

PASSBOOK® SERIES

THE *PASSBOOK® SERIES* has been created to prepare applicants and candidates for the ultimate academic battlefield – the examination room.

At some time in our lives, each and every one of us may be required to take an examination – for validation, matriculation, admission, qualification, registration, certification, or licensure.

Based on the assumption that every applicant or candidate has met the basic formal educational standards, has taken the required number of courses, and read the necessary texts, the *PASSBOOK® SERIES* furnishes the one special preparation which may assure passing with confidence, instead of failing with insecurity. Examination questions – together with answers – are furnished as the basic vehicle for study so that the mysteries of the examination and its compounding difficulties may be eliminated or diminished by a sure method.

This book is meant to help you pass your examination provided that you qualify and are serious in your objective.

The entire field is reviewed through the huge store of content information which is succinctly presented through a provocative and challenging approach – the question-and-answer method.

A climate of success is established by furnishing the correct answers at the end of each test.

You soon learn to recognize types of questions, forms of questions, and patterns of questioning. You may even begin to anticipate expected outcomes.

You perceive that many questions are repeated or adapted so that you can gain acute insights, which may enable you to score many sure points.

You learn how to confront new questions, or types of questions, and to attack them confidently and work out the correct answers.

You note objectives and emphases, and recognize pitfalls and dangers, so that you may make positive educational adjustments.

Moreover, you are kept fully informed in relation to new concepts, methods, practices, and directions in the field.

You discover that you arre actually taking the examination all the time: you are preparing for the examination by "taking" an examination, not by reading extraneous and/or supererogatory textbooks.

In short, this PASSBOOK®, used directedly, should be an important factor in helping you to pass your test.

REAL ESTATE OFFICER I, II

DUTIES

As a Real Estate Officer I, you would manage and direct real estate programs or large portions of real estate programs at State agencies responsible for the following specializations of appraisal, acquisition and/or disposition, control of right-of-way access and land use, or leases and/or easements of real property.

As a Real Estate Officer II, you would manage and direct real estate programs for which the real estate activities include the full range of specializations including appraisal, control of right-of-way access and land use, or leases and/or easements of real property.

SCOPE OF THE EXAMINATION

The written test will cover knowledge, skills and/or abilities in such areas as:

1. **Administration** - These questions test for knowledge of the managerial functions involved in directing an organization or an organizational segment. These questions cover such areas as: developing objectives and formulating policies; making decisions based on the context of the administrator's position and authority; forecasting and planning; organizing; developing personnel; coordinating and informing; guiding and leading; testing and evaluating; and budgeting.

2. **Administrative supervision** - These questions test for knowledge of the principles and practices involved in directing the activities of a large subordinate staff, including subordinate supervisors. Questions relate to the personal interactions between an upper level supervisor and his/her subordinate supervisors in the accomplishment of objectives. These questions cover such areas as assigning work to and coordinating the activities of several units, establishing and guiding staff development programs, evaluating the performance of subordinate supervisors, and maintaining relationships with other organizational sections.

3. **Preparing written material** - These questions test for the ability to present information clearly and accurately, and to organize paragraphs logically and comprehensibly. For some questions, you will be given information in two or three sentences followed by four restatements of the information. You must then choose the best version. For other questions, you will be given paragraphs with their sentences out of order. You must then choose, from four suggestions, the best order for the sentences.

4. **Principles and techniques of real property appraisal** - These questions test for a knowledge of principles and practices used in the appraisal of agricultural, commercial, and residential real property including knowledge of the three approaches to value; sales comparison, income, and cost estimation.

5. **Real property acquisition, appraisal, negotiations, relocation, property management and applicable state and federal law, rules and regulations** - These questions test for knowledge of terms, principles and processes relating to the State's ability to acquire real property. They cover such subjects as the role of negotiators in real property acquisition; right of landowners and tenants when the State acquires property; factors influencing property value determinations and rent determinations; types and characteristics of leasing agreements; eligibility for relocation payments and calculation of payment amounts. The information

needed to answer some of these questions can be found in the Eminent Domain
Procedure Law, Environmental Conservation Law and Public Lands Law.

6. **Understanding and interpreting tax maps and site plans** - These questions
test for the ability to read, analyze and perform computations based on various
types of maps and plans, and may include tax maps, deed descriptions, site plans,
survey maps and building layouts. All the information needed to answer the
questions will be provided in the maps, plans, layouts or related written material.
A calculator and magnifying glass may be helpful for answering some of these
questions. Candidates may bring their own calculator and magnifying glass if they
so choose.

HOW TO TAKE A TEST

I. YOU MUST PASS AN EXAMINATION

A. *WHAT EVERY CANDIDATE SHOULD KNOW*

Examination applicants often ask us for help in preparing for the written test. What can I study in advance? What kinds of questions will be asked? How will the test be given? How will the papers be graded?

As an applicant for a civil service examination, you may be wondering about some of these things. Our purpose here is to suggest effective methods of advance study and to describe civil service examinations.

Your chances for success on this examination can be increased if you know how to prepare. Those "pre-examination jitters" can be reduced if you know what to expect. You can even experience an adventure in good citizenship if you know why civil service exams are given.

B. *WHY ARE CIVIL SERVICE EXAMINATIONS GIVEN?*

Civil service examinations are important to you in two ways. As a citizen, you want public jobs filled by employees who know how to do their work. As a job seeker, you want a fair chance to compete for that job on an equal footing with other candidates. The best-known means of accomplishing this two-fold goal is the competitive examination.

Exams are widely publicized throughout the nation. They may be administered for jobs in federal, state, city, municipal, town or village governments or agencies.

Any citizen may apply, with some limitations, such as the age or residence of applicants. Your experience and education may be reviewed to see whether you meet the requirements for the particular examination. When these requirements exist, they are reasonable and applied consistently to all applicants. Thus, a competitive examination may cause you some uneasiness now, but it is your privilege and safeguard.

C. *HOW ARE CIVIL SERVICE EXAMS DEVELOPED?*

Examinations are carefully written by trained technicians who are specialists in the field known as "psychological measurement," in consultation with recognized authorities in the field of work that the test will cover. These experts recommend the subject matter areas or skills to be tested; only those knowledges or skills important to your success on the job are included. The most reliable books and source materials available are used as references. Together, the experts and technicians judge the difficulty level of the questions.

Test technicians know how to phrase questions so that the problem is clearly stated. Their ethics do not permit "trick" or "catch" questions. Questions may have been tried out on sample groups, or subjected to statistical analysis, to determine their usefulness.

Written tests are often used in combination with performance tests, ratings of training and experience, and oral interviews. All of these measures combine to form the best-known means of finding the right person for the right job.

II. HOW TO PASS THE WRITTEN TEST

A. NATURE OF THE EXAMINATION

To prepare intelligently for civil service examinations, you should know how they differ from school examinations you have taken. In school you were assigned certain definite pages to read or subjects to cover. The examination questions were quite detailed and usually emphasized memory. Civil service exams, on the other hand, try to discover your present ability to perform the duties of a position, plus your potentiality to learn these duties. In other words, a civil service exam attempts to predict how successful you will be. Questions cover such a broad area that they cannot be as minute and detailed as school exam questions.

In the public service similar kinds of work, or positions, are grouped together in one "class." This process is known as *position-classification*. All the positions in a class are paid according to the salary range for that class. One class title covers all of these positions, and they are all tested by the same examination.

B. FOUR BASIC STEPS

1) Study the announcement

How, then, can you know what subjects to study? Our best answer is: "Learn as much as possible about the class of positions for which you've applied." The exam will test the knowledge, skills and abilities needed to do the work.

Your most valuable source of information about the position you want is the official exam announcement. This announcement lists the training and experience qualifications. Check these standards and apply only if you come reasonably close to meeting them.

The brief description of the position in the examination announcement offers some clues to the subjects which will be tested. Think about the job itself. Review the duties in your mind. Can you perform them, or are there some in which you are rusty? Fill in the blank spots in your preparation.

Many jurisdictions preview the written test in the exam announcement by including a section called "Knowledge and Abilities Required," "Scope of the Examination," or some similar heading. Here you will find out specifically what fields will be tested.

2) Review your own background

Once you learn in general what the position is all about, and what you need to know to do the work, ask yourself which subjects you already know fairly well and which need improvement. You may wonder whether to concentrate on improving your strong areas or on building some background in your fields of weakness. When the announcement has specified "some knowledge" or "considerable knowledge," or has used adjectives like "beginning principles of…" or "advanced … methods," you can get a clue as to the number and difficulty of questions to be asked in any given field. More questions, and hence broader coverage, would be included for those subjects which are more important in the work. Now weigh your strengths and weaknesses against the job requirements and prepare accordingly.

3) Determine the level of the position

Another way to tell how intensively you should prepare is to understand the level of the job for which you are applying. Is it the entering level? In other words, is this the position in which beginners in a field of work are hired? Or is it an intermediate or advanced level? Sometimes this is indicated by such words as "Junior" or "Senior" in the class title. Other jurisdictions use Roman numerals to designate the level – Clerk I, Clerk II, for example. The word "Supervisor" sometimes appears in the title. If the level is not indicated by the title, check the description of duties. Will you be working under very close supervision, or will you have responsibility for independent decisions in this work?

4) Choose appropriate study materials

Now that you know the subjects to be examined and the relative amount of each subject to be covered, you can choose suitable study materials. For beginning level jobs, or even advanced ones, if you have a pronounced weakness in some aspect of your training, read a modern, standard textbook in that field. Be sure it is up to date and has general coverage. Such books are normally available at your library, and the librarian will be glad to help you locate one. For entry-level positions, questions of appropriate difficulty are chosen – neither highly advanced questions, nor those too simple. Such questions require careful thought but not advanced training.

If the position for which you are applying is technical or advanced, you will read more advanced, specialized material. If you are already familiar with the basic principles of your field, elementary textbooks would waste your time. Concentrate on advanced textbooks and technical periodicals. Think through the concepts and review difficult problems in your field.

These are all general sources. You can get more ideas on your own initiative, following these leads. For example, training manuals and publications of the government agency which employs workers in your field can be useful, particularly for technical and professional positions. A letter or visit to the government department involved may result in more specific study suggestions, and certainly will provide you with a more definite idea of the exact nature of the position you are seeking.

III. KINDS OF TESTS

Tests are used for purposes other than measuring knowledge and ability to perform specified duties. For some positions, it is equally important to test ability to make adjustments to new situations or to profit from training. In others, basic mental abilities not dependent on information are essential. Questions which test these things may not appear as pertinent to the duties of the position as those which test for knowledge and information. Yet they are often highly important parts of a fair examination. For very general questions, it is almost impossible to help you direct your study efforts. What we can do is to point out some of the more common of these general abilities needed in public service positions and describe some typical questions.

1) General information

Broad, general information has been found useful for predicting job success in some kinds of work. This is tested in a variety of ways, from vocabulary lists to questions about current events. Basic background in some field of work, such as sociology or economics, may be sampled in a group of questions. Often these are principles which have become familiar to most persons through exposure rather than through formal training. It is difficult to advise you how to study for these questions; being alert to the world around you is our best suggestion.

2) Verbal ability

An example of an ability needed in many positions is verbal or language ability. Verbal ability is, in brief, the ability to use and understand words. Vocabulary and grammar tests are typical measures of this ability. Reading comprehension or paragraph interpretation questions are common in many kinds of civil service tests. You are given a paragraph of written material and asked to find its central meaning.

3) Numerical ability

Number skills can be tested by the familiar arithmetic problem, by checking paired lists of numbers to see which are alike and which are different, or by interpreting charts and graphs. In the latter test, a graph may be printed in the test booklet which you are asked to use as the basis for answering questions.

4) Observation

A popular test for law-enforcement positions is the observation test. A picture is shown to you for several minutes, then taken away. Questions about the picture test your ability to observe both details and larger elements.

5) Following directions

In many positions in the public service, the employee must be able to carry out written instructions dependably and accurately. You may be given a chart with several columns, each column listing a variety of information. The questions require you to carry out directions involving the information given in the chart.

6) Skills and aptitudes

Performance tests effectively measure some manual skills and aptitudes. When the skill is one in which you are trained, such as typing or shorthand, you can practice. These tests are often very much like those given in business school or high school courses. For many of the other skills and aptitudes, however, no short-time preparation can be made. Skills and abilities natural to you or that you have developed throughout your lifetime are being tested.

Many of the general questions just described provide all the data needed to answer the questions and ask you to use your reasoning ability to find the answers. Your best preparation for these tests, as well as for tests of facts and ideas, is to be at your physical and mental best. You, no doubt, have your own methods of getting into an exam-taking mood and keeping "in shape." The next section lists some ideas on this subject.

IV. KINDS OF QUESTIONS

Only rarely is the "essay" question, which you answer in narrative form, used in civil service tests. Civil service tests are usually of the short-answer type. Full instructions for answering these questions will be given to you at the examination. But in case this is your first experience with short-answer questions and separate answer sheets, here is what you need to know:

1) Multiple-choice Questions

Most popular of the short-answer questions is the "multiple choice" or "best answer" question. It can be used, for example, to test for factual knowledge, ability to solve problems or judgment in meeting situations found at work.

A multiple-choice question is normally one of three types—

- It can begin with an incomplete statement followed by several possible endings. You are to find the one ending which *best* completes the statement, although some of the others may not be entirely wrong.
- It can also be a complete statement in the form of a question which is answered by choosing one of the statements listed.
- It can be in the form of a problem – again you select the best answer.

Here is an example of a multiple-choice question with a discussion which should give you some clues as to the method for choosing the right answer:

When an employee has a complaint about his assignment, the action which will *best* help him overcome his difficulty is to
   A. discuss his difficulty with his coworkers
   B. take the problem to the head of the organization
   C. take the problem to the person who gave him the assignment
   D. say nothing to anyone about his complaint

In answering this question, you should study each of the choices to find which is best. Consider choice "A" – Certainly an employee may discuss his complaint with fellow employees, but no change or improvement can result, and the complaint remains unresolved. Choice "B" is a poor choice since the head of the organization probably does not know what assignment you have been given, and taking your problem to him is known as "going over the head" of the supervisor. The supervisor, or person who made the assignment, is the person who can clarify it or correct any injustice. Choice "C" is, therefore, correct. To say nothing, as in choice "D," is unwise. Supervisors have and interest in knowing the problems employees are facing, and the employee is seeking a solution to his problem.

2) True/False Questions

The "true/false" or "right/wrong" form of question is sometimes used. Here a complete statement is given. Your job is to decide whether the statement is right or wrong.

SAMPLE: A roaming cell-phone call to a nearby city costs less than a non-roaming call to a distant city.

This statement is wrong, or false, since roaming calls are more expensive.

This is not a complete list of all possible question forms, although most of the others are variations of these common types. You will always get complete directions for answering questions. Be sure you understand *how* to mark your answers – ask questions until you do.

V. RECORDING YOUR ANSWERS

Computer terminals are used more and more today for many different kinds of exams.

For an examination with very few applicants, you may be told to record your answers in the test booklet itself. Separate answer sheets are much more common. If this separate answer sheet is to be scored by machine – and this is often the case – it is highly important that you mark your answers correctly in order to get credit.

An electronic scoring machine is often used in civil service offices because of the speed with which papers can be scored. Machine-scored answer sheets must be marked with a pencil, which will be given to you. This pencil has a high graphite content which responds to the electronic scoring machine. As a matter of fact, stray dots may register as answers, so do not let your pencil rest on the answer sheet while you are pondering the correct answer. Also, if your pencil lead breaks or is otherwise defective, ask for another.

Since the answer sheet will be dropped in a slot in the scoring machine, be careful not to bend the corners or get the paper crumpled.

The answer sheet normally has five vertical columns of numbers, with 30 numbers to a column. These numbers correspond to the question numbers in your test booklet. After each number, going across the page are four or five pairs of dotted lines. These short dotted lines have small letters or numbers above them. The first two pairs may also have a "T" or "F" above the letters. This indicates that the first two pairs only are to be used if the questions are of the true-false type. If the questions are multiple choice, disregard the "T" and "F" and pay attention only to the small letters or numbers.

Answer your questions in the manner of the sample that follows:

32. The largest city in the United States is
    A. Washington, D.C.
    B. New York City
    C. Chicago
    D. Detroit
    E. San Francisco

1) Choose the answer you think is best. (New York City is the largest, so "B" is correct.)
2) Find the row of dotted lines numbered the same as the question you are answering. (Find row number 32)
3) Find the pair of dotted lines corresponding to the answer. (Find the pair of lines under the mark "B.")
4) Make a solid black mark between the dotted lines.

VI. BEFORE THE TEST

Common sense will help you find procedures to follow to get ready for an examination. Too many of us, however, overlook these sensible measures. Indeed, nervousness and fatigue have been found to be the most serious reasons why applicants fail to do their best on civil service tests. Here is a list of reminders:

- Begin your preparation early – Don't wait until the last minute to go scurrying around for books and materials or to find out what the position is all about.
- Prepare continuously – An hour a night for a week is better than an all-night cram session. This has been definitely established. What is more, a night a week for a month will return better dividends than crowding your study into a shorter period of time.
- Locate the place of the exam – You have been sent a notice telling you when and where to report for the examination. If the location is in a different town or otherwise unfamiliar to you, it would be well to inquire the best route and learn something about the building.
- Relax the night before the test – Allow your mind to rest. Do not study at all that night. Plan some mild recreation or diversion; then go to bed early and get a good night's sleep.
- Get up early enough to make a leisurely trip to the place for the test – This way unforeseen events, traffic snarls, unfamiliar buildings, etc. will not upset you.
- Dress comfortably – A written test is not a fashion show. You will be known by number and not by name, so wear something comfortable.
- Leave excess paraphernalia at home – Shopping bags and odd bundles will get in your way. You need bring only the items mentioned in the official notice you received; usually everything you need is provided. Do not bring reference books to the exam. They will only confuse those last minutes and be taken away from you when in the test room.
- Arrive somewhat ahead of time – If because of transportation schedules you must get there very early, bring a newspaper or magazine to take your mind off yourself while waiting.
- Locate the examination room – When you have found the proper room, you will be directed to the seat or part of the room where you will sit. Sometimes you are given a sheet of instructions to read while you are waiting. Do not fill out any forms until you are told to do so; just read them and be prepared.
- Relax and prepare to listen to the instructions
- If you have any physical problem that may keep you from doing your best, be sure to tell the test administrator. If you are sick or in poor health, you really cannot do your best on the exam. You can come back and take the test some other time.

VII. AT THE TEST

The day of the test is here and you have the test booklet in your hand. The temptation to get going is very strong. Caution! There is more to success than knowing the right answers. You must know how to identify your papers and understand variations in the type of short-answer question used in this particular examination. Follow these suggestions for maximum results from your efforts:

1) Cooperate with the monitor

The test administrator has a duty to create a situation in which you can be as much at ease as possible. He will give instructions, tell you when to begin, check to see that you are marking your answer sheet correctly, and so on. He is not there to guard you, although he will see that your competitors do not take unfair advantage. He wants to help you do your best.

2) Listen to all instructions

Don't jump the gun! Wait until you understand all directions. In most civil service tests you get more time than you need to answer the questions. So don't be in a hurry. Read each word of instructions until you clearly understand the meaning. Study the examples, listen to all announcements and follow directions. Ask questions if you do not understand what to do.

3) Identify your papers

Civil service exams are usually identified by number only. You will be assigned a number; you must not put your name on your test papers. Be sure to copy your number correctly. Since more than one exam may be given, copy your exact examination title.

4) Plan your time

Unless you are told that a test is a "speed" or "rate of work" test, speed itself is usually not important. Time enough to answer all the questions will be provided, but this does not mean that you have all day. An overall time limit has been set. Divide the total time (in minutes) by the number of questions to determine the approximate time you have for each question.

5) Do not linger over difficult questions

If you come across a difficult question, mark it with a paper clip (useful to have along) and come back to it when you have been through the booklet. One caution if you do this – be sure to skip a number on your answer sheet as well. Check often to be sure that you have not lost your place and that you are marking in the row numbered the same as the question you are answering.

6) Read the questions

Be sure you know what the question asks! Many capable people are unsuccessful because they failed to *read* the questions correctly.

7) Answer all questions

Unless you have been instructed that a penalty will be deducted for incorrect answers, it is better to guess than to omit a question.

8) Speed tests

It is often better NOT to guess on speed tests. It has been found that on timed tests people are tempted to spend the last few seconds before time is called in marking answers at random – without even reading them – in the hope of picking up a few extra points. To discourage this practice, the instructions may warn you that your score will be "corrected" for guessing. That is, a penalty will be applied. The incorrect answers will be deducted from the correct ones, or some other penalty formula will be used.

9) Review your answers

If you finish before time is called, go back to the questions you guessed or omitted to give them further thought. Review other answers if you have time.

10) Return your test materials

If you are ready to leave before others have finished or time is called, take ALL your materials to the monitor and leave quietly. Never take any test material with you. The monitor can discover whose papers are not complete, and taking a test booklet may be grounds for disqualification.

VIII. EXAMINATION TECHNIQUES

1) Read the general instructions carefully. These are usually printed on the first page of the exam booklet. As a rule, these instructions refer to the timing of the examination; the fact that you should not start work until the signal and must stop work at a signal, etc. If there are any *special* instructions, such as a choice of questions to be answered, make sure that you note this instruction carefully.

2) When you are ready to start work on the examination, that is as soon as the signal has been given, read the instructions to each question booklet, underline any key words or phrases, such as *least, best, outline, describe* and the like. In this way you will tend to answer as requested rather than discover on reviewing your paper that you *listed without describing*, that you selected the *worst* choice rather than the *best* choice, etc.

3) If the examination is of the objective or multiple-choice type – that is, each question will also give a series of possible answers: A, B, C or D, and you are called upon to select the best answer and write the letter next to that answer on your answer paper – it is advisable to start answering each question in turn. There may be anywhere from 50 to 100 such questions in the three or four hours allotted and you can see how much time would be taken if you read through all the questions before beginning to answer any. Furthermore, if you come across a question or group of questions which you know would be difficult to answer, it would undoubtedly affect your handling of all the other questions.

4) If the examination is of the essay type and contains but a few questions, it is a moot point as to whether you should read all the questions before starting to answer any one. Of course, if you are given a choice – say five out of seven and the like – then it is essential to read all the questions so you can eliminate the two that are most difficult. If, however, you are asked to answer all the questions, there may be danger in trying to answer the easiest one first because you may find that you will spend too much time on it. The best technique is to answer the first question, then proceed to the second, etc.

5) Time your answers. Before the exam begins, write down the time it started, then add the time allowed for the examination and write down the time it must be completed, then divide the time available somewhat as follows:

- If 3-1/2 hours are allowed, that would be 210 minutes. If you have 80 objective-type questions, that would be an average of 2-1/2 minutes per question. Allow yourself no more than 2 minutes per question, or a total of 160 minutes, which will permit about 50 minutes to review.
- If for the time allotment of 210 minutes there are 7 essay questions to answer, that would average about 30 minutes a question. Give yourself only 25 minutes per question so that you have about 35 minutes to review.

6) The most important instruction is to *read each question* and make sure you know what is wanted. The second most important instruction is to *time yourself properly* so that you answer every question. The third most important instruction is to *answer every question.* Guess if you have to but include something for each question. Remember that you will receive no credit for a blank and will probably receive some credit if you write something in answer to an essay question. If you guess a letter – say "B" for a multiple-choice question – you may have guessed right. If you leave a blank as an answer to a multiple-choice question, the examiners may respect your feelings but it will not add a point to your score. Some exams may penalize you for wrong answers, so in such cases *only*, you may not want to guess unless you have some basis for your answer.

7) Suggestions
   a. Objective-type questions
      1. Examine the question booklet for proper sequence of pages and questions
      2. Read all instructions carefully
      3. Skip any question which seems too difficult; return to it after all other questions have been answered
      4. Apportion your time properly; do not spend too much time on any single question or group of questions
      5. Note and underline key words – *all, most, fewest, least, best, worst, same, opposite,* etc.
      6. Pay particular attention to negatives
      7. Note unusual option, e.g., unduly long, short, complex, different or similar in content to the body of the question
      8. Observe the use of "hedging" words – *probably, may, most likely,* etc.
      9. Make sure that your answer is put next to the same number as the question
      10. Do not second-guess unless you have good reason to believe the second answer is definitely more correct
      11. Cross out original answer if you decide another answer is more accurate; do not erase until you are ready to hand your paper in
      12. Answer all questions; guess unless instructed otherwise
      13. Leave time for review

   b. Essay questions
      1. Read each question carefully
      2. Determine exactly what is wanted. Underline key words or phrases.
      3. Decide on outline or paragraph answer

4. Include many different points and elements unless asked to develop any one or two points or elements
5. Show impartiality by giving pros and cons unless directed to select one side only
6. Make and write down any assumptions you find necessary to answer the questions
7. Watch your English, grammar, punctuation and choice of words
8. Time your answers; don't crowd material

8) Answering the essay question

Most essay questions can be answered by framing the specific response around several key words or ideas. Here are a few such key words or ideas:

M's: manpower, materials, methods, money, management
P's: purpose, program, policy, plan, procedure, practice, problems, pitfalls, personnel, public relations
 a. Six basic steps in handling problems:
  1. Preliminary plan and background development
  2. Collect information, data and facts
  3. Analyze and interpret information, data and facts
  4. Analyze and develop solutions as well as make recommendations
  5. Prepare report and sell recommendations
  6. Install recommendations and follow up effectiveness

 b. Pitfalls to avoid
  1. *Taking things for granted* – A statement of the situation does not necessarily imply that each of the elements is necessarily true; for example, a complaint may be invalid and biased so that all that can be taken for granted is that a complaint has been registered
  2. *Considering only one side of a situation* – Wherever possible, indicate several alternatives and then point out the reasons you selected the best one
  3. *Failing to indicate follow up* – Whenever your answer indicates action on your part, make certain that you will take proper follow-up action to see how successful your recommendations, procedures or actions turn out to be
  4. *Taking too long in answering any single question* – Remember to time your answers properly

IX. AFTER THE TEST

Scoring procedures differ in detail among civil service jurisdictions although the general principles are the same. Whether the papers are hand-scored or graded by machine we have described, they are nearly always graded by number. That is, the person who marks the paper knows only the number – never the name – of the applicant. Not until all the papers have been graded will they be matched with names. If other tests, such as training and experience or oral interview ratings have been given, scores will be combined. Different parts of the examination usually have different weights. For example, the written test might count 60 percent of the final grade, and a rating of training and experience 40 percent. In many jurisdictions, veterans will have a certain number of points added to their grades.

After the final grade has been determined, the names are placed in grade order and an eligible list is established. There are various methods for resolving ties between those who get the same final grade – probably the most common is to place first the name of the person whose application was received first. Job offers are made from the eligible list in the order the names appear on it. You will be notified of your grade and your rank as soon as all these computations have been made. This will be done as rapidly as possible.

People who are found to meet the requirements in the announcement are called "eligibles." Their names are put on a list of eligible candidates. An eligible's chances of getting a job depend on how high he stands on this list and how fast agencies are filling jobs from the list.

When a job is to be filled from a list of eligibles, the agency asks for the names of people on the list of eligibles for that job. When the civil service commission receives this request, it sends to the agency the names of the three people highest on this list. Or, if the job to be filled has specialized requirements, the office sends the agency the names of the top three persons who meet these requirements from the general list.

The appointing officer makes a choice from among the three people whose names were sent to him. If the selected person accepts the appointment, the names of the others are put back on the list to be considered for future openings.

That is the rule in hiring from all kinds of eligible lists, whether they are for typist, carpenter, chemist, or something else. For every vacancy, the appointing officer has his choice of any one of the top three eligibles on the list. This explains why the person whose name is on top of the list sometimes does not get an appointment when some of the persons lower on the list do. If the appointing officer chooses the second or third eligible, the No. 1 eligible does not get a job at once, but stays on the list until he is appointed or the list is terminated.

X. HOW TO PASS THE INTERVIEW TEST

The examination for which you applied requires an oral interview test. You have already taken the written test and you are now being called for the interview test – the final part of the formal examination.

You may think that it is not possible to prepare for an interview test and that there are no procedures to follow during an interview. Our purpose is to point out some things you can do in advance that will help you and some good rules to follow and pitfalls to avoid while you are being interviewed.

What is an interview supposed to test?
The written examination is designed to test the technical knowledge and competence of the candidate; the oral is designed to evaluate intangible qualities, not readily measured otherwise, and to establish a list showing the relative fitness of each candidate – as measured against his competitors – for the position sought. Scoring is not on the basis of "right" and "wrong," but on a sliding scale of values ranging from "not passable" to "outstanding." As a matter of fact, it is possible to achieve a relatively low score without a single "incorrect" answer because of evident weakness in the qualities being measured.

Occasionally, an examination may consist entirely of an oral test – either an individual or a group oral. In such cases, information is sought concerning the technical knowledges and abilities of the candidate, since there has been no written examination for this purpose. More commonly, however, an oral test is used to supplement a written examination.

Who conducts interviews?

The composition of oral boards varies among different jurisdictions. In nearly all, a representative of the personnel department serves as chairman. One of the members of the board may be a representative of the department in which the candidate would work. In some cases, "outside experts" are used, and, frequently, a businessman or some other representative of the general public is asked to serve. Labor and management or other special groups may be represented. The aim is to secure the services of experts in the appropriate field.

However the board is composed, it is a good idea (and not at all improper or unethical) to ascertain in advance of the interview who the members are and what groups they represent. When you are introduced to them, you will have some idea of their backgrounds and interests, and at least you will not stutter and stammer over their names.

What should be done before the interview?

While knowledge about the board members is useful and takes some of the surprise element out of the interview, there is other preparation which is more substantive. It *is* possible to prepare for an oral interview – in several ways:

1) Keep a copy of your application and review it carefully before the interview

This may be the only document before the oral board, and the starting point of the interview. Know what education and experience you have listed there, and the sequence and dates of all of it. Sometimes the board will ask you to review the highlights of your experience for them; you should not have to hem and haw doing it.

2) Study the class specification and the examination announcement

Usually, the oral board has one or both of these to guide them. The qualities, characteristics or knowledges required by the position sought are stated in these documents. They offer valuable clues as to the nature of the oral interview. For example, if the job involves supervisory responsibilities, the announcement will usually indicate that knowledge of modern supervisory methods and the qualifications of the candidate as a supervisor will be tested. If so, you can expect such questions, frequently in the form of a hypothetical situation which you are expected to solve. NEVER go into an oral without knowledge of the duties and responsibilities of the job you seek.

3) Think through each qualification required

Try to visualize the kind of questions you would ask if you were a board member. How well could you answer them? Try especially to appraise your own knowledge and background in each area, *measured against the job sought*, and identify any areas in which you are weak. Be critical and realistic – do not flatter yourself.

4) Do some general reading in areas in which you feel you may be weak

For example, if the job involves supervision and your past experience has NOT, some general reading in supervisory methods and practices, particularly in the field of human relations, might be useful. Do NOT study agency procedures or detailed manuals. The oral board will be testing your understanding and capacity, not your memory.

5) Get a good night's sleep and watch your general health and mental attitude

You will want a clear head at the interview. Take care of a cold or any other minor ailment, and of course, no hangovers.

What should be done on the day of the interview?

Now comes the day of the interview itself. Give yourself plenty of time to get there. Plan to arrive somewhat ahead of the scheduled time, particularly if your appointment is in the fore part of the day. If a previous candidate fails to appear, the board might be ready for you a bit early. By early afternoon an oral board is almost invariably behind schedule if there are many candidates, and you may have to wait. Take along a book or magazine to read, or your application to review, but leave any extraneous material in the waiting room when you go in for your interview. In any event, relax and compose yourself.

The matter of dress is important. The board is forming impressions about you – from your experience, your manners, your attitude, and your appearance. Give your personal appearance careful attention. Dress your best, but not your flashiest. Choose conservative, appropriate clothing, and be sure it is immaculate. This is a business interview, and your appearance should indicate that you regard it as such. Besides, being well groomed and properly dressed will help boost your confidence.

Sooner or later, someone will call your name and escort you into the interview room. *This is it.* From here on you are on your own. It is too late for any more preparation. But remember, you asked for this opportunity to prove your fitness, and you are here because your request was granted.

What happens when you go in?

The usual sequence of events will be as follows: The clerk (who is often the board stenographer) will introduce you to the chairman of the oral board, who will introduce you to the other members of the board. Acknowledge the introductions before you sit down. Do not be surprised if you find a microphone facing you or a stenotypist sitting by. Oral interviews are usually recorded in the event of an appeal or other review.

Usually the chairman of the board will open the interview by reviewing the highlights of your education and work experience from your application – primarily for the benefit of the other members of the board, as well as to get the material into the record. Do not interrupt or comment unless there is an error or significant misinterpretation; if that is the case, do not hesitate. But do not quibble about insignificant matters. Also, he will usually ask you some question about your education, experience or your present job – partly to get you to start talking and to establish the interviewing "rapport." He may start the actual questioning, or turn it over to one of the other members. Frequently, each member undertakes the questioning on a particular area, one in which he is perhaps most competent, so you can expect each member to participate in the examination. Because time is limited, you may also expect some rather abrupt switches in the direction the questioning takes, so do not be upset by it. Normally, a board member will not pursue a single line of questioning unless he discovers a particular strength or weakness.

After each member has participated, the chairman will usually ask whether any member has any further questions, then will ask you if you have anything you wish to add. Unless you are expecting this question, it may floor you. Worse, it may start you off on an extended, extemporaneous speech. The board is not usually seeking more information. The question is principally to offer you a last opportunity to present further qualifications or to indicate that you have nothing to add. So, if you feel that a significant qualification or characteristic has been overlooked, it is proper to point it out in a sentence or so. Do not compliment the board on the thoroughness of their examination – they have been sketchy, and you know it. If you wish, merely say, "No thank you, I have nothing further to add." This is a point where you can "talk yourself out" of a good impression or fail to present an important bit of information. Remember, *you close the interview yourself.*

The chairman will then say, "That is all, Mr. _____, thank you." Do not be startled; the interview is over, and quicker than you think. Thank him, gather your belongings and take your leave. Save your sigh of relief for the other side of the door.

How to put your best foot forward

Throughout this entire process, you may feel that the board individually and collectively is trying to pierce your defenses, seek out your hidden weaknesses and embarrass and confuse you. Actually, this is not true. They are obliged to make an appraisal of your qualifications for the job you are seeking, and they want to see you in your best light. Remember, they must interview all candidates and a non-cooperative candidate may become a failure in spite of their best efforts to bring out his qualifications. Here are 15 suggestions that will help you:

1) Be natural – Keep your attitude confident, not cocky

If you are not confident that you can do the job, do not expect the board to be. Do not apologize for your weaknesses, try to bring out your strong points. The board is interested in a positive, not negative, presentation. Cockiness will antagonize any board member and make him wonder if you are covering up a weakness by a false show of strength.

2) Get comfortable, but don't lounge or sprawl

Sit erectly but not stiffly. A careless posture may lead the board to conclude that you are careless in other things, or at least that you are not impressed by the importance of the occasion. Either conclusion is natural, even if incorrect. Do not fuss with your clothing, a pencil or an ashtray. Your hands may occasionally be useful to emphasize a point; do not let them become a point of distraction.

3) Do not wisecrack or make small talk

This is a serious situation, and your attitude should show that you consider it as such. Further, the time of the board is limited – they do not want to waste it, and neither should you.

4) Do not exaggerate your experience or abilities

In the first place, from information in the application or other interviews and sources, the board may know more about you than you think. Secondly, you probably will not get away with it. An experienced board is rather adept at spotting such a situation, so do not take the chance.

5) If you know a board member, do not make a point of it, yet do not hide it

Certainly you are not fooling him, and probably not the other members of the board. Do not try to take advantage of your acquaintanceship – it will probably do you little good.

6) Do not dominate the interview

Let the board do that. They will give you the clues – do not assume that you have to do all the talking. Realize that the board has a number of questions to ask you, and do not try to take up all the interview time by showing off your extensive knowledge of the answer to the first one.

7) Be attentive

You only have 20 minutes or so, and you should keep your attention at its sharpest throughout. When a member is addressing a problem or question to you, give him your undivided attention. Address your reply principally to him, but do not exclude the other board members.

8) Do not interrupt

A board member may be stating a problem for you to analyze. He will ask you a question when the time comes. Let him state the problem, and wait for the question.

9) Make sure you understand the question

Do not try to answer until you are sure what the question is. If it is not clear, restate it in your own words or ask the board member to clarify it for you. However, do not haggle about minor elements.

10) Reply promptly but not hastily

A common entry on oral board rating sheets is "candidate responded readily," or "candidate hesitated in replies." Respond as promptly and quickly as you can, but do not jump to a hasty, ill-considered answer.

11) Do not be peremptory in your answers

A brief answer is proper – but do not fire your answer back. That is a losing game from your point of view. The board member can probably ask questions much faster than you can answer them.

12) Do not try to create the answer you think the board member wants

He is interested in what kind of mind you have and how it works – not in playing games. Furthermore, he can usually spot this practice and will actually grade you down on it.

13) Do not switch sides in your reply merely to agree with a board member

Frequently, a member will take a contrary position merely to draw you out and to see if you are willing and able to defend your point of view. Do not start a debate, yet do not surrender a good position. If a position is worth taking, it is worth defending.

14) Do not be afraid to admit an error in judgment if you are shown to be wrong

The board knows that you are forced to reply without any opportunity for careful consideration. Your answer may be demonstrably wrong. If so, admit it and get on with the interview.

15) Do not dwell at length on your present job

The opening question may relate to your present assignment. Answer the question but do not go into an extended discussion. You are being examined for a *new* job, not your present one. As a matter of fact, try to phrase ALL your answers in terms of the job for which you are being examined.

Basis of Rating

Probably you will forget most of these "do's" and "don'ts" when you walk into the oral interview room. Even remembering them all will not ensure you a passing grade. Perhaps you did not have the qualifications in the first place. But remembering them will help you to put your best foot forward, without treading on the toes of the board members.

Rumor and popular opinion to the contrary notwithstanding, an oral board wants you to make the best appearance possible. They know you are under pressure – but they also want to see how you respond to it as a guide to what your reaction would be under the pressures of the job you seek. They will be influenced by the degree of poise you display, the personal traits you show and the manner in which you respond.

ABOUT THIS BOOK

This book contains tests divided into Examination Sections. Go through each test, answering every question in the margin. At the end of each test look at the answer key and check your answers. On the ones you got wrong, look at the right answer choice and learn. Do not fill in the answers first. Do not memorize the questions and answers, but understand the answer and principles involved. On your test, the questions will likely be different from the samples. Questions are changed and new ones added. If you understand these past questions you should have success with any changes that arise. Tests may consist of several types of questions. We have additional books on each subject should more study be advisable or necessary for you. Finally, the more you study, the better prepared you will be. This book is intended to be the last thing you study before you walk into the examination room. Prior study of relevant texts is also recommended. NLC publishes some of these in our Fundamental Series. Knowledge and good sense are important factors in passing your exam. Good luck also helps. So now study this Passbook, absorb the material contained within and take that knowledge into the examination. Then do your best to pass that exam.

––––––––

EXAMINATION SECTION

EXAMINATION SECTION
TEST 1

DIRECTIONS: Each question or incomplete statement is followed by several suggested answers or completions. Select the one that BEST answers the question or completes the statement. *PRINT THE LETTER OF THE CORRECT ANSWER IN THE SPACE AT THE RIGHT.*

1. When a supervisor in a large office introduces a change in the regular office procedure, it is USUAL to expect   1._____

    A. immediate acceptance by office staff, unless the change is unnecessary
    B. an immediate production increase, since new procedures are more stimulating than old ones
    C. a temporary production loss, even if the change is really an overall improvement
    D. resistance to the change only if it has been put into writing

2. A supervisor evaluates the performance of subordinates and then applies measures, where needed, which result in bringing performance up to desired standards. Which of the following functions of management might he BEST be described as performing?   2._____

    A. Organizing   B. Controlling   C. Directing   D. Planning

3. Assume that, as a supervisor, you have been assigned responsibility for a new and complex project which entails collection and analysis of data. You have prepared general written instructions which explain the project and procedures to be followed by several statisticians.
Which of the procedures below would be MOST advisable for you, as the supervisor, to follow?   3._____

    A. Distribute the instructions to your subordinates to come to you with any important questions
    B. Distribute the instructions and advise subordinates to come to you with any important questions
    C. Meet with subordinates as a group and explain the project using the written instructions as a handout
    D. Delegate responsibility for further explanation of the project to an immediate qualified subordinate to free you for concentration on research design

4. Supervisors have an obligation to make careful and thorough appraisals and reports of probationary employees. Of the following, the MOST important justification for this statement is that the probationary period   4._____

    A. should be used for positive development of the employee's understanding of the organization
    B. is the most effective period for changing a new employee's knowledges, skills, and attitudes
    C. insures that the employee will meet work standard requirements on future assignments
    D. should be considered as the final step in the selection process

5. Many studies of management indicate that a principal reason for failure of supervisors lies in their ability to delegate duties effectively.
Which one of the following practices by a supervisor would NOT be a block to successful delegation?

    A. Instructing the delegatee to follow a set procedure in carrying out the assignment
    B. Maintaining point by point control over the process delegated
    C. Transferring ultimate responsibility for the duties assigned to the delegatee
    D. Requiring the delegatee to keep the delegator informed of his progress

5.____

6. Crosswise communication occurs between personnel at lower or middle levels of different organizational units. It often speeds information and improves understanding, but has certain dangers.
Of the following proposed policies, which would NOT be important as a safeguard in crosswise communication?

    A. Supervisors should agree as to how crosswise communication should occur.
    B. Crosswise relationships must exist only between employees of equal status.
    C. Subordinates must keep their superiors informed about their interdepartmental communications.
    D. Subordinates must refrain from making commitments beyond their authority.

6.____

7. *Systems* theory has given us certain principles which are as applicable to organizational and social activities as they are to those of science. With regard to the training of employees in an organization, which of the following is likely to be most consistent with the modern *systems* approach?
Training can be effective ONLY when it is

    A. related to the individual abilities of the employees
    B. done on all levels of the organizational hierarchy
    C. evaluated on the basis of experimental and control groups
    D. provided on the job by the immediate supervisor

7.____

8. The management of a large agency, before making a decision as to whether or not to computerize its operations, should have a feasibility study made.
Of the following, the one which is LEAST important to include in such a study is

    A. the current abilities of management and staff to use a computer
    B. projected workloads and changes in objectives of functional units in the agency
    C. the contributions expected of each organizational unit towards achievement of agency objectives
    D. the decision-making activity and informational needs of each management function

8.____

9. Managing information covers the creation, collection, processing, storage and transmission of information that appears in a variety of forms. A supervisor responsible for a statistical unit can be considered, in many respects, an information manager.
Of the following, which would be considered the LEAST important aspect of the information manager's job?

    A. Establishing better information standards and formats
    B. Reducing the amount of unnecessary paper work performed
    C. Producing progressively greater numbers of informational reports
    D. Developing a greater appreciation for information among management members

9.____

10. Because of the need for improvement in information systems throughout industry and government, various techniques for improving these systems have been developed. Of these, *systems simulation* is a technique for improving systems which

    A. creates new ideas and concepts through the use of a computer
    B. deals with time controlling of interrelated systems which make up an overall project
    C. permits experimentation with various ideas to see what results might be obtained
    D. does not rely on assumptions which condition the value of the results

10.____

11. The one of the following which it is NOT advisable for a supervisor to do when dealing with individual employees is to

    A. recognize a person's outstanding service as well as his mistakes
    B. help an employee satisfy his need to excel
    C. encourage an efficient employee to seek better opportunities even if this action may cause the supervisor to lose a good worker
    D. take public notice of an employee's mistakes so that fewer errors will be made in the future

11.____

12. Suppose that you are in a department where you are given the responsibility for teaching seven new assistants a number of routine procedures that all assistants should know. Of the following, the BEST method for you to follow in teaching these procedures is to

    A. separate the slower learners from the faster learners and adapt your presentation to their level of ability
    B. instruct all the new employees in a group without attempting to assess differences in learning rates
    C. restrict your approach to giving them detailed written instructions in order to save time
    D. avoid giving the employees written instructions in order to force them to memorize job procedures quickly

12.____

13. Suppose that you are a supervisor to whom several assistants must hand in work for review. You notice that one of the assistants gets very upset whenever you discover an error in his work, although all the assistants make mistakes from time to time. Of the following, it would be BEST for you to

    A. arrange discreetly for the employee's work to be reviewed by another supervisor
    B. ignore his reaction since giving attention to such behavior increases its intensity
    C. suggest that the employee seek medical help since he has such great difficulty in accepting normal criticism
    D. try to build the employee's self-confidence by emphasizing those parts of his work that are done well

13.____

14. Suppose you are a supervisor responsible for supervising a number of assistants in an agency where each assistant receives a manual of policies and procedures when he first reports for work. You have been asked to teach your subordinates a new procedure which requires knowledge of several items of policy and procedure found in the manual. The one of the following techniques which it would be BEST for you to employ is to

    A. give verbal instructions which include a review of the appropriate standard procedures as well as an explanation of new tasks
    B. give individual instruction restricted to the new procedure to each assistant as the need arises
    C. provide written instructions for new procedural elements and refer employees to their manuals for explanation of standard procedures
    D. ask employees to review appropriate sections of their manual and then explain those aspects of the new procedure which the manual did not cover

14.____

15. Suppose that you are a supervisor in charge of a unit in which changes in work procedures are about to be instituted. The one of the following which you, as the supervisor, should anticipate as being MOST likely to occur during the changeover is

    A. a temporary rise in production because of interest in the new procedures
    B. uniform acceptance of these procedures on the part of your staff
    C. varying interpretations of the new procedures by your staff
    D. general agreement among staff members that the new procedures are advantageous

15.____

16. Suppose that a supervisor and one of the assistants under his supervision are known to be friends who play golf together on weekends.
The maintenance of such a friendship on the part of the supervisor is GENERALLY

    A. *acceptable* as long as this assistant continues to perform his duties satisfactorily
    B. *unacceptable* since the supervisor will find it difficult to treat the assistant as a subordinate
    C. *acceptable* if the supervisor does not favor this assistant above other employees
    D. *unacceptable* because the other assistants will resent the friendship regardless of the supervisor's behavior on the job

16.____

17. Suppose that you are a supervisor assigned to review the financial records of an agency which has recently undergone a major reorganization.
Which of the following would it be best for you to do FIRST?

    A. Interview the individual in charge of agency financial operations to determine whether the organizational changes affect the system of financial review
    B. Discuss the nature of the reorganization with your own supervisor to anticipate and plan a new financial review procedure.
    C. Carry out the financial review as usual, and adjust your methods to any problems arising from the reorganization.
    D. Request a written report from the agency head explaining the nature of the reorganization and recommending changes in the system of financial review.

17.____

18. Suppose that a newly assigned supervisor finds that he must delegate some of his duties   18.____
to subordinates in order to get the work done.
Which one of the following would NOT be a block to his delegating these duties effectively?

    A. Inability to give proper directions as to what he wants done
    B. Reluctance to take calculated risks
    C. Lack of trust in his subordinates
    D. Retaining ultimate responsibility for the delegated work

19. A supervisor sometimes performs the staff function of preparing and circulating reports   19.____
among bureau chiefs. Which of the following is LEAST important as an objective in
designing and writing such reports?

    A. Providing relevant information on past, present, and future actions
    B. Modifying his language in order to insure goodwill among the bureau chiefs
    C. Helping the readers of the report to make appropriate decisions
    D. Summarizing important information to help readers see trends or outstanding
       points.

20. Suppose you are a supervisor assigned to prepare a report to be read by all bureau   20.____
chiefs in your agency.
The MOST important reason for avoiding highly technical accounting terminology in
writing this report is to

    A. ensure the accuracy and relevancy of the text
    B. insure winning the readers' cooperation
    C. make the report more interesting to the readers
    D. make it easier for the readers to understand

21. Which of the following conditions is MOST likely to cause low morale in an office?   21.____

    A. Different standards of performance for individuals in the same title
    B. A requirement that employees perform at full capacity
    C. Standards of performance that vary with titles of employees
    D. Careful attention to the image of the division or department

22. A wise supervisor or representative of management realizes that, in the relationship   22.____
between supervisor and subordinates, all power is not on the side of management, and
that subordinates do sometimes react to restrictive authority in such a manner as to seriously retard management's objectives. A wise supervisor does not stimulate such
reactions.
In the subordinate's attempt to retaliate against an unusually authoritative management style, which of the following actions would generally be LEAST successful for the
subordinate? He

    A. joins with other employees in organizations to deal with management
    B. obviously delays in carrying out instructions which are given in an arrogant or inci-
       sive manner
    C. performs assignments exactly as instructed even when he recognizes errors in
       instructions
    D. holds back the flow of feedback information to superiors

23. Which of the following is the MOST likely and costly effect of vague and indefinite instruc-   23._____
tions given to subordinates by a supervisor?

   A.   Misunderstanding and ineffective work on the part of the subordinates
   B.   A necessity for the supervisor to report identical instructions with each assignment
   C.   A failure of the supervisor to adequately keep the attention of subordinates
   D.   Inability of subordinates to assist each other in the absence of the supervisor

24. At the professional level, there is a kind of informal authority which exercises itself even   24._____
though no delegation of authority has taken place from higher management. It occurs
within the context of knowledge required and professional competence in a special area.
An example of the kind of authority described in this statement is MOST clearly exem-
plified in the situation where a senior supervisor influences associates and subordinates by virtue of the

   A.   salary level fixed for his particular set of duties
   B.   amount of college training he possesses
   C.   technical position he has gained and holds on the work team
   D.   initiative and judgment he has demonstrated to his supervisor

25. An assistant under your supervision attempts to conceal the fact that he has made an   25._____
error.
Under this circumstance, it would be BEST for you, as the supervisor, to proceed on
the assumption that

   A.   this evasion indicates something wrong in the fundamental relationship between
        you and the assistant
   B.   this evasion is not deliberate, if the error is subsequently corrected by the assistant
   C.   this evasion should be overlooked if the error is not significant
   D.   detection and correction of errors will come about as an automatic consequence of
        internal control procedures

_____

KEY (CORRECT ANSWERS)

1.	C	11.	D
2.	B	12.	B
3.	C	13.	D
4.	D	14.	A
5.	D	15.	C
6.	B	16.	C
7.	B	17.	A
8.	A	18.	D
9.	C	19.	B
10.	C	20.	D

21.	A
22.	B
23.	A
24.	C
25.	A

TEST 2

DIRECTIONS: Each question or incomplete statement is followed by several suggested answers or completions. Select the one that BEST answers the question or completes the statement. *PRINT THE LETTER OF THE CORRECT ANSWER IN THE SPACE AT THE RIGHT.*

1. The unit which you supervise has a number of attorneys, accountants, examiners, statisticians, and clerks who prepare some of the routine papers required to be filed.
   In order to be certain that nothing goes out of your office that is improper, you have instituted a system that requires that you review and initial all moving papers, memoranda of law and briefs that are prepared. As a result, you put in a great deal of overtime and even must take work home with you frequently.
   A situation such as this is

   A. inevitable if you are to keep proper controls over the quality of the office work product
   B. indicative of the fact that the agency must provide an additional position within your office for an assistant supervisor who would do all the reviewing, leaving you free for other pressing administrative work and to handle the most difficult work in your unit
   C. the logical result of an ever-increasing case load
   D. symptomatic of poor supervision and management

   1.____

2. Your unit has been assigned a new employee who has never worked for the city.
   To orient him to his job in your unit, of the following, the BEST procedure is first to

   A. assign him to another employee to whatever work that employee gives him so that he can become familiar with your work and at the same time be productive
   B. give him copies of the charter and code provisions affecting your operations plus any in-office memoranda or instructions that are available and have him read them
   C. assign him to work on a relatively simple problem and then, after he has finished it, tell him politely what he did wrong
   D. explain to him the duties of his position and the functions of the office

   2.____

3. A bureau chief who supervises other supervisors makes it a practice to assign them more cases than they can possibly handle.
   This approach is

   A. *right,* because it results in getting more work done than would otherwise be the case
   B. *right,* because it relieves the bureau chief making the assignments of the responsibility of getting the work done
   C. *wrong,* because it builds resistance on the part of those called upon to handle the case load
   D. *wrong,* because superiors lose track of cases

   3.____

4. Assume you are a supervisor and are expected to exercise *authority* over subordinates.
   Which of the following BEST defines *authority?* The

   A. ability to control the nature of the contribution a subordinate is desirous of making
   B. innate inability to get others to do for you what you want to get done irrespective of their own wishes
   C. legal right conferred by the agency to control the actions of others
   D. power to determine a subordinate's attitude toward his agency and his superiors

   4.____

5. Paternalistic leadership stresses a paternal or fatherly influence in the relationships between the leader and the group and is manifest in a watchful care for the comfort and welfare of the followers.
   Which one of the following statements regarding paternalistic leadership is MOST accurate?

   A. Employees who work well under paternalistic leadership come to expect such leadership even when the paternal leader has left the organization.
   B. Most disputes arising out of supervisor-subordinate relationships develop because group leaders do not understand the principles of paternalistic leadership.
   C. Paternalistic leadership frequently destroys office relationships because most employees are turned into non-thinking dependent robots.
   D. Paternalistic leadership is rarely, if ever, successful because employees resent paternalistic leadership which they equate with weakness.

   5.____

6. Employees who have extensive dealings with members of the public should have, as much as possible, *real acceptance* of all people and a willingness to serve everyone impartially and objectively.
   Assuming that this statement is correct, the one of the following which would be the BEST demonstration of *real acceptance* is

   A. condoning antisocial behavior
   B. giving the appearance of agreeing with everyone encountered
   C. refusing to give opinions on anyone's behavior
   D. understanding the feelings expressed through a person's behavior

   6.____

7. Assume that the agency chief has requested you to help plan a public relations program because of recent complaints from citizens about the unbecoming conduct and language of various groups of city employees who have dealings with the public.
   In carrying out this assignment, the one of the following steps which should be undertaken FIRST is to

   A. study the characteristics of the public clientele dealt with by employees in your agency
   B. arrange to have employees attend several seminars on human relations
   C. develop several procedures for dealing with the public and allow the staff to choose the one which is best
   D. find out whether the employees in your agency may oppose any plan proposed by you

   7.____

8. The one of the following statements which BEST expresses the relationship between the morale of government employees and the public relations aspects of their work is:

   A. There is little relationship between employee morale and public relations, chiefly because public opinion is shaped primarily by response to departmental policy formulation.
   B. Employee morale is closely related to public relations, chiefly because the employee's morale will largely determine the manner in which he deals with the public.
   C. There is little relationship between employee morale and public relations, chiefly because public relations is primarily a function of the agency's public relations department.
   D. Employee morale is closely related to public relations, chiefly because employee morale indicates the attitude of the agency's top officials toward the public.

   8.____

9. As a supervisor, you are required to deal extensively with the public. The agency chief   9.____
has indicated that he is considering holding a special in-service training course for
employees in communications skills.
Holding this training course would be

    A. *advisable,* chiefly because government employees should receive formal training
       in public relations skills
    B. *inadvisable,* chiefly because the public regards such training as a *waste of the tax-
       payers' money*
    C. *advisable,* chiefly because such training will enable the employee to aid in drafting
       departmental press releases
    D. *inadvisable,* chiefly because of the great difficulty involved in developing such skills
       through formal instruction

10. Assume that you have extensive contact with the public. In dealing with the public, sensi-   10.____
tivity to an individual's attitudes is important because these attitudes can be used to predict behavior.
However, the MAIN reason that attitudes CANNOT successfully predict all behavior is
that

    A. attitudes are highly resistant to change
    B. an individual acquires attitudes as a function of growing up in a particular cultural
       environment
    C. attitudes are only one of many factors which determine a person's behavior
    D. an individual's behavior is not always observable

11. Rotation of employees from assignment to assignment is sometimes advocated by man-   11.____
agement experts.
Of the following, the MOST probable advantage to the organization of this practice is
that it leads to

    A. higher specialization of duties so that excessive identification with the overall orga-
       nization is reduced
    B. increased loyalty of employees to their immediate supervisors
    C. greater training and development of employees
    D. intensified desire of employees to obtain additional, outside formal education

12. Usually, a supervisor should attempt to standardize the work for which he is responsible.   12.____
The one of the following which is a BASIC reason for doing this is to

    A. eliminate the need to establish priorities
    B. permit the granting of exceptions to rules and special circumstances
    C. facilitate the taking of action based on applicable standards
    D. learn the identity of outstanding employees

13. The differences between line and staff authority are often quite ambiguous.   13.____
Of the following, the ESSENTIAL difference is that

    A. *line authority* is exercised by first-level supervisors; staff authority is exercised by
       higher-level supervisors and managerial staff
    B. *staff authority* is the right to issue directives; line authority is entirely consultative
    C. *line authority* is the power to make decisions regarding intra-agency matters; staff
       authority involves decisions regarding inter-agency matters
    D. *staff authority* is largely advisory; line authority is the right to command

14. Modern management theory stresses work-centered motivation as one way of increasing the productivity of employees.
    The one of the following which is PARTICULARLY characteristic of such motivation is that it

    A. emphasizes the crucial role of routinization of procedures
    B. stresses the satisfaction to be found in performing work
    C. features the value of wages and fringe benefits
    D. uses a firm but fair method of discipline

14.____

15. The agency's informal communications network is called the *grapevine*.
    If employees are learning about important organizational developments primarily through the grapevine, this is MOST likely an indication that

    A. official channels of communication are not functioning so efficiently as they should
    B. supervisory personnel are making effective use of the grapevine to communicate with subordinates
    C. employees already have a clear understanding of the agency's policies and procedures
    D. upward formal channels of communication within the agency are informing management of employee grievances

15.____

16. Of the following, a flow chart is BEST described as a chart which shows

    A. the places through which work moves in the course of the job process
    B. which employees perform specific functions leading to the completion of a job
    C. the schedules for production and how they eliminate waiting time between jobs
    D. how work units are affected by the actions of related work units

16.____

17. Evaluation of the results of training is necessary in order to assess its value.
    Of the following, the BEST technique for the supervisor to use in determining whether the training under consideration actually resulted in the desired modification of the behavior of the employee concerned is through

    A. inference   B. job analysis
    C. observation   D. simulation

17.____

18. The usual distinction between line and staff authority is that staff authority is mainly advisory, whereas line authority is the right to command. However, a third category has been suggested–prescriptive–to distinguish those personnel whose functions may be formally defined as staff but in practice exercise considerable authority regarding decisions relating to their specialties.
    The one of the following which indicates the MAJOR purpose of creating this third category is to

    A. develop the ability of each employee to perform a greater number of tasks
    B. reduce line-staff conflict
    C. prevent over-specialization of functions
    D. encourage decision-making by line personnel

18.____

11

19. It is sometimes considered desirable to train employees to a standard of proficiency   19._____
    higher than that deemed necessary for actual job performance.
    The MOST likely reason for such overtraining would be to

    A. eliminate the need for standards
    B. increase the value of refresher training
    C. compensate for previous lack of training
    D. reduce forgetting or loss of skill

20. Assume that you have been directed to immediately institute various new procedures in   20._____
    the handling of records.
    Of the following, the BEST method for you to use to insure that your subordinates
    know exactly what to do is to

    A. circulate a memorandum explaining the new procedures and have your subordi-
       nates initial it
    B. explain the new procedures to one or two subordinates and ask them to tell the
       others
    C. have a meeting with your subordinates to give them copies of the procedures and
       discuss it with them
    D. post the new procedures where they can be referred to by all those concerned

21. A supervisor decided to hold a problem-solving conference with his entire staff and dis-   21._____
    tributed an announcement and agenda one week before the meeting.
    Of the following, the BEST reason for providing each participant with an agenda is that

    A. participants will feel that something will be accomplished
    B. participants may prepare for the conference
    C. controversy will be reduced
    D. the top man should state the expected conclusions

22. In attempting to motivate employees, rewards are considered preferable to punishment   22._____
    PRIMARILY because

    A. punishment seldom has any effect on human behavior
    B. punishment usually results in decreased production
    C. supervisors find it difficult to punish
    D. rewards are more likely to result in willing cooperation

23. In an attempt to combat the low morale in his organization, a high-level supervisor publi-   23._____
    cized an *open–door* policy to allow employees who wished to do so to come to him with
    their complaints.
    Which of the following is LEAST likely to account for the fact that no employee came in
    with a complaint?

    A. Employees are generally reluctant to go over the heads of their immediate supervi-
       sors.
    B. The employees did not feel that management would help them.
    C. The low morale was not due to complaints associated with the job.
    D. The employees felt that, they had more to lose than to gain.

24. It is MOST desirable to use written instructions rather than oral instructions for a particu-   24._____
    lar job when

    A. a mistake on the job will not be serious
    B. the job can be completed in a short time
    C. there is no need to explain the job minutely
    D. the job involves many details

25. You have been asked to prepare for public distribution a statement dealing with a contro-   25._____
    versial matter.
    Of the following approaches, the one which would usually be MOST effective is to
    present your department's point of view

    A. as tersely as possible with no reference to any other matters
    B. developed from ideas and facts well known to most readers
    C. and show all the statistical data and techniques which were used in arriving at it
    D. in such a way that the controversial parts are omitted

_____

KEY (CORRECT ANSWERS)

1.	D	11.	C
2.	D	12.	C
3.	C	13.	D
4.	C	14.	B
5.	A	15.	A
6.	D	16.	A
7.	A	17.	C
8.	B	18.	B
9.	A	19.	D
10.	C	20.	C

21.	B
22.	D
23.	C
24.	D
25.	B

_____

13

TEST 3

1. An administrator who supervises other supervisors makes it a practice to set deadline dates for completion of assignments.
A NATURAL consequence of setting deadline dates is that

    A. supervisors will usually wait until the deadline date before they give projects their wholehearted attention
    B. projects are completed sooner than if no deadline dates are set
    C. such dates are ignored even though they are conspicuously posted
    D. the frequency of errors sharply increases resulting in an inability to meet deadlines

1.____

2. Assume that you are chairing a meeting of the members of your staff. You throw out a question to the group. No one answers your question immediately, so that you find yourself faced with silence.
In the circumstances, it would probably be BEST for you to

    A. ask the member of the group who appears to be least attentive to repeat the question
    B. change the topic quickly
    C. repeat the question carefully, pronouncing each word, and if there is still no response, repeat the question an additional time
    D. wait for an answer since someone will usually say something to break the tension

2.____

3. Assume that you are holding a meeting with the members of your staff. John, a member of the unit, keeps sidetracking the subject of the discussion by bringing up extraneous matters. You deal with the situation by saying to him after he has raised an immaterial point, *"That's an interesting point John, but can you show me how it ties in with what we're talking about?"*
Your approach in this situation would GENERALLY be considered

    A. *bad;* you have prevented the group from discussing not only extraneous matters but pertinent material as well
    B. *bad;* you have seriously humiliated John in front of the entire group
    C. *good;* you have pointed out how the discussion is straying from the main topic
    D. *good;* you have prevented John from presenting extraneous matters at future meetings

3.____

4. Assume that a senior supervisor is asked to supervise a group of staff personnel. The work of one of these staff men meets minimum standards of acceptability. However, this staff man constantly looks for something at which to take offense. In any conversation with either a fellow staff man or with a superior, he views the slightest criticism as a grave insult.
In this case, the senior supervisor should

    A. advise the staff man that the next time he refuses to accept criticism, he will be severely reprimanded
    B. ask members of the group for advice on how to deal with this staff man
    C. make it a practice to speak calmly, slowly, and deliberately to this staff man and question him frequently to make sure that there is no breakdown in communications
    D. recognize that professional help may be required and that this problem may not be conducive to a solution by a supervisor

4.____

5. Assume that you discover that one of the staff in preparing certain papers has made a serious mistake which has become obvious.
In dealing with this situation, it would be BEST for you to begin by

    A. asking the employee how the mistake happened
    B. asking the employee to read through the papers to see whether he can correct the mistake
    C. pointing out to the employee that, while an occasional error is permissible, frequent errors can prove a source of embarrassment to all concerned
    D. pointing to the mistake and asking the employee whether he realizes the consequences of the mistake

5.____

6. You desire to develop teamwork among the members of your staff. You are assigned a case which will require that two of the staff work together if the papers are to be prepared in time. You decided to assign two employees, whom you know to be close friends, to work on these papers. Your action in this regard would GENERALLY be considered

    A. *bad;* friends working together tend to do as little as they can get away with
    B. *bad;* people who are friends socially often find that the bonds of friendship disintegrate in work situations
    C. *good;* friends who are permitted to work together show their appreciation by utilizing every opportunity to reinforce the group leader's position of authority
    D. *good;* the evidence suggests that more work can be done in this way

6.____

7. You notice that all of the employees, without exception, take lunch hours which in your view are excessively long. You call each of them to your desk and point out that unless this practice is brought to a stop, appropriate action will be taken.
The way in which you handled this problem would GENERALLY be considered

    A. *proper,* primarily because a civil servant, no matter what his professional status, owes the public a full day's work for a full day's pay
    B. *proper,* primarily because employees need to have a clear picture of the rewards and penalties that go with public employment
    C. *improper,* primarily because group problems require group discussion which need not be formal in character
    D. *improper,* primarily because professional personnel resent having such matters as lunch hours brought to their attention.

7.____

8. In communicating with superiors or subordinates, it is well to bear in mind a phenomenon known as the *halo effect.* An example of this *halo effect* occurs when we

    A. employ informal language in a formal setting as a means of attracting attention
    B. ignore the advice of someone we distrust without evaluating the advice
    C. ask people to speak up who have a tendency to speak softly or occasionally indistinctly
    D. react to a piece of good work by inquiring into the motivations of those who did the work

8.____

9. Which of the following dangers is MOST likely to arise when a work group becomes too tightly knit? The

    A. group may appoint an informal leader who gradually sets policies and standards for the group to the detriment of the agency
    B. group may be reluctant to accept new employees as members
    C. quantity and quality of work produced may tend to diminish sharply despite the group's best efforts
    D. group may focus too strongly on employee benefits at inappropriate times

9.____

10. The overall managerial problem has become more complex because each group of management specialists will tend to view the interests of the enterprise in terms which are compatible with the survival or the increase of its special function. That is, each group will have a trained capacity for its own function and a *trained incapacity* to see its relation to the whole.
The *trained incapacity* to which the foregoing passage refers PROBABLY results from

    A. an imbalance in the number of specialists as compared with the number of generalists
    B. development by each specialized group of a certain dominant value or goal that shapes its entire way of doing things
    C. low morale accompanied by lackadaisical behavior by large segments of the managerial staff
    D. supervisory failure to inculcate pride in workmanship

10.____

11. Of the following, the MOST important responsibility of a supervisor in charge of a section is to

    A. establish close personal relationships with each of his subordinates in the section
    B. insure that each subordinate in the section knows the full range of his duties and responsibilities
    C. maintain friendly relations with his immediate supervisor
    D. protect his subordinates from criticism from any source

11.____

12. The BEST way to get a good work output from employees is to

    A. hold over them the threat of disciplinary action or removal
    B. maintain a steady, unrelenting pressure on them
    C. show them that you can do anything they can do faster and better
    D. win their respect and liking so they want to work for you

12.____

13. Supervisors should GENERALLY

    A. lean more toward management than toward their subordinates
    B. lean neither toward subordinates nor management
    C. lean more toward their subordinates than toward their management
    D. maintain a proper balance between management and subordinates

13.____

14. For a supervisor in charge of a section to ask occasionally the opinion of a subordinate concerning a problem is   14.____

    A. *desirable;* but it would be even better if the subordinate were consulted routinely on every problem
    B. *desirable;* subordinates may make good suggestions and will be pleased by being consulted
    C. *undesirable;* subordinats may be resentful if their advice is not followed
    D. *undesirable;* the supervisor should not attempt to shift his responsibilities to subordinates

15. The PRIMARY responsibility of a supervisor is to   15.____

    A. gain the confidence and make friends of all his subordinates
    B. get the work done properly
    C. satisfy his superior and gain his respect
    D. train the men in new methods for doing the work

16. In starting a work simplification study, the one of the following steps that should be taken FIRST is to   16.____

    A. break the work down into its elements
    B. draw up a chart of operations
    C. enlist the interest and cooperation of the personnel
    D. suggest alternative procedures

17. Of the following, the MOST important value of a manual of procedures is that it usually   17.____

    A. eliminates the need for on-the-job training
    B. decreases the span of control which can be exercised by individual supervisory personnel
    C. outlines methods of operation for ready reference
    D. provides concrete examples of work previously performed by employees

18. Reprimanding a subordinate when he has done something wrong should be done PRIMARILY in order to   18.____

    A. deter others from similar acts
    B. improve the subordinate in future performance
    C. maintain discipline
    D. uphold departmental rules

19. Most of the training of new employees in a public agency is USUALLY accomplished by   19.____

    A. formal classes   B. general orientation
    C. internship   D. on-the-job activities

20. You find that delivery of a certain item cannot possibly be made to a using agency by the date the using agency requested.
Of the following, the MOST advisable course of action for you to take FIRST is to

    A. cancel the order and inform the using agency
    B. discuss the problem with the using agency
    C. notify the using agency to obtain the item through direct purchase
    D. schedule the delivery for the earliest possible date

20.____

21. Assume that one of your subordinates has gotten into the habit of regularly and routinely referring every small problem which arises in his work to you.
In order to help him overcome this habit, it is generally MOST advisable for you to

    A. advise him that you do not have time to discuss each problem with him and that he should do whatever he wants
    B. ask your subordinate for his solution and approve any satisfactory approach that he suggests
    C. refuse to discuss such routine problems with him
    D. tell him that he should consider looking for another position if he does not feel competent to solve such routine problems

21.____

22. The BEST of the following reasons for developing understudies to supervisory staff is that this practice

    A. assures that capable staff will not leave their jobs since they are certain to be promoted
    B. helps to assure continued efficiency when persons in important positions leave their jobs
    C. improves morale by demonstrating to employees the opportunities for advancement
    D. provides an opportunity for giving on-the-job training

22.____

23. When a supervisor delegates some of his work to a subordinate, the

    A. supervisor retains final responsibility for the work
    B. supervisor should not check on the work until it has been completed
    C. subordinate assumes full responsibility for the successful completion of the work
    D. subordinate is likely to lose interest and get less satisfaction from the work

23.____

24. Sometimes it is necessary to give out written orders or to post written or typed information on a bulletin board rather than to merely give spoken orders. The supervisor must decide how he will do it.
In which of the following situations would it be BETTER for him to give written rather than spoken orders?

    A. He is going to reassign a man from one unit to another under his supervision.
    B. His staff must be informed of a permanent change in a complicated operating procedure.
    C. A man must be transferred from a clerical unit to an operating unit.
    D. He must order a group of staff men to do a difficult and tedious inventory job to which most of them are likely to object.

24.____

25. Of the following symbolic patterns, which one is NOT representative of a normal direction   25.____
in which formal organizational communications flow.

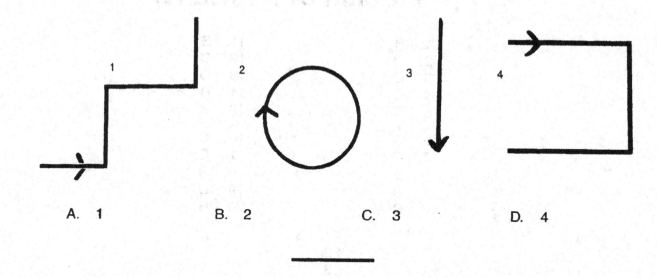

A. 1   B. 2   C. 3   D. 4

____

KEY (CORRECT ANSWERS)

1.	B		11.	B
2.	D		12.	D
3.	C		13.	D
4.	D		14.	B
5.	A		15.	B
6.	D		16.	C
7.	C		17.	C
8.	B		18.	B
9.	B		19.	D
10.	B		20.	B

21. B
22. B
23. A
24. B
25. B

EXAMINATION SECTION
TEST 1

DIRECTIONS: Each question or incomplete statement is followed by several suggested answers or completions. Select the one that BEST answers the question or completes the statement. *PRINT THE LETTER OF THE CORRECT ANSWER IN THE SPACE AT THE RIGHT.*

1. *Which one* of the following generalizations is *most likely* to be INACCURATE and lead to judgmental errors in communication?   1._____

    A. A supervisor must be able to read with understanding
    B. Misunderstanding may lead to dislike
    C. Anyone can listen to another person and understand what he means
    D. It is usually desirable to let a speaker talk until he is finished

2. Assume that, as a supervisor, you have been directed to inform your subordinates about the implementation of a new procedure which will affect their work. While communicating this information, you should do all of the following EXCEPT   2._____

    A. obtain the approval of your subordinates regarding the new procedure
    B. explain the reason for implementing the new procedure
    C. hold a staff meeting at a time convenient to most of your subordinates
    D. encourage a productive discussion of the new procedure

3. Assume that you are in charge of a section that handles requests for information on matters received from the public. One day, you observe that a clerk under your supervision is using a method to log-in requests for information that is different from the one specified by you in the past. Upon questioning the clerk, you discover that instructions changing the old procedure were delivered orally by your supervisor on a day on which you were absent from the office.
Of the following, the *most appropriate* action for you to take is to   3._____

    A. tell the clerk to revert to the old procedure at once
    B. ask your supervisor for information about the change
    C. call your staff together and tell them that no existing procedure is to be changed unless you direct that it be done
    D. write a memo to your supervisor suggesting that all future changes in procedure are to be in writing and that they be directed to you

4. At the first meeting with your staff after appointment as a supervisor, you find considerable indifference and some hostility among the participants.
Of the following, the *most appropriate* way to handle this situation is to   4._____

    A. disregard the attitudes displayed and continue to make your presentation until you have completed it
    B. discontinue your presentation but continue the meeting and attempt to find out the reasons for their attitudes
    C. warm up your audience with some good natured statements and anecdotes and then proceed with your presentation
    D. discontinue the meeting and set up personal interviews with the staff members to try to find out the reason for their attitude

5. In order to start the training of a new employee, it has been a standard practice to have him read a manual of instructions or procedures.
   This method is currently being replaced by the _____ method.   5.____

   A. audio-visual
   C. lecture
   B. conference
   D. programmed instruction

6. Of the following subjects, the *one* that can usually be *successfully* taught by a first-line supervisor who is training his subordinates is: 6.____

   A. Theory and philosophy of manage-ment
   C. Responsibilities of a supervisor
   B. Human relations
   D. Job skills

7. Assume that as a supervisor you are training a clerk who is experiencing difficulty learning a new task.   7.____
   Which one of the following would be the LEAST effective approach to take when trying to solve this problem? To

   A. ask questions which will reveal the clerk's understanding of the task
   B. take a different approach in explaining the task
   C. give the clerk an opportunity to ask questions about the task
   D. make sure the clerk knows you are watching his work closely

8. One school of management and supervision involves participation by employees in the setting of group goals and in the sharing of responsibility for the operation of the unit.   8.____
   If this philosophy were applied to a unit consisting of professional and clerical personnel, one should expect

   A. the professional and clerical personnel to participate with equal effectiveness in operating areas and policy areas
   B. the professional personnel to participate with greater effectiveness than the clerical personnel in policy areas
   C. the clerical personnel to participate with greater effectiveness than the professional personnel in operating areas
   D. greater participation by clerical personnel but with less responsibility for their actions

9. With regard to productivity, high morale among employees *generally* indicates a   9.____

   A. history of high productivity
   B. nearly absolute positive correlation with high productivity
   C. predisposition to be productive under facilitating leadership and circumstances
   D. complacency which has little effect on productivity

10. Assume that you are going to organize the professionals and clerks under your supervision into work groups or teams of two or three employees.   10.____
    Of the following, the step which is LEAST likely to foster the successful development of each group is to

    A. allow friends to work together in the group
    B. provide special help and attention to employees with no friends in their group
    C. frequently switch employees from group to group
    D. rotate jobs within the group in order to strengthen group identification

11. Following are four statements which might be made by an employee to his supervisor during a performance evaluation interview.
Which of the statements BEST provides a basis for developing a plan to improve the employee's performance?

    A. *I understand that you are dissatisfied with my work and I will try harder in the future.*
    B. *I feel that I've been making too many careless clerical errors recently.*
    C. *I am aware that I will be subject to disciplinary action if my work does not improve within one month.*
    D. *I understand that this interview is simply a requirement of your job, and not a personal attack on me.*

11.____

12. Three months ago, Mr. Smith and his supervisor, Mrs. Jones, developed a plan which was intended to correct Mr. Smith's inadequate job performance. Now, during a follow-up interview, Mr. Smith, who thought his performance had satisfactorily improved, has been informed that Mrs. Jones is still dissatisfied with his work.
Of the following, it is *most likely* that the disagreement occurred because, when formulating the plan ,they did NOT

    A. set realistic goals for Mr. Smith Is performance
    B. set a reasonable time limit for Mr. Smith to effect his improvement in performance
    C. provide for adequate training to improve Mr. Smith's skills
    D. establish performance standards for measuring Mr. Smith's progress

12.____

13. When a supervisor delegates authority to subordinates, there are usually many problems to overcome, such as inadequately trained subordinates and poor planning.
All of the following are means of increasing the effectiveness of delegation EXCEPT:

    A. Defining assignments in the light of results expected
    B. Maintaining open lines of communication
    C. Establishing tight controls so that subordinates will stay within the bounds of the area of delegation
    D. Providing rewards for successful assumption of authority by a subordinate

13.____

14. Assume that one of your subordinates has arrived late for work several times during the current month. The last time he was late you had warned him that another unexcused lateness would result in formal disciplinary action.
If the employee arrives late for work again during this month, the FIRST action you should take is to

    A. give the employee a chance to explain this lateness
    B. give the employee a written copy of your warning
    C. tell the employee that you are recommending formal disciplinary action
    D. tell the employee that you will give him only one more chance before recommending formal disciplinary action

14.____

15. In trying to decide how many subordinates a manager can control directly, one of the determinants is how much the manager can reduce the frequency and time consumed in contacts with his subordinates.
Of the following, the factor which LEAST influences the number and direction of these contacts is:

    A. How well the manager delegates authority
    B. The rate at which the organization is changing
    C. The control techniques used by the manager
    D. Whether the activity is line or staff

15.____

16. Systematic rotation of employees through lateral transfer within a government organization to provide for managerial development is

    A. *good*, because systematic rotation develops specialists who learn to do many jobs well
    B. *bad*, because the outsider upsets the status quo of the existing organization
    C. *good*, because rotation provides challenge and organizational flexibility
    D. *bad*, because it is upsetting to employees to be transferred within a service

16.____

17. Assume that you are required to provide an evaluation of the performance of your subordinates.
Of the following factors, it is MOST important that the performance evaluation include a rating of each employees

    A. initiative   B. productivity   C. intelligence   D. personality

17.____

18. When preparing performance evaluations of your subordinates, *one* way to help assure that you are rating each employee fairly is to

    A. prepare a list of all employees and all the rating factors and rate all employees on one rating factor before going on to the next factor
    B. prepare a list of all your employees and all the rating factors and rate each employee on all factors before going on to the next employee
    C. discuss all the ratings you anticipate giving with another supervisor in order to obtain an unbiased opinion
    D. discuss each employee with his co-workers in order to obtain peer judgment of worth before doing any rating

18.____

19. A managerial plan which would include the GREATEST control is a plan which is

    A. spontaneous and geared to each new job that is received
    B. detailed and covering an extended time period
    C. long-range and generalized, allowing for various interpretations
    D. specific and prepared daily

19.____

20. Assume that you are preparing a report which includes statistical data covering increases in budget allocations of four agencies for the past ten years.
For you to represent the statistical data pictorially or graphically within the report is a

    20.____

    A. *poor idea*, because you should be able to make statistical data understandable through the use of words

    B. *good idea*, because it is easier for the reader to understand pictorial representation rather than quantities of words conveying statistical data

    C. *poor idea*, because using pictorial representation in a report may make the report too expensive to print

    D. *good idea*, because a pictorial representation makes the report appear more attractive than the use of many words to convey the statistical data

---

KEY (CORRECT ANSWERS)

1.	C		11.	A
2.	A		12.	B
3.	B		13.	C
4.	D		14.	A
5.	D		15.	D
6.	D		16.	C
7.	D		17.	B
8.	B		18.	A
9.	C		19.	B
10.	C		20.	B

TEST 2

DIRECTIONS: Each question or incomplete statement is followed by several suggested answers or completions. Select the one that BEST answers the question or completes the statement. *PRINT THE LETTER OF THE CORRECT ANSWER IN THE SPACE AT THE RIGHT.*

1. Research studies have shown that supervisors of groups with high production records USUALLY

    1.____

   A. give detailed instructions, constantly check on progress, and insist on approval of all decisions before implementation

   B. do considerable paperwork and other work similar to that performed by subordinates

   C. think of themselves as team members on the same level as others in the work group

   D. perform tasks traditionally associated with managerial functions

2. Mr. Smith, a bureau chief, is summoned by his agency's head in a conference to discuss Mr. Jones, an accountant who works in one of the divisions of his bureau. Mr. Jones has committed an error of such magnitude as to arouse the agency head's concern.
After agreeing with the other conferees that a severe reprimand would be the appropriate punishment, Mr. Smith should

    2.____

   A. arrange for Mr. Jones to explain the reasons for his error to the agency head

   B. send a memorandum to Mr. Jones, being careful that the language emphasizes the nature of the error rather than Mr. Jones' personal faults

   C. inform Mr. Jones' immediate supervisor of the conclusion reached at the conference, and let the supervisor take the necessary action

   D. suggest to the agency head that no additional action be taken against Mr. Jones because no further damage will be caused by the error

3. Assume that Ms. Thomson, a unit chief, has determined that the findings of an internal audit have been seriously distorted as a result of careless errors. The audit had been performed by a group of auditors in her unit and the errors were overlooked by the associate accountant in charge of the audit. Ms. Thomson has decided to delay discussing the matter with the associate accountant and the staff who performed the audit until she verifies certain details, which may require prolonged investigation.
Ms. Thomson's method of handling this situation is

    3.____

   A. *appropriate;* employees should not be accused of wrongdoing until all the facts have been determined

   B. *inappropriate;* the employees involved may assume that the errors were considered unimportant

   C. *appropriate;* employees are more likely to change their behavior as a result of disciplinary action taken after a *cooling off* period

   D. *inappropriate;* the employees involved may have forgotten the details and become emotionally upset when confronted with the facts

4. After studying the financial situation in his agency, an administrative accountant decides to recommend centralization of certain accounting functions which are being performed in three different bureaus of the organization.
   The one of the following which is *most likely* to be a DISADVANTAGE if this recommendation is implemented is that

    4.____

   A. there may be less coordination of the accounting procedure because central direction is not so close to the day-to-day problems as the personnel handling them in each specialized accounting unit
   B. the higher management levels would not be able to make emergency decisions in as timely a manner as the more involved, lower-level administrators who are closer to the problem
   C. it is more difficult to focus the attention of the top management in order to resolve accounting problems because of the many other activities top management is involved in at the same time
   D. the accuracy of upward and inter-unit communication may be reduced because centralization may require insertion of more levels of administration in the chain of command

5. Of the following assumptions about the role of conflict in an organization, the *one* which is the MOST accurate statement of the approach of modern management theorists is that conflict

    5.____

   A. can usually be avoided or controlled
   B. serves as a vital element in organizational change
   C. works against attainment of organizational goals
   D. provides a constructive outlet for problem employees

6. Which of the following is generally regarded as the BEST approach for a supervisor to follow in handling grievances brought by subordinates?

    6.____

   A. Avoid becoming involved personally
   B. Involve the union representative in the first stage of discussion
   C. Settle the grievance as soon as possible
   D. Arrange for arbitration by a third party

7. Assume that supervisors of similar-sized accounting units in city, state, and federal offices were interviewed and observed at their work. It was found that the ways they acted in and viewed their roles tended to be very similar, regardless of who employed them.
   Which of the following is the BEST explanation of this similarity?

    7.____

   A. A supervisor will ordinarily behave in conformance to his own self-image
   B. Each role in an organization, including the supervisory role, calls for a distinct type of personality
   C. The supervisory role reflects an exceptionally complex pattern of human response
   D. The general nature of the duties and responsibilities of the supervisory position determines the role

8. Which of the following is NOT consistent with the findings of recent research about the characteristics of successful top managers?

    A. They are *inner-directed* and not overly concerned with pleasing others
    B. They are challenged by situations filled with high risk and ambiguity
    C. They tend to stay on the same job for long periods of time
    D. They consider it more important to handle critical assignments successfully than to do routine work well

8.____

9. As a supervisor you have to give subordinate operational guidelines.
Of the following, the BEST reason for providing them with information about the overall objectives within which their operations fit is that the subordinates will

    A. be more likely to carry out the operation according to your expectations
    B. know that there is a legitimate reason for carrying out the operation in the way you have prescribed
    C. be more likely to handle unanticipated problems that may arise without having to take up your time
    D. more likely to transmit the operating instructions correctly to their subordinates

9.____

10. A supervisor holds frequent meetings with his staff.
Of the following, the BEST approach he can take in order to elicit productive discussions at these meetings is for him to

    A. ask questions of those who attend
    B. include several levels of supervisors at the meetings
    C. hold the meetings at a specified time each week
    D. begin each meeting with a statement that discussion is welcomed

10.____

11. Of the following, the MOST important action that a supervisor can take to increase the productivity of a subordinate is to

    A. increase his uninterrupted work time
    B. increase the number of reproducing machines available in the office
    C. provide clerical assistance whenever he requests it
    D. reduce the number of his assigned tasks

11.____

12. Assume that, as a supervisor, you find that you often must countermand or modify your original staff memos. If this practice continues, *which one* of the following situations is MOST likely to occur? The

    A. staff will not bother to read your memos   B. office files will become cluttered
    C. staff will delay acting on your memos   D. memos will be treated routinely

12.____

13. In making management decisions the committee approach is often used by managers.
Of the following, the BEST reason for using this approach is to

    A. prevent any one individual from assuming too much authority
    B. allow the manager to bring a wider range of experience and judgment to bear on the problem
    C. allow the participation of all staff members, which will make them feel more committed to the decisions reached
    D. permit the rapid transmission of information about decisions reached to the staff members concerned

13.____

14. In establishing standards for the measurement of the performance of a management   14.____
project team, it is MOST important for the project manager to

    A. identify and define the objectives of the project
    B. determine the number of people who will be assigned to the project team
    C. evaluate the skills of the staff who will be assigned to the project team
    D. estimate fairly accurately the length of time required to complete each phase of the
       project

15. It is virtually impossible to tell an employee either that he is not so good as another   15.____
employee or that he does not measure up to a desirable level of performance, without
having him feel threatened, rejected, and discouraged.
In accordance with the foregoing observation, a supervisor who is concerned about
the performance of the less efficient members of his staff should realize that

    A. he might obtain better results by not discussing the quality and quantity of their
       work with them, but by relying instead on the written evaluation of their perfor-
       mance to motivate their improvement
    B. since he is required to discuss their performance with them, he should do so in
       words of encouragement and in so friendly a manner as to not destroy their morale
    C. he might discuss their work in a general way, without mentioning any of the specif-
       ics about the quality of their performance, with the expectation that they would
       understand the full implications of his talk
    D. he should make it a point, while telling them of their poor performance, to mention
       that their work is as good as that of some of the other employees in the unit

16. Some advocates of management-by-objectives procedures in public agencies have   16.____
been urging that this method of operations be expanded to encompass all agencies of
the government, for one or more of the following reasons, not all of which may be correct:
    I. The MBO method is likely to succeed because it embraces the practice of
       setting near-term goals for the subordinate manager, reviewing accomplish-
       ments at an appropriate time, and repeating this process indefinitely
    II. Provision for authority to perform the tasks assigned as goals in the MBO
       method is normally not needed because targets are set in quantitative or
       qualitative terms and specific times for accomplishment are arranged in
       short-term, repetitive intervals
    III. Many other appraisal-of-performance programs failed because both super-
       visors and subordinates resisted them, while the MBO approach is not insti-
       tuted until there is an organizational commitment to it
    IV. Personal accountability is clearly established through the MBO approach
       because verifiable results are set up in the process of formulating the targets
Which of the choices below includes ALL of the foregoing statements that are COR-
RECT?

    A. I and III   B. II and IV
    C. I,II,III,IV   D. I,III,IV

29

17. In preparing an organizational structure, the PRINCIPAL guideline for locating staff units is to place them 17.____

    A. all under a common supervisor
    B. as close as possible to the activities they serve
    C. as close to the chief executive as possible without over–extending his span of control
    D. at the lowest operational level

18. The relative importance of any unit in a department can be LEAST reliably judged by the 18.____

    A. amount of office space allocated to the unit
    B. number of employees in the unit
    C. rank of the individual who heads the unit
    D. rank of the individual to whom the unit head reports directly

19. Those who favor Planning-Programming-Budgeting Systems (PPBS) as a new method of governmental financial administration emphasize that PPBS 19.____

    A. applies statistical measurements which correlate highly with criteria
    B. makes possible economic systems analysis, including an explicit examination of alternatives
    C. makes available scarce government resources which can be coordinated on a government-wide basis and shared between local units of government
    D. shifts the emphasis in budgeting methods to an automated system of data processing

20. The term applied to computer processing which processes data concurrently with a given activity and provides results soon enough to influence the selection of a course of action is 20.____

    A. realtime processing
    B. batch processing
    C. random access processing
    D. integrated data processing

KEY (CORRECT ANSWERS)

1.	D	11.	A
2.	C	12.	C
3.	B	13.	B
4.	D	14.	A
5.	B	15.	B
6.	C	16.	D
7.	D	17.	B
8.	C	18.	B
9.	C	19.	B
10.	A	20.	A

SUPERVISION, ADMINISTRATION, MANAGEMENT AND ORGANIZATION

EXAMINATION SECTION
TEST 1

DIRECTIONS: Each question or incomplete statement is followed by several suggested answers or completions. Select the one that BEST answers the question or completes the statement. *PRINT THE LETTER OF THE CORRECT ANSWER IN THE SPACE AT THE RIGHT.*

1. One of the responsibilities of the supervisor is to provide top administration with information about clients and their problems that will help in the evaluation of existing policies and indicate the need for modifications.
   In order to fulfill this responsibility, it would be MOST essential for the supervisor to

   A. routinely forward all regularly prepared and recurrent reports from his subordinates to his immediate superior
   B. regularly review agency rules, regulations and policies to make sure that he has sufficient knowledge to make appropriate analyses
   C. note repeated instances of failure of staff to correctly administer a policy and schedule staff conferences for corrective training
   D. analyze reports on cases submitted by subordinates, in order to select relevant trend material to be forwarded to his superiors

1.____

2. You find that your division has a serious problem because of unusually long delays in filing reports and overdue approvals to private agencies under contract for services.
   The MOST appropriate step to take FIRST in this situation would be to

   A. request additional staff to work on reports and approvals
   B. order staff to work overtime until the backlog is eliminated
   C. impress staff with the importance of expeditious handling of reports and approvals
   D. analyze present procedures for handling reports and approvals

2.____

3. When a supervisor finds that he must communicate orally information that is significant enough to affect the entire staff, it would be MOST important to

   A. distribute a written summary of the information to his staff before discussing it orally
   B. tell his subordinate supervisors to discuss this information at individual conferences with their subordinates
   C. call a follow-up meeting of absentees as soon as they return
   D. restate and summarize the information in order to make sure that everyone understands its meaning and implications

3.____

4. Of the following, the BEST way for a supervisor to assist a subordinate who has unusually heavy work pressures is to

   A. point out that such pressures go with the job and must be tolerated
   B. suggest to him that the pressures probably result from poor handling of his workload
   C. help him to be selective in deciding on priorities during the period of pressure
   D. ask him to work overtime until the period of pressure is over

4.____

5. Leadership is a basic responsibility of the supervisor. The one of the following which would be the LEAST appropriate way to fulfill this role is for the supervisor to

    A. help staff to work up to their capacities in every possible way
    B. encourage independent judgment and actions by staff members
    C. allow staff to participate in decisions within policy limits
    D. take over certain tasks in which he is more competent than his subordinates

5.____

6. Assume that you have assigned a very difficult administrative task to one of your best subordinate supervisors, but he is reluctant to take it on because he fears that he will fail in it. It is your judgment, however, that he is quite capable of performing this task.
The one of the following which is the MOST desirable way for you to handle this situation is to

    A. reassure him that he has enough skill to perform the task and that he will not be penalized if he fails
    B. reassign the task to another supervisor who is more achievement-oriented and more confident of his skills
    C. minimize the importance of the task so that he will feel it is safe for him to attempt it
    D. stress the importance of the task and the dependence of the other staff members on his succeeding in it

6.____

7. Assume that a member of your professional staff deliberately misinterprets a new state directive because he fears that its enforcement will have an adverse effect on clients. Although you consider him to be a good supervisor and basically agree with him, you should direct him to comply.
Of the following, the MOST desirable way for you to handle this situation would be to

    A. avoid a confrontation with him by transferring responsibility for carrying out the directive to another member of your staff
    B. explain to him that you are in a better position than he to assess the implications of the new directive
    C. discuss with him the basic reasons for his misinterpretation and explain why he must comply with the directive
    D. allow him to interpret the directive in his own way as long as he assumes full responsibility for his actions

7.____

8. Of the following, the MAIN reason it is important for an administrator in a large organization to properly coordinate the work delegated to subordinates is that such coordination

    A. makes it unnecessary to hold frequent staff meetings and conferences with key staff members
    B. reduces the necessity for regular evaluation of procedures and programs, production and performance of personnel
    C. results in greater economy and stricter accountability for the organization's resources
    D. facilitates integration of the contributions of the numerous staff members who are responsible for specific parts of the total workload

8.____

9. The one of the following which would NOT be an appropriate reason for the formulation of an entirely NEW policy is that it would

    A. serve as a positive affirmation of the agency's function and how it is to be carried out

    B. give focus and direction to the work of the staff, particularly in decision-making

    C. inform the public of the precise conditions under which services will be rendered

    D. provide procedures which constitute uniform methods of carrying out operations

9.____

10. Of the following, it is MOST difficult to formulate policy in an organization where

    A. work assignments are narrowly specialized by units

    B. staff members have varied backgrounds and a wide range of competency

    C. units implementing the same policy are in the same geographic location

    D. staff is experienced and fully trained

10.____

11. For a supervisor to feel that he is responsible for influencing the attitudes of his staff members is GENERALLY considered

    A. *undesirable;* attitudes of adults are emotional factors which usually cannot be changed

    B. *desirable;* certain attitudes can be obstructive and should be modified in order to provide effective service to clients

    C. *undesirable;* the supervisor should be nonjudgmental and accepting of widely different attitudes and social patterns of staff members

    D. *desirable;* influencing attitudes is a teaching responsibility which the supervisor shares with the training specialist

11.____

12. The one of the following which is NOT generally a function of the higher-level supervisor is

    A. projecting the budget and obtaining financial resources

    B. providing conditions conducive to optimum employee production

    C. maintaining records and reports as a basis for accountability and evaluation

    D. evaluating program achievements and personnel effectiveness in accordance with goals and standards

12.____

13. As a supervisor in a recently decentralized services center offering multiple services, you are given responsibility for an orientation program for professional staff on the recent reorganization of the Department.
Of the following, the MOST appropriate step to take FIRST would be to

    A. organize a series of workshops for subordinate supervisors

    B. arrange a tour of the new geographic area of service

    C. review supervisors' reports, statistical data and other relevant material

    D. develop a resource manual for staff on the reorganized center

13.____

14. Experts generally agree that the content of training sessions should be closely related to workers' practice.
Of the following, the BEST method of achieving this aim is for the training conference leader to

    A. encourage group discussion of problems that concern staff in their practice

    B. develop closer working relationships with top administration

14.____

    C.   coordinate with central office to obtain feedback on problems that concern staff
    D.   observe workers in order to develop a pattern of problems for class discussion

15.   The one of the following which is generally the MOST useful teaching tool for profes-   15._____
sional staff development is

    A.   visual aids and tape recordings
    B.   professional literature
    C.   agency case material
    D.   lectures by experts

16.   The one of the following which is NOT a good reason for using group conferences as a   16._____
method of supervision is to

    A.   give workers a feeling of mutual support through sharing common problems
    B.   save time by eliminating the need for individual conferences
    C.   encourage discussion of certain problems that are not as likely to come up in indi-
        vidual conferences
    D.   provide an opportunity for developing positive identification with the department
        and its programs

17.   The supervisor, in his role as teacher, applies his teaching in line with his understanding   17._____
of people and realizes that teaching is a highly individualized process, based on understanding of the worker as a person and as a learner. This statement implies, MOST
NEARLY, that the supervisor must help the worker to

    A.   overcome his biases
    B.   develop his own ways of working
    C.   gain confidence in his ability
    D.   develop the will to work

18.   Of the following, the circumstance under which it would be MOST appropriate to divide a   18._____
training conference for professional staff into small workshops is when

    A.   some of the trainees are not aware of the effect of their attitudes and behavior on
        others
    B.   the trainees need to look at human relations problems from different perspectives
    C.   the trainees are faced with several substantially different types of problems in their
        job assignments
    D.   the trainees need to know how to function in many different capacities

19.   Of the following, the MAIN reason why it is important to systemically evaluate a specific   19._____
training program while it is in progress is to

    A.   collect data that will serve as a valid basis for improving the agency's overall train-
        ing program and maintaining control over its components
    B.   insure that instruction by training specialists is conducted in a manner consistent
        with the planned design of the training program
    C.   identify areas in which additional or remedial training for the training specialists can
        be planned and implemented
    D.   provide data which are usable in effecting revisions of specific components of the
        training program

20. Staff development has been defined as an educational process which seeks to provide agency staff with knowledge about specific job responsibilities and to effect changes in staff attitudes and behavior patterns. Assume that you are assigned to define the educational objectives of a specific training program.
In accordance with the above concept, the MOST helpful formulation would be a statement of the

    A. purpose and goals of each training session
    B. generalized patterns of behavior to be developed in the trainees
    C. content material to be presented in the training sessions
    D. kind of behavior to be developed in the trainees and the situations in which this behavior will be applied

21. In teaching personnel under your supervision how to gather and analyze facts before attempting to solve a problem, the one of the following training methods which would be MOST effective is

    A. case study   B. role playing
    C. programmed learning   D. planned experience'

22. The importance of analyzing functions traditionally included in the position of caseworker, with a view toward identifying and separating those activities to be performed by the most highly skilled personnel, has been widely discussed.
Of the following, an IMPORTANT *secondary* gain which can result from such differential use of staff is that

    A. supporting job assignments can be given to persons unable to meet the demands of casework, to the satisfaction of all concerned
    B. documentation will be provided on workers who are not suited for all the duties now part of the caseworker's job
    C. caseworkers with a high level of competence in working with people can be rewarded through promotion or merit increases
    D. incompetent workers can be identified and categorized, as a basis for transfer or separation from the service

23. Of the following, a serious DISADVANTAGE of a performance evaluation system based on standardized evaluation factors is that such a system tends to

    A. exacerbate the anxieties of those supervisors who are apprehensive about determining what happens to another person
    B. subject the supervisor to psychological stress by emphasizing the incompatibility of his dual role as both judge and counselor
    C. create organizational conflict by encouraging personnel who wish to enhance their standing to become too aggressive in the performance of their duties
    D. lead many staff members to concentrate on measuring up in terms of the evaluation factors and to disregard other aspects of their work

24. Which of the following would contribute MOST to the achievement of conformity of staff activities and goals to the intent of agency policies and procedures?

    A. Effective communications and organizational discipline
    B. Changing nature of the underlying principles and desired purpose of the policies and procedures

C. Formulation of specific criteria for implementing the policies and procedures
D. Continuous monitoring of the essential effectiveness of agency operations

25. Job enlargement, a management device used by large organizations to counteract the adverse effects of specialization on employee performance, is LEAST likely to improve employee motivation if it is accomplished by

25._____

A. lengthening the job cycle and adding a large number of similar tasks
B. allowing the employee to use a greater variety of skills
C. increasing the scope and complexity of the employee's job
D. giving the employee more opportunities to make decisions

KEY (CORRECT ANSWERS)

1.	D		11.	B
2.	D		12.	A
3.	D		13.	A
4.	C		14.	A
5.	D		15.	C
6.	A		16.	B
7.	C		17.	B
8.	D		18.	C
9.	D		19.	A
10.	B		20.	D

21.	A
22.	A
23.	D
24.	A
25.	A

TEST 2

DIRECTIONS: Each question or incomplete statement is followed by several suggested answers or completions. Select the one that BEST answers the question or completes the statement. *PRINT THE LETTER OF THE CORRECT ANSWER IN THE SPACE AT THE RIGHT.*

1. When a supervisor requires approval for case action on a higher level, the process used is known as   1.____

     A. administrative clearance   B. going outside channels
     C. administrative consultation   D. delegation of authority

2. In delegating authority to his subordinates, the one of the following to which a GOOD supervisor should give PRIMARY consideration is the   2.____

     A. results expected of them
     B. amount of power to be delegated
     C. amount of responsibility to be delegated
     D. their skill in the performance of present tasks

3. Of the following, the type of decision which could be SAFELY delegated to LOWER-LEVEL staff without undermining basic supervisory responsibility is one which   3.____

     A. involves a commitment that can be fulfilled only over a long period of time
     B. has fairly uncertain goals and premises
     C. has the possibility of modification built into it
     D. may generate considerable resistance from those affected by it

4. Of the following, the MOST valuable contribution made by the informal organization in a large public service agency is that such an organization   4.____

     A. has goals and values which are usually consistent with and reinforce those of the formal organization
     B. is more flexible than the formal organization and more adaptable to changing conditions
     C. has a communications system which often contributes to the efficiency of the formal organization
     D. represents a sound basis on which to build the formal organizational structure

5. Of the following, the condition under which it would be MOST useful for an agency to develop detailed procedures is when   5.____

     A. subordinate supervisory personnel need a structure to help them develop greater independence
     B. employees have little experience or knowledge of how to perform certain assigned tasks
     C. coordination of agency activities is largely dependent upon personal contact
     D. agency activities must continually adjust to changes in local circumstances

6. Assume that a certain administrator has the management philosophy that his agency's responsibility is to routinize existing operations, meet each day's problems as they arise, and resolve problems with a minimum of residual effect upon himself or his agency. The possibility that this official would be able to administer his agency without running into serious difficulties would be MORE likely during a period of   6.____

     A. economic change   B. social change
     C. economic crisis   D. social and economic stability

7. Some large organizations have adopted the practice of allowing each employee to estab-   7.____
lish his own performance goals, and then later evaluate himself in an individual conference with his immediate supervisor.
Of the following, a DRAWBACK of this approach is that the employee

    A. may set his goals too low and rate himself too highly
    B. cannot control those variables which may improve his performance
    C. has no guidelines for improving his performance
    D. usually finds it more difficult to criticize himself than to accept criticism from others

8. Decentralization of services cannot completely eliminate the requirement of central office   8.____
approval for certain case actions. The MOST valid reason for complaint about this
requirement is that

    A. unavoidable delay created by referral to central office may cause serious problems
      for the client
    B. it may lower morale of supervisors who are not given the authority to take final
      action on urgent cases
    C. the concept of role responsibility is minimized
    D. the objective of delegated responsibility tends to be negated

9. Which of the following would be the MOST useful administrative tool for the purpose of   9.____
showing the sequence of operations and staff involved? A(n)

    A. organization chart   B. flow chart
    C. manual of operating procedures   D. statistical review

10. The prevailing pattern of organization in large public agencies consists of a limited span   10.____
of control and organization by function or, at lower levels, process.
Of the following, the PRINCIPAL effect which this pattern of organization has on the
management of work is that it

    A. reduces the management burden in significant ways
    B. creates a time lag between the perception of a problem and action on it
    C. makes it difficult to direct and observe employee performance
    D. facilitates the development of employees with managerial ability

11. The one of the following which would be the MOST appropriate way to reduce tensions   11.____
between line and staff personnel in public service agencies is to

    A. provide in-service training that will increase the sensitivity of line and staff person-
      nel to their respective roles
    B. assign to staff personnel the role of providing assistance only when requested by
      line personnel
    C. separate staff from line personnel and provide staff with its own independent
      reward structure
    D. give line and staff personnel equal status in making decisions

12. In determining the appropriate span of control for subordinate supervisors, which of the   12.____
following principles should be followed? The more

    A. complex the work, the broader the effective span of control
    B. similar the jobs being supervised, the more narrow the effective span of control

    C.   interdependent the jobs being supervised, the more narrow the effective span of control
    D.   unpredictable the work, the broader the effective span of control

13.   A method sometimes used in public service agencies to improve upward communication is to require subordinate supervisory staff to submit to top management monthly narrative reports of any problems which they deem important for consideration.
Of the following, a major DISADVANTAGE of this method is that it may   13.____

    A.   enable subordinate supervisors to avoid thinking about their problems by simply referring such matters to their superiors
    B.   obscure important issues so that they are not given appropriate attention
    C.   create a need for numerous staff conferences in order to handle all of the reported problems
    D.   encourage some subordinate supervisors to focus on irrelevant matters and compete with each other in the length and content of their reports

14.   The use of a committee as an approach to the problem of coordinating interdepartmental activities can present difficulties if the committee functions PRIMARILY as a(n)   14.____

    A.   means of achieving personal objectives and goals
    B.   instrument for coordinating activities that flow across departmental lines
    C.   device for involving subordinate personnel in the decision-making process
    D.   means of giving representation to competing interest groups

15.   A study was recently made of the attitudes and perceptions of a sample of workers who had experienced a major organizational change and redefinition of their jobs as a result of separation of certain functions.
Questionnaires administered to these workers indicated that a disproportionate number of workers in the larger agencies were dissatisfied with the reorganization and their new assignments.
Of the following, the MOST plausible reason for this dissatisfaction is that workers in larger agencies are   15.____

    A.   less likely to be known to management and to be personally disciplined if they expressed dissatisfaction with their new roles
    B.   less likely to have the opportunity to participate in planning a reorganization and to be given consideration for the assignments they preferred
    C.   given a shorter lead period to implement the changes and therefore had insufficient time to plan the reorganization and carry it out efficiently
    D.   usually made up of more older members who have had routinized their work according to habit and find it more difficult to adjust to change

16.   An article which recently appeared in a professional journal presents a proposal for participatory leadership, in which the goal of supervision would be development of subordinates' self-reliance, with the premise that each staff member is held accountable for his own performance.
The one of the following which would NOT be a desirable outcome of this type of supervision is the   16.____

    A.   necessity for subordinates to critically examine their performance
    B.   development by some subordinates of skills not possessed by the supervisor

C. establishment of a quality control unit for sample checking and identification of errors

D. relaxation of demands made on the supervisor

17. The "management by objectives" concept is a major development in the administration of services organizations. The purpose of this approach is to establish a system for 17._____

A. reduction of waiting time
B. planning and controlling work output
C. consolidation of organizational units
D. work measurement

18. Assume that you encounter a serious administrative problem in implementing a new pro- 18._____
gram. After consulting with the members of your staff individually, you come up with several alternate solutions.
Of the following, the procedure which would be MOST appropriate for evaluating the relative merits of each solution would be to

A. try all of them on a limited experimental basis
B. break the problem down into its component parts and analyze the effect of each solution on each component in terms of costs and benefits
C. break the problem down into its component parts, eliminate all intangibles, and measure the effect of the tangible aspects of each solution on each component in terms of costs and benefits
D. bring the matter before your weekly staff conference, discuss the relative merits of each alternate solution, and then choose the one favored by the majority of the conference

19. When establishing planning objectives for a service program under your supervision, the 19._____
one of the following principles which should be followed is that objectives

A. are rarely verifiable if they are qualitative
B. should be few in number and of equal importance
C. should cover as many of the activities of the program as possible
D. should be set in the light of assumptions about future funding

20. Assume that you have been assigned responsibility for coordinating various aspects of a 20._____
program in a community services center. Which of the following administrative concepts would NOT be applicable to this assignment?

A. Functional job analysis   B. Peer group supervision
C. Differential use of staff   D. Systems design

21. Good administrative practice includes the use of outside consultants as an effective tech- 21._____
nique in achieving agency objectives. However, the one of the following which would NOT be an appropriate role for the consultant is

A. provision of technical or professional expertise not otherwise available in the agency
B. administrative direction of a new program activity
C. facilitating coordination and communication among agency staff
D. objective measurement of the effectiveness of agency services

22. Of the following, the MOST common fault of research projects attempting to measure the effectiveness of social programs has been their

    A. questionable methodology
    B. inaccurate findings
    C. unrealistic expectations
    D. lack of objectivity

22.____

23. One of the most difficult tasks of supervision in a modern public agency is teaching workers to cope with the hostile reactions of clients. In order to help the disconcerted worker analyze and understand a client's hostile behavior, the supervisor should FIRST

    A. encourage the worker to identify with the client's frustrations and deprivations
    B. give the worker a chance to express and accept his feelings about the client
    C. ask the worker to review his knowledge of the client and his circumstances
    D. explain to the worker that the client's anger is not directed at the worker personally

23.____

24. Determination of the level of participation, or how much of the public should participate in a given project, is a vital step in community organization.
    In order to make this determination, the FIRST action that should be taken is to

    A. develop the participants
    B. fix the goals of the project
    C. evaluate community interest in the project
    D. enlist the cooperation of community leaders

24.____

25. The one of the following which would be the MOST critical factor for SUCCESSFUL operation of a decentralized system of programs and services is

    A. periodic review and evaluation of services delivered at the community level
    B. transfer of decision-making authority to the community level wherever feasible
    C. participation of indigenous non-professionals in service delivery
    D. formulation of quantitative plans for dealing with community problems wherever feasible

25.____

KEY (CORRECT ANSWERS)

1.	A	11.	A
2.	A	12.	C
3.	C	13.	D
4.	C	14.	A
5.	B	15.	B
6.	D	16.	D
7.	A	17.	B
8.	A	18.	C
9.	B	19.	D
10.	B	20.	B

21.	B
22.	C
23.	B
24.	B
25.	B

———

TEST 3

DIRECTIONS: Each question or incomplete statement is followed by several suggested answers or completions. Select the one that BEST answers the question or completes the statement. *PRINT THE LETTER OF THE CORRECT ANSWER IN THE SPACE AT THE RIGHT.*

1. Douglas McGregor's theory of human motivation classifies worker behavior into two distinct categories: Theory X and Theory Y. Theory X, the traditional view, states that the average man dislikes to work and will avoid work if he can, unless coerced. Theory Y holds essentially the opposite view. The executive can apply both of these theories to worker behavior BEST if he   1._____

   A. follows an "open-door" policy only with respect to his immediate subordinates
   B. recognizes his subordinates' mental and social needs as well as agency needs
   C. recognizes that executive responsibility is primarily limited to fulfillment of agency productivity goals
   D. directs his subordinate managers to follow a policy of close supervision

2. In interpersonal communications it is of paramount importance to determine whether or not what has been said has been understood by others. One of the MOST important sources of such information is known as   2._____

   A. the halo effect   B. evaluation
   C. feedback   D. quantitative analysis

3. The grapevine most often provides a USEFUL service by   3._____

   A. correcting some of the deficiencies of the formal communication system
   B. rapidly conveying a true picture of events
   C. involving staff in current organizational changes
   D. interfering with the operation of the formal communication system

4. People who are in favor of a leadership style in which the subordinates help make decisions, contend that it produces favorable effects in a work unit. According to these people, which of the following is NOT likely to be an effect of such "participative management"?   4._____

   A. Reduced turnover
   B. Accelerated learning of duties
   C. Greater acceptance of change
   D. Reduced acceptance of the work unit's goals

5. Employees of a public service agency will be MOST likely to develop meaningful goals for both the agency and the employee and become committed to attaining them if supervisors   5._____

   A. allow them unilaterally to set their own goals
   B. provide them with a clear understanding of the premises underlying the agency's goals
   C. encourage them to concentrate on setting only short-range goals for themselves
   D. periodically review the agency's goals in order to suggest changes in accordance with current conditions

6. The insights of Chester Barnard have influenced the development of management   6.____
   thought in significant ways. He is MOST closely identified with a position that has
   become known as the

   A. acceptance theory of authority
   B. principle of the manager's or executive's span of control
   C. "Theory X" and "Theory Y" dichotomy
   D. unity of command principle

7. If a manager believes that man is primarily motivated by economic incentives and,above   7.____
   all,seeks security, he MOST usually should operate on the assumption that his subordinates

   A. need to be closely directed and have relatively little ambition
   B. are more responsive to the social forces of their peer group than to the incentives
      of management
   C. are capable of learning not only to accept but to seek responsibility
   D. are capable of responding favorably to many different kinds of managerial strate-
      gies

8. Of the following, the MOST important reason why it is in the interest of public service   8.____
   agencies to involve subordinate personnel in setting goals is that the more committed
   employees are to the goals of their agency the

   A. *more* likely they are to develop a desire for the agency's achievement of success
   B. *more* likely they are to prefer difficult rather than easy tasks
   C. *more* likely they are to perceive their individual performance as a reliable indicator
      of the agency's performance
   D. *less* likely they are to choose unreasonably difficult goals

9. As a result of gaining more recent knowledge about motivation, modern executives have   9.____
   had to rethink their notions about what motivates their subordinate managers. Which of
   the following factors is GENERALLY considered MOST important in modern motivation
   theory?

   A. Fringe benefits
   B. Working conditions
   C. Recognition of good work performance
   D. Education and experience required for the job

10. Of the following, the MAIN reason why cooperative interrelationships among personnel   10.____
    are more likely than competitive interrelationships to promote efficiency in the operation
    of a public service agency is that cooperation

    A. allows for a greater degree of specialization by function
    B. increases the opportunities for employees to check on each others' work
    C. provides a feeling of identification with the organization and enhances the desire
       for accomplishment
    D. improves the capacity of employees to acquire knowledge and learn new skills

11. Four statements are given below. Three of them describe approaches which are desirable in developing a program of employee motivation. The one which does NOT describe such an approach is:

    A. "Establish attainable goals to give employees a sense of achievement."
    B. "Largely discount the self-interest motive because it is impractical to consider it."
    C. "Allow for the participation of persons included in the plans."
    D. "Base plans on group considerations as well as individual considerations."

11.____

12. It is GENERALLY acknowledged that certain conditions should exist to insure that a subordinate will decide to accept a communication as being authoritative. Which of the following is LEAST valid as a condition which should exist?

    A. The subordinate understands the communication
    B. At the time of the subordinate's decision, he views the communication as consistent with the organization's purpose and his personal interest
    C. At the time of the subordinate's decision, he views the communication as more consistent with his personal purpose than with the organization's interests
    D. The subordinate is mentally and physically able to comply with the communication

12.____

13. In exploring the effects that employee participation has on putting changes in work methods into effect, certain relationships have been established between participation and productivity. It has MOST generally been found that HIGHEST productivity occurs in groups that are given

    A. participation in the process of change only through representatives of their group
    B. no participation in the change process
    C. full participation in the change process
    D. intermittent participation in the process of change

13.____

14. Of the following statements, the one which represents a trend LEAST likely to occur in the area of employee-management relations is that:

    A. Employees will exert more influence on decisions affecting their interests.
    B. Technological change will have a stronger impact on organizations' human resources.
    C. Labor will judge management according to company profits.
    D. Government will play a larger role in balancing the interests of the parties in labor-management affairs.

14.____

15. Members of an organization must satisfy several fundamental psychological needs in order to be happy and productive. The broadest and MOST basic needs are

    A. achievement, recognition and acceptance
    B. competition, recognition and accomplishment
    C. salary increments and recognition
    D. acceptance of competition and economic reward

15.____

16. Morale has been defined as the capacity of a group of people to pull together steadily for a common purpose. Morale thus defined is MOST generally dependent on which one of the following conditions?

    A. Job security
    B. Group and individual self-confidence
    C. Organizational efficiency
    D. Physical health of the individuals

16.____

17. Assume that consideration is being given to forming a committee for the purpose of get- 17._____
ting a. new program under way which requires the coordination of several organizational
units. Which one of the following would be a MAJOR weakness of using the "committee"
approach in this situation?

    A. Its inappropriateness for decision-making
    B. The necessity to include line and staff employees
    C. The difficulty of achieving proper representation
    D. Its independence from the formal organization

18. Which of the following techniques is NOT used as an approach to encourage communi- 18._____
cation between individuals at the same level?

    A. The informal organization
    C. Committee meetings
    B. The chain of command
    D. Distribution of written reports

19. In everyday actual operations, downward communications MOST often concern 19._____

    A. specific directives about job performance
    B. information about worker performance
    C. information about the rationale of the job
    D. information to indoctrinate the organization's staff on goals to be achieved

20. Communication has been thought of for a long time as a vital process in a formal organi- 20._____
zation system. Of the following, the MOST accurate statement that can be made concerning this process is that

    A. decision-making depends on communication and organizational structure
    B. communication does not interact but is interdependent with organizational struc-
ture and decision-making
    C. effective decision-making is dependent on organizational structure but not on com-
munication
    D. communication is dependent on the decision-making process but not on organiza-
tional structure

21. In coaching a subordinate manager in the use of the type of management in which sub- 21._____
ordinate employees participate, an executive would be MOST accurate in emphasizing
that participative management

    A. uses consultative as opposed to democratic techniques
    B. uses democratic as opposed to consultative techniques
    C. requires the involvement of subordinates while reserving for the superior the right
to make decisions
    D. requires involving subordinates and giving them the right to make most decisions

22. In most work situations, employees tend to form informal groups and relationships. The 22._____
BEST way for a supervisor interested in high productivity to deal with such groups and
relationships is to

    A. take them into account as much as possible when making work assignments and
schedules
    B. ignore them, since such relationships and groups usually have no effect on work
productivity

C. attempt to destroy such groups and relationships since they are usually counter-productive

D. ignore them, even though they are usually counterproductive, since nothing can be done about them

23. Assume that in an office an entirely new method has been introduced in the handling of applications for service and related information. Employees USUALLY approach such a sudden change in their work routine with an attitude of   23.____

    A. *apprehension*, chiefly because such a change makes them uncertain of their position

    B. *indifference*, chiefly because most people don't care what they are doing, as long as they are paid

    C. *approval*, chiefly because such a change provides a welcome change of pace in their work

    D. *acceptance*, mainly because most people prefer changes to the same routines

24. In what order should the following steps be taken when revising office procedure?   24.____
    I. To develop the improved method as determined by time and motion studies and effective workplace layout
    II. To find out how the task is now performed
    III. To apply the new method
    IV. To analyze the current method
The CORRECT order is:

    A. IV, II, I, III   B. II, I, III, IV
    C. I, II, IV, III   D. II, IV, I, III

25. In contrast to broad spans of control, narrow spans of control are MOST likely to   25.____

    A. provide opportunity for more personal contact between superior and subordinate
    B. encourage decentralization
    C. stress individual initiative
    D. foster group or team effort

KEY (CORRECT ANSWERS)

1.	B		11.	B
2.	C		12.	C
3.	A		13.	C
4.	D		14.	C
5.	B		15.	A
6.	A		16.	B
7.	A		17.	A
8.	A		18.	B
9.	C		19.	A
10.	C		20.	A

21.	C
22.	A
23.	A
24.	D
25.	A

———

PREPARING WRITTEN MATERIALS

EXAMINATION SECTION
TEST 1

DIRECTIONS: Each question or incomplete statement is followed by several suggested answers or completions. Select the one that BEST answers the question or completes the statement. *PRINT THE LETTER OF THE CORRECT ANSWER IN THE SPACE AT THE RIGHT.*

Questions 1-21.

DIRECTIONS: In each of the following sentences, which were taken from students' transcripts, there may be an error. Indicate the appropriate correction in the space at the right. If the sentence is correct as is, indicate this choice. Unnecessary changes will be considered incorrect.

1. In that building there seemed to be representatives of Teachers College, the Veterans Bureau, and the Businessmen's Association.   1._____

    A. Teacher's College   B. Veterans' Bureau
    C. Businessmens Association   D. Correct as is

2. In his travels, he visited St. Paul, San Francisco, Springfield, Ohio, and Washington, D.C.   2._____

    A. Ohio and   B. Saint Paul
    C. Washington, D.C.   D. Correct as is

3. As a result of their purchasing a controlling interest in the syndicate, it was well-known that the Bureau of Labor Statistics' calculations would be unimportant.   3._____

    A. of them purchasing   B. well known
    C. Statistics   D. Correct as is

4. Walter Scott, Jr.'s, attempt to emulate his father's success was doomed to failure.   4._____

    A. Junior's,   B. Scott's, Jr.
    C. Scott, Jr.'s attempt   D. Correct as is

5. About B.C. 250 the Romans invaded Great Britain, and remains of their highly developed civilization can still be seen.   5._____

    A. 250 B.C.   B. Britain and
    C. highly-developed   D. Correct as is

6. The two boss's sons visited the children's department.   6._____

    A. bosses   B. bosses'
    C. childrens'   D. Correct as is

7. Miss Amex not only approved the report, but also decided that it needed no revision.   7._____

    A. report; but   B. report but
    C. report. But   D. Correct as is

8. Here's brain food in a jiffy—economical, too!　　　　　　　　　　8.____

    A.　economical too!　　　　　　　　B.　'brain food'
    C.　jiffy-economical　　　　　　　　D.　Correct as is

9. She said, "He likes the "Gatsby Look" very much."　　　　　　　　9.____

    A.　said "He　　　　　　　　　　B.　"he
    C.　'Gatsby Look'　　　　　　　　D.　Correct as is

10. We anticipate that we will be able to visit them briefly in Los Angeles on Wednesday after　　10.____
a five-day visit.

    A.　Wednes-　　　　　　　　　　B.　5 day
    C.　five day　　　　　　　　　　D.　Correct as is

11. She passed all her tests, and, she now has a good position.　　　　11.____

    A.　tests, and she　　　　　　　　B.　past
    C.　tests;　　　　　　　　　　　D.　Correct as is

12. The billing clerk said, "I will send the bill today"; however, that was a week ago, and it　　12.____
hasn't arrived yet!

    A.　today;"　　　　　　　　　　B.　today,"
    C.　ago and　　　　　　　　　　D.　Correct as is

13. "She types at more-than-average speed," Miss Smith said, "but I feel that it is a result of　　13.____
marvelous concentration and self control on her part."

    A.　more than average　　　　　　B.　"But
    C.　self-control　　　　　　　　D.　Correct as is

14. The state of Alaska, the largest state in the union, is also the northernmost state.　　14.____

    A.　Union　　　　　　　　　　　B.　Northernmost State
    C.　State of Alaska　　　　　　　D.　Correct as is

15. The memoirs of Ex-President Nixon, according to figures, sold more copies than <u>Six Cri-</u>　　15.____
<u>ses</u>, the book he wrote in the 60's.

    A.　Six Crises　　　　　　　　　B.　ex-President
    C.　60s　　　　　　　　　　　D.　Correct as is

16. "There are three principal elements, determining the hazard of buildings: the contents　　16.____
hazard, the fire resistance of the structure, and the character of the interior finish," concluded the speaker.
The one of the following statements that is MOST acceptable is that, in the above passage,

    A.　the comma following the word *elements* is incorrect
    B.　the colon following the word *buildings* is incorrect
    C.　the comma following the word *finish* is incorrect
    D.　there is no error in the punctuation of the sentence

17. He spoke on his favorite topic, "Why We Will Win." (How could I stop him?)　　17.____

    A.　Win".　　　　　　　　　　　B.　him?).
    C.　him)?　　　　　　　　　　　D.　Correct as is

18. "All any insurance policy is, is a contract for services," said my insurance agent, Mr. Newton.

    A.   Insurance Policy   B.   Insurance Agent
    C.   policy is is a   D.   Correct as is

18._____

19. Inasmuch as the price list has now been up dated, we should send it to the printer.

    A.   In as much   B.   updated
    C.   pricelist   D.   Correct as is

19._____

20. We feel that "Our know-how" is responsible for the improvement in technical developments.

    A.   "our   B.   know how
    C.   that,   D.   Correct as is

20._____

21. Did Cortez conquer the Incas? the Aztecs? the South American Indians?

    A.   Incas, the Aztecs, the South American Indians?
    B.   Incas; the Aztecs; the South American Indians?
    C.   south American Indians?
    D.   Correct as is

21._____

22. Which one of the following forms for the typed name of the dictator in the closing lines of a letter is generally MOST acceptable in the United States?

    A.   (Dr.) James F. Farley
    B.   Dr. James F. Farley
    C.   Mr. James F. Farley, Ph.D.
    D.   James F. Farley

22._____

23. The plural of

    A.   turkey is turkies
    B.   cargo is cargoes
    C.   bankruptcy is bankruptcys
    D.   son-in-law is son-in-laws

23._____

24. The abbreviation *viz.* means MOST NEARLY

    A.   namely   B.   for example
    C.   the following   D.   see

24._____

25. In the sentence, *A man in a light-gray suit waited thirty-five minutes in the ante-room for the all-important document,* the word IMPROPERLY hyphenated is

    A.   light-gray   B.   thirty-five
    C.   ante-room   D.   all-important

25._____

KEY (CORRECT ANSWERS)

1.	D	11.	A
2.	C	12.	D
3.	B	13.	D
4.	D	14.	A
5.	A	15.	B
6.	B	16.	A
7.	B	17.	D
8.	D	18.	D
9.	C	19.	B
10.	C	20.	A

21. D
22. D
23. B
24. A
25. C

TEST 2

DIRECTIONS: Each question or incomplete statement is followed by several suggested answers or completions. Select the one that BEST answers the question or completes the statement. *PRINT THE LETTER OF THE CORRECT ANSWER IN THE SPACE AT THE RIGHT.*

Questions 1-10.

DIRECTIONS: In each of the following groups of four sentences, one sentence contains an error in sentence structure, grammar, usage, diction, or punctuation. Indicate the INCORRECT sentence.

1.   A.   The lecture finished, the audience began asking questions.   1.____
      B.   Any man who could accomplish that task the world would regard as a hero.
      C.   Our respect and admiration are mutual.
      D.   George did like his mother told him, despite the importunities of his playmates.

2.   A.   I cannot but help admiring you for your dedication to your job.   2.____
      B.   Because they had insisted upon showing us films of their travels, we have lost many friends whom we once cherished.
      C.   I am constrained to admit that your remarks made me feel bad.
      D.   My brother having been notified of his acceptance by the university of his choice, my father immediately made plans for a vacation.

3.   A.   In no other country is freedom of speech and assembly so jealously guarded.   3.____
      B.   Being a beatnik, he felt that it would be a betrayal of his cause to wear shoes and socks at the same time.
      C.   Riding over the Brooklyn Bridge gave us an opportunity to see the Manhattan skyline.
      D.   In 1961, flaunting SEATO, the North Vietnamese crossed the line of demarcation.

4.   A.   I have enjoyed the study of the Spanish language not only because of its beauty   4.____
and the opportunity it offers to understand the Hispanic culture but also to make use of it in the business associations I have in South America.
      B.   The opinions he expressed were decidedly different from those he had held in his youth.
      C.   Had he actually studied, he certainly would have passed.
      D.   A supervisor should be patient, tactful, and firm.

5.   A.   At this point we were faced with only three alternatives: to push on, to remain   5.____
where we were, or to return to the village.
      B.   We had no choice but to forgive so venial a sin.
      C.   In their new picture, the Warners are flouting tradition.
      D.   Photographs taken revealed that 2.5 square miles had been burned.

6.   A.   He asked whether he might write to his friends.   6.____
       B.   There are many problems which must be solved before we can be assured of world peace.
       C.   Each person with whom I talked expressed his opinion freely.
       D.   Holding on to my saddle with all my strength the horse galloped down the road at a terrifying pace.

7.   A.   After graduating high school, he obtained a position as a runner in Wall Street.   7.____
       B.   Last night, in a radio address, the President urged us to subscribe to the Red Cross.
       C.   In the evening, light spring rain cooled the streets.
       D.   "Un-American" is a word which has been used even by those whose sympathies may well have been pro-Nazi.

8.   A.   It is hard to conceive of their not doing good work.   8.____
       B.   Who won - you or I?
       C.   He having read the speech caused much comment.
       D.   Their finishing the work proves that it can be done.

9.   A.   Our course of study should not be different now than it was five years ago.   9.____
       B.   I cannot deny myself the pleasure of publicly thanking the mayor for his actions.
       C.   The article on "Morale" has appeared in the Times Literary Supplement.
       D.   He died of tuberculosis contracted during service with the Allied Forces.

10.   A.   If it wasn't for a lucky accident, he would still be an office-clerk.   10.____
       B.   It is evident that teachers need help.
       C.   Rolls of postage stamps may be bought at stationery stores.
       D.   Addressing machines are used by firms that publish magazines.

11.   The one of the following sentences which contains NO error in usage is: 11.____

       A.   After the robbers left, the proprietor stood tied in his chair for about two hours before help arrived.
       B.   In the cellar I found the watchmans' hat and coat.
       C.   The persons living in adjacent apartments stated that they had heard no unusual noises.
       D.   Neither a knife or any firearms were found in the room.

12.   The one of the following sentences which contains NO error in usage is: 12.____

       A.   The policeman lay a firm hand on the suspect's shoulder.
       B.   It is true that neither strength nor agility are the most important requirement for a good patrolman.
       C.   Good citizens constantly strive to do more than merely comply the restraints imposed by society.
       D.   Twenty years is considered a severe sentence for a felony.

13.   Select the sentence containing an adverbial objective.   13.____

       A.   Concepts can only acquire content when they are connected, however indirectly, with sensible experience.
       B.   The cloth was several shades too light to match the skirt which she had discarded.

C. The Gargantuan Hall of Commons became a tri-daily horror to Kurt, because two youths discerned that he had a beard and courageously told the world about it.
D. Brooding morbidly over the event, Elsie found herself incapable of engaging in normal activity.

14. Select the sentence containing a verb in the subjunctive mood.   14._____

A. Had he known of the new experiments with penicillin dust for the cure of colds, he might have been tempted to try them in his own office.
B. I should be very much honored by your visit.
C. Though he has one of the highest intelligence quotients in his group, he seems far below the average in actual achievement.
D. Long had I known that he would be the man finally selected for such signal honors.

15. Select the sentence containing one (or more) passive perfect participle(s).   15._____

A. Having been apprised of the consequences of his refusal to answer, the witness finally revealed the source of his information.
B. To have been placed in such an uncomfortable position was perhaps unfair to a journalist of his reputation.
C. When deprived of special immunity he had, of course, no alternative but to speak.
D. Having been obdurate until now, he was reluctant to surrender under this final pressure exerted upon him.

16. Select the sentence containing a predicate nominative.   16._____

A. His dying wish, which he expressed almost with his last breath, was to see that justice was done toward his estranged wife.
B. So long as we continue to elect our officials in truly democratic fashion, we shall have the power to preserve our liberties.
C. We could do nothing, at this juncture, but walk the five miles back to camp.
D. There was the spaniel, wet and cold and miserable, waiting silently at the door.

17. Select the sentence containing exactly TWO adverbs.   17._____

A. The gentlemen advanced with exasperating deliberateness, while his lonely partner waited.
B. If you are well, will you come early?
C. I think you have guessed right, though you were rather slow, I must say.
D. The last hundred years have seen more change than a thousand years of the Roman Empire, than a hundred thousand years of the stone age.

Questions 18-24.

DIRECTIONS: Select the choice describing the error in the sentence.

18. If us seniors do not support school functions, who will?   18._____

A. Unnecessary shift in tense
B. Incomplete sentence
C. Improper case of pronoun
D. Lack of parallelism

19. The principal has issued regulations which, in my opinion, I think are too harsh.   19.____

     A. Incorrect punctuation   B. Faulty sentence structure
     C. Misspelling   D. Redundant expression

20. The freshmens' and sophomores' performances equaled those of the juniors and   20.____
seniors.

     A. Ambiguous reference
     B. Incorrect placement of punctuation
     C. Misspelling of past tense
     D. Incomplete comparison

21. Each of them, Anne and her, is an outstanding pianist; I can't tell you which one is best.   21.____

     A. Lack of agreement
     B. Improper degree of comparison
     C. Incorrect case of pronoun
     D. Run-on sentence

22. She wears clothes that are more expensive than my other friends.   22.____

     A. Misuse of *than*   B. Incorrect relative pronoun
     C. Shift in tense   D. Faulty comparison

23. At the very end of the story it implies that the children's father died tragically.   23.____

     A. Misuse of *implies*   B. Indefinite use of pronoun
     C. Incorrect spelling   D. Incorrect possessive

24. At the end of the game both of us, John and me, couldn't scarcely walk because we were   24.____
so tired.

     A. Incorrect punctuation
     B. Run-on sentence
     C. Incorrect case of pronoun
     D. Double negative

Questions 25-30.

DIRECTIONS: Questions 25 through 30 consist of a sentence lacking certain needed punctuation. Pick as your answer the description of punctuation which will COR-
RECTLY complete the sentence.

25. If you take the time to keep up your daily correspondence you will no doubt be most effi-   25.____
cient.

     A. Comma only after *doubt*
     B. Comma only after *correspondence*
     C. Commas after *correspondence, will,* and *be*
     D. Commas after *if, correspondence,* and *will*

26. Because he did not send the application soon enough he did not receive the up to date copy of the book.   26.____

    A. Commas after *application* and *enough*, and quotation marks before *up* and after *date*
    B. Commas after *application* and *enough*, and hyphens between *to* and *date*
    C. Comma after *enough*, and hyphens between *up* and *to* and between *to* and *date*
    D. Comma after *application*, and quotation marks before *up* and after *date*

27. The coordinator requested from the department the following items a letter each week summarizing progress personal forms and completed applications for tests.   27.____

    A. Commas after *items* and *completed*
    B. Semi-colon after *items* and *progress*, comma after *forms*
    C. Colon after *items*, commas after *progress* and *forms*
    D. Colon after *items*, commas after *forms* and *applications*

28. The supervisor asked Who will attend the conference next month.   28.____

    A. Comma after *asked*, period after *month*
    B. Period after *asked*, question mark after *month*
    C. Comma after *asked*, quotation marks before *Who*, quotation marks after *month*, and question mark after the quotation marks
    D. Comma after *asked*, quotation marks before *Who*, question mark after *month*, and quotation marks after the question mark

29. When the statistics are collected, we will forward the results to you as soon as possible.   29.____

    A. Comma after *you*
    B. Commas after *forward* and *you*
    C. Commas after *collected*, *results*, and *you*
    D. Comma after *collected*

30. The ecology of our environment is concerned with mans pollution of the atmosphere.   30.____

    A. Comma after *ecology*
    B. Apostrophe after *n* and before *s* in *mans*
    C. Commas after *ecology* and *environment*
    D. Apostrophe after *s* in *mans*

KEY (CORRECT ANSWERS)

1.	D	16.	A
2.	A	17.	C
3.	D	18.	C
4.	A	19.	D
5.	B	20.	B
6.	D	21.	B
7.	A	22.	D
8.	C	23.	B
9.	A	24.	D
10.	A	25.	B
11.	C	26.	C
12.	D	27.	C
13.	B	28.	D
14.	A	29.	D
15.	A	30.	B

TEST 3

DIRECTIONS: Each question or incorrect statement is followed by several suggested answers or completions. Select the one that BEST answers the question or completes the statement. *PRINT THE LETTER OF THE CORRECT ANSWER IN THE SPACE AT THE RIGHT.*

Questions 1-6.

DIRECTIONS: From the four choices offered in Questions 1 through 6, select the one which is INCORRECT.

1. A. Before we try to extricate ourselves from this struggle in which we are now engaged in, we must be sure that we are not severing ties of honor and duty.
    B. Besides being an outstanding student, he is also a leader in school government and a trophy-winner in school sports.
    C. If the framers of the Constitution were to return to life for a day, their opinion of our amendments would be interesting.
    D. Since there are three m's in the word, it is frequently misspelled.

    1.____

2. A. It was a college with an excellance beyond question.
    B. The coach will accompany the winners, whomever they may be.
    C. The dean, together with some other faculty members, is planning a conference.
    D. The jury are arguing among themselves.

    2.____

3. A. This box is less nearly square than that one.
    B. Wagner is many persons' choice as the world's greatest composer.
    C. The habits of Copperheads are different from Diamond Backs.
    D. The teacher maintains that the child was insolent.

    3.____

4. A. There was a time when the Far North was unknown territory. Now American soldiers manning radar stations there wave to Boeing jet planes zooming by overhead.
    B. Exodus, the psalms, and Deuteronomy are all books of the Old Testament.
    C. Linda identified her china dishes by marking their bottoms with india ink.
    D. Harry S. Truman, former president of the United States, served as a captain in the American army during World War I.

    4.____

5. A. The sequel of their marriage was a divorce.
    B. We bought our car secondhand.
    C. His whereabouts is unknown.
    D. Jones offered to use his own car, providing the company would pay for gasoline, oil, and repairs.

    5.____

6. A. I read Golding's "Lord of the Flies".
    B. The orator at the civil rights rally thrilled the audience when he said, "I quote Robert Burns's line, 'A man's a man for a' that.'"
    C. The phrase "producer to consumer" is commonly used by market analysts.
    D. The lawyer shouted, "Is not this evidence illegal?"

    6.____

Questions 7-9.

DIRECTIONS: In answering Questions 7 through 9, mark the letter A if faulty because of incorrect grammar, mark the letter B if faulty because of incorrect punctuation, mark the letter C if correct.

7. Mr. Brown our accountant, will audit the accounts next week.   7.____

8. Give the assignment to whomever is able to do it most efficiently.   8.____

9. The supervisor expected either your or I to file these reports.   9.____

Questions 10-14.

DIRECTIONS: In each of the following groups of four sentences, one sentence contains an error in sentence structure, grammar, usage, diction, or punctuation. Indicate the INCORRECT sentence.

10. A. The agent asked, "Did you say, 'Never again?"   10.____
    B. Kindly let me know whether you can visit us on the 17th.
    C. "I cannot accept that!" he exploded. "Please show me something else."
    D. Ed, will you please lend me your grass shears for an hour or so.

11. A. Recalcitrant though he may have been, Alexander was wilfully destructive.   11.____
    B. Everybody should look out for himself.
    C. John is one of those students who usually spends most of his time in the princi-
       pal's office.
    D. She seems to feel that what is theirs is hers.

12. A. Be he ever so much in the wrong, I'll support the man while deploring his actions. 12.____
    B. The schools' lack of interest in consumer education is shortsighted.
    C. I think that Fitzgerald's finest stanza is one which includes the reference to
       youth's "sweet-scented manuscript."
    D. I never would agree to Anderson having full control of the company's policies.

13. A. We had to walk about five miles before finding a gas station.   13.____
    B. The willful sending of a false alarm has, and may, result in homicide.
    C. Please bring that book to me at once!
    D. Neither my sister nor I am interested in bowling.

14. A. He is one of the very few football players who doesn't wear a helmet with a face   14.____
       guard.
    B. But three volunteers appeared at the recruiting office.
    C. Such consideration as you can give us will be appreciated.
    D. When I left them, the group were disagreeing about the proposed legislation.

Question 15.

DIRECTIONS: Question 15 contains two sentences concerning criminal law. The sentences could contain errors in English grammar or usage. A sentence does not contain an error simply because it could be written in a different manner. In answering this question, choose answer
    A.   if only sentence I is correct
    B.   if only sentence II is correct
    C.   if both sentences are correct
    D.   if neither sentence is correct

15.   I.   The use of fire or explosives to destroy tangible property is proscribed by the criminal mischief provisions of the Revised Penal Law.   15.____
    II. The defendant's taking of a taxicab for the immediate purpose of affecting his escape did not constitute grand larceny.

———

KEY (CORRECT ANSWERS)

1.	A		6.	A
2.	B		7.	B
3.	C		8.	A
4.	B		9.	A
5.	D		10.	A

11.	C
12.	D
13.	B
14.	A
15.	A

———

PREPARING WRITTEN MATERIAL

PARAGRAPH REARRANGEMENT
COMMENTARY

The sentences which follow are in scrambled order. You are to rearrange them in proper order and indicate the letter choice containing the correct answer at the space at the right.

Each group of sentences in this section is actually a paragraph presented in scrambled order. Each sentence in the group has a place in that paragraph; no sentence is to be left out. You are to read each group of sentences and decide upon the best order in which to put the sentences so as to form as well-organized paragraph.

The questions in this section measure the ability to solve a problem when all the facts relevant to its solution are not given.

More specifically, certain positions of responsibility and authority require the employee to discover connections between events sometimes, apparently, unrelated. In order to do this, the employee will find it necessary to correctly infer that unspecified events have probably occurred or are likely to occur. This ability becomes especially important when action must be taken on incomplete information.

Accordingly, these questions require competitors to choose among several suggested alternatives, each of which presents a different sequential arrangement of the events. Competitors must choose the MOST logical of the suggested sequences.

In order to do so, they may be required to draw on general knowledge to infer missing concepts or events that are essential to sequencing the given events. Competitors should be careful to infer only what is essential to the sequence. The plausibility of the wrong alternatives will always require the inclusion of unlikely events or of additional chains of events which are NOT essential to sequencing the given events.

It's very important to remember that you are looking for the best of the four possible choices, and that the best choice of all may not even be one of the answers you're given to choose from.

There is no one right way to solve these problems. Many people have found it helpful to first write out the order of the sentences, as they would have arranged them, on their scrap paper before looking at the possible answers. If their optimum answer is there, this can save them some time. If it isn't, this method can still give insight into solving the problem. Others find it most helpful to just go through each of the possible choices, contrasting each as they go along. You should use whatever method feels comfortable, and works, for you.

While most of these types of questions are not that difficult, we've added a higher percentage of the difficult type, just to give you more practice. Usually there are only one or two questions on this section that contain such subtle distinctions that you're unable to answer confidently, and you then may find yourself stuck deciding between two possible choices, neither of which you're sure about.

EXAMINATION SECTION
TEST 1

DIRECTIONS: The sentences listed below are part of a meaningful paragraph, but they are not given in their proper order. You are to decide what would be the BEST order to put sentences to form a well-organized paragraph. Each sentence has a place in the paragraph; there are no extra sentences. *PRINT THE LETTER OF THE CORRECT ANSWER IN THE SPACE AT THE RIGHT.*

Questions 1-3.

DIRECTIONS: Questions 1 through 3 are to be answered on the basis of the following passage.

Almost half of the increase in Chicago came from five neighborhoods, including West Garfield Park. He was 12 years old and had just been recruited into a gang by his older brothers and cousin. A decade later, he sits in Cook County jail, held without bail and awaiting trial on three cases, including felony drug charges and possession of a weapon. Violence in Chicago erupted last year, with the city recording 771 murders—a 58% jump from 2015. They point to a $95 million police-training center in West Garfield Park, public-transit improvements on Chicago's south side and efforts to get major corporations such as Whole Foods and Wal-Mart to invest. Chicago city officials say that they are making strategic investments in ailing neighborhoods. Amarley Coggins remembers the first time he dealt heroin, discreetly approaching a car coming off an interstate highway and into West Garfield park, the neighborhood where he grew up on Chicago's west side.

1.   When organized correctly, the first sentence of the paragraph begins with   1.____
     A. "Amarley Coggins remembers…"   B. "He was 12 years old…"
     C. "They point to a…"   D. "Violence in Chicago…"

2.   After correctly organizing the paragraph, the author wishes to replace a word   2.____
     in the last sentence with its synonym *enterprises*. Which word does the author
     wish to replace?
     A. murders   B. neighborhoods
     C. corporations   D. improvements

3.   If put together correctly, the second to last sentence would end with the words   3.____
     A. "…Chicago's west side."   B. "…in ailing neighborhoods."
     C. "…older brother and cousins."   D. "…and Wal-Mart to invest."

Questions 4-6.

DIRECTIONS: Questions 4 through 6 are to be answered on the basis of the following passage.

Critics argue that driverless vehicles pose too many risks, including cyberattacks, computer malfunctions, relying on algorithms to make ethical decisions, and fewer transportation jobs. Driverless vehicles, also called autonomous vehicles and self-driving vehicles, are vehicles that can operate without human intervention. And algorithms make decisions based on data obtained from sensors and connectivity. Driverless vehicles rely primarily on three technologies: sensors, connectivity, and algorithms. Sensors observe multiple directions simultaneously. Connectivity accesses information on traffic, weather, road hazards, and navigation. Supporters argue that driverless vehicles have many benefits, including fewer traffic accidents and fatalities, more efficient traffic flows, greater mobility for those who cannot drive, and less pollution. Once the realm of science fiction, driverless vehicles could revolutionize automotive travel over the next few decades.

4.   When all of the sentences are organized in correct order, the first sentence starts with
    A.   "Connectivity accesses information..."
    B.   "Critics argue that..."
    C.   "Once the realm of..."
    D.   "Driverless vehicles, also called..."

4._____

5.   If the above paragraph appeared in correct order, which of the following transition words would be MOST appropriate in the beginning of the sentence that starts "Critics argue that..."
    A.   Additionally   B.   To begin,
    C.   In conclusion,   D.   Conversely,

5._____

6.   When the paragraph is properly arranged, it ends with the words
    A.   "...over the next few decades."   B.   "...fewer transportation jobs."
    C.   "...and less pollution."   D.   "...without human intervention"

6._____

Questions 7-10.

DIRECTIONS: Questions 7 through 10 are to be answered on the basis of the following passage.

This method had some success, but also carried fatal risks. Various people across Europe independently developed vaccination as an alternative during the later years of the eighteenth century, but Edward Jenner (1749-1823) popularized the practice. Vaccination has been called a miracle of modern medicine, but it has a long and controversial history stretching back to the ancient world. In 1803 the Royal Jennerian Institute was founded in England, and vaccination programs initially drew enormous public support. In 429 BCE in Greece, the historian Thucydides (c.460-c.395 BCE) noted that survivors of smallpox did not become reinfected in subsequent epidemics. Variolation as a means of preventing severe smallpox infection became an accepted practice in China in the tenth century CE, and its popularity spread across Asia,

Europe, and to the Americas by the seventeenth century. Variolation required either inhalation of smallpox dust, or putting scabs or parts of the smallpox pustules under the skin. Widespread inoculation against smallpox was purported to have been part of Ayurvedic tradition as far back as at least 1000 BCE, when Indian doctors traveled to households before the rainy season each year.

7. When arranged properly, what does "This method" refer to in the sentence   7.____
   that begins "This method had some success..."?
     A. Vaccination   B. Inoculation
     C. Variolation   D. Hybridization

8. When organized correctly, the paragraph's third sentence should begin   8.____
     A. "In 429 BCE in Greece..."   B. "Variolation required..."
     C. "In 1803 the..."   D. "Vaccination has been called..."

9. If put in the correct order, this paragraph should end with the words   9.____
     A. "...under the skin."   B. "...to the ancient world."
     C. "...enormous public support."   D. "...by the seventeenth century."

10. In the second sentence, the author is thinking about using the word   10.____
    immunization instead of which of its synonyms?
      A. Variolation   B. Vaccination   C. Inhalation   D. Inoculation

Questions 11-13.

DIRECTIONS: Questions 11 through 13 are to be answered on the basis of the following
           passage.

Summers are hot—often north of 100 degrees—and because it lies at the far end of a San Diego Gas & Electric transmission line, the town has suffered frequent power outages. Another way is that microgrids can ease the entry of intermittent renewable energy sources, like wind and solar, into the modern grid. Utilities are also interested in microgrids because of the money they can save by deferring the need to build new transmission lines. "If you're on the very end of a utility line, everything that happens, happens 10 times worse for you," says Mike Gravely, team leader for energy systems integration at the California Energy Commission. The town has a lot of senior citizens, who can be frail in the heat. Borrego Springs, California, is a quaint town of about 3,400 people set against the Anza-Borrego Desert about 90 miles east of San Diego. High winds, lightning strikes, forest fires and flash floods can bust up that line and kill the electricity. But today, Borrego Springs has a failsafe against power outages: a microgrid. Resiliency is one of the main reasons the market in microgrids is booming, with installed capacity in the United States projected to be more than double between 2017 and 2022, according to a new report on microgrids from GTM Research. "Without air conditioning," says Linda Haddock, head of the local Chamber of Commerce, "people will die."

11. When the sentences above are organized correctly, the paragraph should   11.____
    start with the sentence that begins
      A. "Borrego Springs, California..."   B. "But today, Borrego Springs..."
      C. "Summers are hot..."   D. "Utilities are also interested..."

12. If the author wanted to split this paragraph into two smaller paragraphs, the   12.____
    first sentence of the second paragraph would start with the words
    A. "High winds, lightning strikes, forest fires…"
    B. "But today, Borrego Springs…"
    C. "Resiliency is one of the main…"
    D. "If you're on the very end…"

13. Assuming the paragraph were organized correctly, the second to last   13.____
    sentence would end
    A. "…to build new transmission lines."
    B. "…be frail in the heat."
    C. "…into the modern grid."
    D. "…east of San Diego."

Questions 14-17.

DIRECTIONS: Questions 14 through 17 are to be answered on the basis of the following
              passage.

Exhaustive search is not typically a successful approach to problem solving because most
interesting problems have search spaces that are simply too large to be dealt with in this
manner, even by the fastest computers. Thus, in order to ignore a portion of a search space,
some guiding knowledge or insight must exist so that the solution will not be overlooked. This
partial understanding is reflected in the fact that a rigid algorithmic solution—a routine and
predetermined number of computational steps—cannot be applied. A large part of the
intelligence of chess players resides in the heuristics they employ. When search is used to
explore the entire solution space, it is said to be exhaustive. Chess is a classic example where
humans routinely employ sophisticated heuristics in a search space. Therefore, if one hopes to
find a solution (or a reasonably good approximation of a solution) to such a problem, one must
selectively explore the problem's search space. Rather, the concept of search is used to solve
such problems. Heuristics is a major area of AI that concerns itself with how to limit effectively
the exploration of a search space. Many problems that humans are confronted with are not fully
understood. The difficulty here is that if part of the search space is not explored, one runs the
risk that the solution one seeks will be missed. A chess player will typically search through a
small number of possible moves before selecting a move to play. Not every possible move and
countermove sequence is explored. Only reasonable sequences are examined.

14. When correctly organized, the paragraph above should begin with the words   14.____
    A. "Many problems that…"
    B. "Therefore, if one hopes to…"
    C. "Only reasonable sequences are…"
    D. "The difficulty here is…"

15. If the paragraph was organized correctly, the fourth sentence would begin   15.____
    with the words
    A. "Chess is a classic…"   B. "Heuristics is a major…"
    C. "Exhaustive search is not…"   D. "The difficulty here is…"

16. If the author wished to separate this paragraph into two equally sized paragraphs, the sentence that begins the second paragraph would END with the words
    A. "…heuristics they employ."
    B. "…in a search space."
    C. "…are not fully employed."
    D. "…will be missed."

16.____

17. When organized correctly, the paragraph would end with the words
    A. "…the heuristics they employ."
    B. "…will not be overlooked."
    C. "…said to be exhaustive."
    D. "…are not fully understood."

17.____

Questions 18-21.

DIRECTIONS: Questions 18 through 21 are to be answered on the basis of the following passage.

Asian-Americans soon found themselves the targets of ridicule and attacks. Prior to the bombing he had tried to enlist in the military but was turned down due to poor health. His case, Korematsu v. The United States, is still considered a blemish on the record of the Supreme Court and has received heightened scrutiny given the indefinite confinement of many prisoners after the terrorist attacks on September 11, 2001. On February 19, 1942, President Franklin D. Roosevelt issued Executive Order 9066, which granted the leaders of the armed forces permission to create Military Areas and authorizing the removal of any and all persons from those areas. Fred Korematsu was a 22-year-old welder when the Japanese bombed Pearl Harbor on December 7, 1941. A Nisei—which means an American citizen born to Japanese parents—he was one of four brothers and grew up working in his parents' plant nursery in Oakland, California. This statement effectively pronounced Japanese-Americans on the West Coast as traitors because even though Executive Order 9066 allowed the military to remove any person from designated areas, only those of Japanese descent were ordered to leave. Before Pearl Harbor, he was employed by a defense contractor in California. At the time of the attack, he was having a picnic with his Italian-American girlfriend. Asian-American Fred Korematsu (1919-2005) is most remembered for challenging the legality of Japanese internment during World War II. It was for this simple reason that he eventually became known as a civil rights leader. American reaction to an attack on United States' soil was both swift and harsh. Awarded the Presidential Medal of Honor, he is considered a leader of the civil rights movement in the United States. Roosevelt justified these actions in the opening paragraph of the order by declaring, "the successful prosecution of the war requires every possible protection against espionage, and against sabotage to national-defense material, national-defenses premises and national-defense utilities." Years later he told the San Francisco Chronicle, "I was just living my life, and that's what I wanted to do."

18. When put together correctly, the above paragraph would begin with the words
    A. "It was for this simple reason…"
    B. "A Nisei—which means…"
    C. "Awarded the Presidential Medal of Honor…"
    D. "Asian-American Fred Korematsu…"

18.____

19. If the author wished to separate this piece into two separate paragraphs, the sentence that would be the BEST way to start the second paragraph would begin with the words 19.____
    A. "Awarded the Presidential Medal of Honor..."
    B. "Fred Korematsu was a..."
    C. "Roosevelt justified these actions..."
    D. "Before Pearl Harbor, he was..."

20. In the sentence that begins "A Nisei—which means...", who does "he" refer to in the paragraph? 20.____
    A. Roosevelt
    B. A sibling of Korematsu
    C. Fred Korematsu
    D. Japanese-Americans on the West Coast

21. If organized correctly, the fourth sentence should begin with the words 21.____
    A. "At the time of the attack..."
    B. "His case, Korematsu v. The United States..."
    C. "Fred Korematsu was a..."
    D. "This statement effectively pronounced..."

22. When put together correctly, the last sentence of the paragraph should end with the words 22.____
    A. "...that's what I wanted to do."   B. "...were ordered to leave."
    C. "...during World War II."   D. "...was both swift and harsh."

Questions 23-25.

DIRECTIONS: Questions 23 through 25 are to be answered on the basis of the following passage.

Over the past two decades, her personal finances have been eroded by illness, divorce, the cost of raising two children, the housing bust, and the economic downturn. "There are more people attending college, more people taking out loans, and more people taking out a higher dollar amount of loans," says Matthew Ward, associate director of media relations at the New York Fed. Anderson, who is 57, told her complicated story at a recent Senate Aging Committee hearing (she's previously appeared on the CBS Evening News). Some 3 percent of U.S. households that are headed by a senior citizen now hold federal student debt, mostly debt they took on to finance their own educations, according to a new report from the Government Accountability Office (GAO), an independent agency. She hasn't been able to afford payments on her loans for nearly eight years. Rosemary Anderson has a master's degree, a good job at the University of California (Santa Cruz), and student loans that she could be paying off until she's 81. Student debt has risen across every age group over the past decade, according to a Federal Reserve Bank of New York analysis of credit report data... "As the baby boomers continue to move into retirement, the number of older Americans with defaulted loans will only continue to increase," the report warned. She first enrolled in college in her thirties.

23. When organized correctly, the first sentence should begin with the words
    A. "She first enrolled..."   B. "Anderson, who is 57..."
    C. "Some 3 percent of..."   D. "Rosemary Anderson has..."

23.____

24. If the author wished to split the paragraph into two paragraphs (not necessarily equal in length), the first sentence of the second paragraph would begin with the words
    A. "Some 3 percent of..."   B. "There are more people..."
    C. "Over the past two decades..." D. "She first enrolled..."

24.____

25. When put in the correct order, the second to last sentence should end with the words
    A. "...an independent agency."   B. "...of credit report data."
    C. "...at the New York Fed."   D. "...in her thirties."

25.____

KEY (CORRECT ANSWERS)

1.	A		11.	A
2.	C		12.	B
3.	B		13.	C
4.	D		14.	A
5.	D		15.	C
6.	B		16.	D
7.	C		17.	A
8.	A		18.	D
9.	C		19.	B
10.	D		20.	C

21.	C
22.	B
23.	D
24.	A
25.	B

TEST 2

DIRECTIONS: The sentences listed below are part of a meaningful paragraph, but they are not given in their proper order. You are to decide what would be the BEST order to put sentences to form a well-organized paragraph. Each sentence has a place in the paragraph; there are no extra sentences. *PRINT THE LETTER OF THE CORRECT ANSWER IN THE SPACE AT THE RIGHT.*

Questions 1-3.

DIRECTIONS: Questions 1 through 3 are to be answered on the basis of the following passage.

According to the World Health Organization (WHO), exposure to ambient (outdoor) air pollution causes 3 million premature deaths around the world each year, largely due to heart and lung diseases. Air pollution also contributes to such environmental threats as smog, acid rain, depletion of the ozone layer, and global climate change. The U.S. Environmental Protection Agency (EPA) sets National Ambient Air Quality Standards (NAAQS) for those four pollutants as well as carbon monoxide (CO) and lead. The EPA also regulates 187 toxic air pollutants, such as asbestos, benzene, dioxin, and mercury. Finally, the EPA places limits on emissions of greenhouse gases like carbon dioxide (CO_2) and methane, which contribute to global climate change. The WHO has established Air Quality Guidelines (ACGs) to identify safe levels of exposure to the emission of four harmful air pollutants worldwide: particulate matter (PM), ozone (O_3), nitrogen dioxide (NO_2), and sulfur dioxide (SO_2). Since EPA criteria define the allowable concentrations of these six substances in ambient air throughout the United States, they are known as criteria air pollutants. Air pollution refers to the release into the air of chemicals and other substances, known as pollutants, that are potentially harmful to human health and the environment.

1.   When organized correctly, the first sentence of this paragraph should begin   1.____
     A. "Air pollution refers…"
     B. "The EPA also regulates..,"
     C. "The WHO has established…"
     D. "According to the…"

2.   When put in the correct order, the fourth sentence should end with the words   2.____
     A. "…to global climate change."
     B. "…as criteria air pollutants."
     C. "…nitrogen dioxide (NO_2), and sulfur dioxide (SO_2)."
     D. "…health and the environment."

3.   If put in the most logical order, the paragraph would end with the words   3.____
     A. "…as criteria air pollutants."
     B. "…to global climate change."
     C. "…benzene, dioxin, and mercury."
     D. "…human health and the environment."

Questions 4-6.

DIRECTIONS: Questions 4 through 6 are to be answered on the basis of the following passage.

Although gentrification has been associated with some positive impacts, such as urban revitalization and lower crime rates, critics charge that it marginalizes racial and ethnic minorities and destroys the character of urban neighborhoods. British sociologist Ruth Glass is credited with coining the term "gentrification" in her 1964 book *London: Aspects of Change*, which described the transformation that occurred when members of the gentry (an elite or privileged social class) took over working-class districts of London. Gentrification is a type of neighborhood change, a broader term that encompasses various physical, demographic, social, and economic processes that affect distinct residential areas. The arrival of wealthier people leads to new economic development and an increase in property values and rent, which often makes housing unaffordable for longtime residents. Gentrification is a transformation process that typically occurs in urban neighborhoods when higher-income people move in and displace lower-income existing residents.

4. When organized in the correct order, the first sentence of the paragraph should begin with the words

    A. "Gentrification is a type of..."   B. "British sociologist Ruth..."
    C. "The arrival of..."   D. "Gentrification is a transformation..."

4.____

5. If put together in the correct order, the second to last sentence in the paragraph would end with the words

    A. "...lower-income existing residents."
    B. "...that affect distinct residential areas."
    C. "...character of urban neighborhoods."
    D. "...working-class districts of London."

5.____

6. If the author wished to change the beginning of the final sentence to "in the end." to better signal the finish of the paragraph, which of the following words would the phrase appear in front of?

    A. British   B. Gentrification
    C. Although   D. The

6.____

Questions 7-11.

DIRECTIONS: Questions 7 through 11 are to be answered on the basis of the following passage.

The primary signs of ADHD include a persistent pattern of inattention or hyperactivity lasting in duration for six months or longer with an onset before 12 years of age. Children with ADHD often experience peer rejection, neglect, or teasing and family interactions may contain high levels of discord and negative interactions (APA, 2013). Two primary types of the disorder include inattentive and hyperactive/impulsive, with a combined type when both inattention and hyperactivity occur together. Inattentive ADHD is evidenced by executive functioning deficits such as being off task, lacking sustained focus, and being disorganized. Hyperactive ADHD is evidenced by excessive talkativeness and fidgeting, with an inability to control impulses that may result in harm. Attention Deficit Hyperactivity Disorder (ADHD) is a commonly diagnosed childhood behavioral disorder affecting millions of children in the U.S. every year (National Institute of Mental Health [NIMH], 2012), with prevalence rates between 5% and 11% of the population. Other research has examined singular traits such as executive function deficits in the school setting, task performance in the school setting (Berk, 1986), driving and awareness of time. However, researching academic aspects of the school experience does not provide a comprehensive understanding of the systemic effects of ADHD in the school environment. Historically, much research on ADHD has focused on the academic impact of behavioral symptoms such as reading and mathematics. These behaviors are inappropriate for the child's age level and symptoms typically interfere with functioning in multiple environments.

7. If the author put the paragraph into a logical order, the first sentence would begin with the words   7.____
     A. "Inattentive ADHD is…"
     B. "Historically, much research…"
     C. "These behaviors are…"
     D. "Attention Deficit Hyperactivity Disorder…"

8. When put in the correct order, what does the author mean by "These behaviors" in the sentence that begins "These behaviors are…"?   8.____
     A. Inattention or hyperactivity   B. Reading and Mathematics
     C. Peer rejection   D. Sustained focus

9. If the author wished to split this paragraph into two paragraphs (not necessarily equal parts), the first sentence of the second paragraph would BEGIN with the words   9.____
     A. "Historically, much research…"
     B. "Other research has examined…"
     C. "Two primary types of…"
     D. "Inattentive ADHD is evidenced…"

10. When put in the correct order, the third sentence in the paragraph would END with the words   10.____
     A. "…an onset before 12 years of age."
     B. "…5% and 11% of the population."
     C. "…such as reading and mathematics."
     D. "…in multiple environments."

11. If the above paragraph was organized correctly, its ending words of the last sentence would be   11.____
     A. "…sustained focus, and being disorganized."
     B. "…an onset before 12 years of age."
     C. "…in the school environment."
     D. "…inattention and hyperactivity occur together."

Questions 12-15.

DIRECTIONS: Questions 12 through 15 are to be answered on the basis of the following
passage.

Health care fraud imposes huge costs on society. In prosecutions of fraud, the DOJ employs
the resources of its own criminal and civil divisions, as well as those of the U.S. Attorneys'
Offices, HHS, and the FBI. The FBI estimates that health care fraud accounts for at least three
and possibly up to ten percent of total health care expenditures, or somewhere between $82
billion and $272 billion each year. Providers are also careful to screen hires for excluded
persons or entities lest they be subject to civil monetary penalties. Several government
agencies are involved in fighting health care fraud. Individual states assist the HHS Office of
the Inspector General ("OIG") and Centers for Medicare & Medicaid Services ("CMS") to initiate
and pursue investigations of Medicare and Medicaid fraud. In addition, the OIG uses its
permissive exclusion authority to exclude individuals and entities convicted of health care
related crimes from federally funded health care services in order to induce providers to help
track fraud through a voluntary disclosure program. $30 to $98 billion dollars of that
(approximately 36%) is fraud against the public health programs Medicare and Medicaid. The
Department of Justice ("DOJ") and the Department of Health and Human Services ("HHS")
enforce federal health care fraud law and regulations.

12.   When put together in a logical order, the second sentence of the paragraph   12.____
would end with the words
    A. "...in fighting health care fraud."
    B. "...$272 billion each year."
    C. "...voluntary disclosure program."
    D. "...to civil monetary penalties."

13.   In order to organize the paragraph correctly, the sentence that begins "In   13.____
addition, the OIG..." should FOLLOW the sentence that begins with the words
    A. "$30 to $98 billion dollars of that..."
    B. "Health care fraud..."
    C. "Individual states assist..."
    D. "In prosecutions of fraud..."

14.   The author wishes to split the paragraph into a smaller introductory paragraph   14.____
followed by a slightly longer body paragraph. Which of the following sentences
would be BEST to start the second paragraph?
    A. "$30 to $98 billion dollars of that (approximately 36%) is fraud against the
        public health care programs Medicare and Medicaid."
    B. "Several government agencies are involved in fighting health care fraud."
    C. "In prosecutions of fraud, the DOJ employs the resources of its own
        criminal and civil divisions, as well as those of the U.S. Attorneys' Offices,
        HHS, and the FBI."
    D. "Health care fraud imposes huge costs on society."

15. If put together correctly, the paragraph should end with the words   15._____
    A. "...Attorneys' Offices, HHS, and the FBI."
    B. "...huge costs on society."
    C. "...fighting health care fraud."
    D. "...of Medicare and Medicaid fraud."

Questions 16-19.

DIRECTIONS: Questions 16 through 19 are to be answered on the basis of the following
             passage.

President Abraham Lincoln advocated for granting amnesty to former Confederates to heal the country after the devastating war. Adams and his fellow Federalist Party members in Congress used the law to jail more than a dozen of his political rivals. In 1977, President Jimmy Carter lifted the restrictions on draft dodgers, granting them unconditional amnesty. The issue of amnesty again arose shortly after the U.S. Civil War (1861-1865). Some U.S. government officials, including Vice President Andrew Johnson, advocating placing severe punishments on the military and civilian leaders of the secessionist Confederate States of America. A century later, the controversial nature of the Vietnam War (1964-1975), combined with the compulsory draft for military service, compelled many young men of eligible age to violate the law to avoid the draft. When Thomas Jefferson, Adams' Vice President and opponent of the Alien and Sedition Acts, won the 1800 presidential election, he declared amnesty for those found to have violated the law. Other young men who were drafted deserted the army and refused to serve. In May 1865, when serving as president following Lincoln's assassination, Johnson issued the Proclamation of Amnesty and Reconstruction, which granted the rights of voting and holding office to most former Confederates. In 1974, President Gerald Ford granted amnesty to deserters and "draft dodgers" on the condition that they swear allegiance to the United States and engage in two years of community service. In 1798, President John Adams signed the Alien and Sedition Acts, a set of four laws that restricted criticism of the federal government.

16. When put in the correct order, the paragraph would begin with the following words.   16._____
    A. "Some U.S. government..."   B. "In May 1865, when..."
    C. "A century later, the..."   D. "In 1798, President..."

17. If put in logical order, what sentence number would the sentence that begins   17._____
    "President Abraham Lincoln..." be?
    A. One   B. Six   C. Five   D. Two

18. The author wants to split this paragraph into three separate paragraphs. The   18._____
    THIRD paragraph should begin with the words
    A. "The issue of amnesty again..."   B. "In 1798, President..."
    C. "In 1977, President Jimmy..."   D. "A century later, the..."

19. When organized in sequential order, the last sentence of the paragraph   19._____
    would end with the words
    A. "...of his political rivals."   B. "...after the devastating war."
    C. "...them unconditional amnesty."   D. "...of the federal government."

Questions 20-22.

DIRECTIONS: Questions 20 through 22 are to be answered on the basis of the following passage.

Throughout history, militias have played an important role in national defense against foreign invaders or oppressors. In the original American colonies, state militias served to keep order and played an important role in the fight for independence from the British during the American Revolutionary War. Since that time, state-level militias have continued to exist in the United States alongside a national standing army, providing additional reserve defense and emergency assistance when needed. Some countries still rely almost entirely on public militias for civil defense. In Switzerland, for example, all able-bodied males must serve as part of the Swiss military or civilian service for several months starting when they turn 20 years old and remain reserve militia for years after. Similarly, in Israel, all non-Arab citizens over the age of 18 are required to serve in the Israel Defense Forces for at least two years; Israel is unique in that it requires military service from female citizens as well as males.

20.   When put into the correct order, the paragraph should begin with the words   20.____
     A. "Throughout history, militias..."   B. "Similarly, in Israel..."
     C. "Some countries still rely..."   D. "Since that time, state-level..."

21.   The fifth sentence of the paragraph should end with the words   21.____
     A. "...against foreign invaders or oppressors."
     B. "...militias for civil defense."
     C. "...reserve militia for years after."
     D. "...citizens as well as males."

22.   The last sentence of the paragraph should end with the words   22.____
     A. "...militias for civil defense."
     B. "...citizens as well as males."
     C. "...against foreign invaders or oppressors."
     D. "...during the American Revolutionary War."

Questions 23-25.

DIRECTIONS: Questions 23 through 25 are to be answered on the basis of the following passage.

Medicines such as herbal and homeopathic remedies differ radically from those typically prescribed by mainstream physicians. These practices derive from different cultural traditions and scientific premises. As of 2012, the Memorial Sloan-Kettering Cancer Center offered hypnosis and tai chi, which is an ancient Chinese exercise, to help eases the pains associated with conventional cancer treatments. Some medical professionals staunchly dismiss a number of alternative techniques and theories as quackery. The concept of alternative medicine encompasses an extremely wide range of therapeutic modalities, from acupuncture to yoga. As of 2012, nearly 40 percent of Americans use some alternative medicines or therapies, according to the National Institutes of Health's National Center for Complementary and Alternative Medicine. Alternative approaches to health, fitness, disease prevention, and treatment are sometimes referred to as holistic health care or natural medicine. These names suggest some of the philosophical foundations shared by traditions such as homeopathy, naturopathy, traditional Chinese medicine and herbal medicine. A University of Pennsylvania study in 2010 found that more than 70 percent of U.S. cancer centers offered information on complementary therapies. Increasingly, health care providers are encouraging patients to combine alternative and conventional (or allopathic) treatments, a practice known as complementary or integrative medicine. In the contemporary United States, the phrase alternative medicine has come to mean virtually any healing or wellness practice not based within the conventional system of medical doctors, nurses, and hospitals. Some of these alternative treatments include acupuncture to alleviate pain and nausea and yoga to help reduce stress and manage pain. Yet taken as a whole, the alternative sector of the health field is enormously popular and rapidly growing. The Health Services Research Journal reported in 2011 that three out of four U.S. health care workers used complementary or alternative medicine practices themselves. Other studies have shown that more medical professionals are recommending that cancer patients seek alternative treatments to deal with the side effects of conventional treatments, such as chemotherapy, radiation, and surgery.

23. When put in the correct order, the first sentence should begin with the words   23.____
    A. "A University of Pennsylvania study…"
    B. "Other studies have shown that…"
    C. "Increasingly, health care providers…"
    D. "In the contemporary United States…"

24. If the author were to split the paragraph into two separate ones, the first   24.____
sentence of the second paragraph should begin with the words
    A. "Alternative approaches to health…"
    B. "The concept of alternative medicine…"
    C. "As of 2012, nearly 40%…"
    D. "These names suggest some…"

25. When put into the correct logical sequence, the paragraph should end with   25.____
the words
    A. "…Complementary and Alternative Medicine."
    B. "…system of medical doctors, nurses, and hospitals."
    C. "…associated with conventional cancer treatments."
    D. "…health care or natural medicine."

KEY (CORRECT ANSWERS)

1.	A		11.	C
2.	C		12.	B
3.	B		13.	C
4.	D		14.	B
5.	B		15.	A
6.	C		16.	D
7.	D		17.	B
8.	A		18.	D
9.	A		19.	C
10.	D		20.	A

21.	C
22.	B
23.	D
24.	A
25.	C

EXAMINATION SECTION
TEST 1

DIRECTIONS: The sentences listed below are part of a meaningful paragraph, but they are not given in their proper order. You are to decide what would be the BEST order to put sentences to form a well-organized paragraph. Each sentence has a place in the paragraph; there are no extra sentences. *PRINT THE LETTER OF THE CORRECT ANSWER IN THE SPACE AT THE RIGHT.*

1.   I.   He came on a winter's eve.
     II. Akira came directly, breaking all tradition.
     III. He pounded on the door while a cold rain beat on the shuttered veranda, so at first Chie thought him only the wind.
     IV. Was that it?
     V.   Had he followed form—had he asked his mother to speak to his father to approach a go-between—would Chie have been more receptive?
     The CORRECT answer is:
        A. II, IV, V, I, III   B. I, III, II, IV, V   C. V, IV, II, III, I   D. III, V, I, II, IV

1.____

2.   I.   We have an understanding.
     II. Either method comes down to the same thing: a matter of parental approval.
     III. If you give your consent, I become Naomi's husband.
     IV. Please don't judge my candidacy by the unseemliness of this proposal.
     V.   I ask directly because the use of a go-between takes much time.
     The CORRECT answer is:
        A. III, IV, II, V, I   B. I, V, II, III, IV   C. I, IV, V, II, III   D. V, III, I, IV, II

2.____

3.   I.   Many relish the opportunity to buy presents because gift-giving offers a powerful means to build stronger bonds with one's closest peers.
     II. Aside from purchasing holiday gifts, most people regularly buy presents for other occasions throughout the year, including weddings, birthdays, anniversaries, graduations, and baby showers.
     III. Last year, Americans spent over $30 billion at retail stores in the month of December alone.
     IV. This frequent experience of gift-giving can engender ambivalent feelings in gift-givers.
     V.   Every day, millions of shoppers hit the stores in full force—both online and on foot—searching frantically for the perfect gift.
     The CORRECT answer is:
        A. II, III, V, I, IV   B. IV, V, I, III, II   C. III, II, V, I, IV   D. V, III, II, IV, I

3.____

4. I.   Why do gift-givers assume that gift price is closely linked to gift-recipients' feelings of appreciation?
    II. Perhaps givers believe that bigger (i.e., more expensive) gifts convey stronger signals of thoughtfulness and consideration.
    III. In this sense, gift-givers may be motivated to spend more money on a gift in order to send a "stronger signal" to their intended recipient.
    IV. According to Camerer (1988) and others, gift-giving represents a symbolic ritual, whereby gift-givers attempt to signal their positive attitudes toward the intended recipient and their willingness to invest resources in a future relationship.
    V.   As for gift-recipients, they may not construe smaller and larger gifts as representing smaller and larger signals of thoughtfulness and consideration.
    The CORRECT answer is:
       A. V, III, II, IV, I   B. I, II, IV, III, V   C. IV, I, III, V, II   D. II, V, I, IV, III

4.____

5. I.   But when the spider is not hungry, the stimulation of its hairs merely causes it to shake the touched limb.
    II. Touching this body hair produces one of two distinct reactions.
    III. The entire body of a tarantula, especially its legs, is thickly clothed with hair.
    IV. Some of it is short and wooly, some long and stiff.
    V.   When the spider is hungry, it responds with an immediate and swift attack.
    The CORRECT answer is:
       A. IV, II, I, III, V   B. V, I, III, IV, II   C. III, IV, II, V, I   D. I, II, IV, III, V

5.____

6. I.   That tough question may be just one question away from an easy one.
    II. They tend to be arranged sequentially: questions on the first paragraph come before questions on the second paragraph.
    III. In summation, it is important not to forget that there is no penalty for guessing.
    IV. Try *all* questions on the passage.
    V.   Remember, the critical reading questions after each passage are not arranged in order of difficulty.
    The CORRECT answer is:
       A. I, III, IV, II, V   B. II, I, V, III, IV   C. III, IV, I, V, II   D. V, II, IV, I, III

6.____

7. I.   This time of year clients come to me with one goal in mind: losing weight.
    II. I usually tell them that their goal should be focused on fat loss instead of weight loss.
    III. Converting and burning fat while maintaining or building muscle is an art, which also happens to be my job.
    IV. What I love about this line of work is that *everyone* benefits from healthy eating and supplemental nutrition.
    V.   This is because most of us have more stored fat than we prefer, but we do not want to lose muscle in addition to the fat.
    The CORRECT answer is:
       A. V, III, I, II, IV   B. I, IV, V, III, IV   C. II, I, III, IV, V   D. II, V, IV, I, II

7.____

8. I.   In Tierra del Fuego, "invasive" describes the beaver perfectly.
    II. What started as a small influx of 50 beavers has since grown to a number over 200,000.
    III. Unlike in North America where the beaver has several natural predators that help to maintain manageable population numbers, Tierra del Fuego has no such luxury.
    IV. An invasive species is a non-indigenous animal, fungus, or plant species introduced to an area that has the potential to inflict harm upon the native ecosystem.
    V.   It was first introduced in 1946 by the Argentine government in an effort to catalyze a fur trading industry in the region.
    The CORRECT answer is:
       A. IV, I, V, II, III   B. I, IV, II, III, V   C. II, V, III, I, IV   D. V, II, IV, III, I

8._____

9. I.   The words ensure that we are all part of something much larger than the here and now.
    II. Literature might be thought of as the creative measure of history.
    III. It seems impossible to disconnect most literary works from their historical context.
    IV. Great writers, poets, and playwrights mold their sense of life and the events of their time into works of art.
    V.   However, the themes that make their work universal and enduring perhaps do transcend time.
    The CORRECT answer is:
       A. I, III, II, V, IV   B. IV, I, V, II, III   C. II, IV, III, V, I   D. III, V, I, IV, II

9._____

10. I.   If you don't already have an exercise routine, try to build up to a good 20- to 45-minute aerobic workout.
    II. When your brain is well oxygenated, it works more efficiently, so you do your work better and faster.
    III. Your routine will help you enormously when you sit down to work on homework or even on the day of a test.
    IV. Twenty minutes of cardiovascular exercise is a great warm-up before you start your homework.
    V.   Exercise does not just help your muscles; it also helps your brain.
    The CORRECT answer is:
       A. I, IV, II, IV, III   B. IV, V, II, I, III   C. V, III, IV, II, I   D. III, IV, I, V, II

10._____

11. I.   Experts often suggest that crime resembles an epidemic, but what kind?
    II. If it travels along major transportation routes, the cause is microbial.
    III. Economics professor Karl Smith has a good rule of thumb for categorizing epidemics: if it is along the lines of communication, he says the cause is information.
    IV. However, if it spreads everywhere all at once, the cause is a molecule.
    V.   If it spreads out like a fan, the cause is an insect.
    The CORRECT answer is:
       A. I, III, II, V, IV   B. II, I, V, IV, III   C. V, III, I, II, IV   D. IV, V, I, III, II

11._____

12. I. A recent study had also suggested a link between childhood lead exposure and juvenile delinquency later on.
     II. These ideas all caused Nevin to look into other sources of lead-based items as well, such as gasoline.
     III. In 1994, Rick Nevin was a consultant working for the U.S Department of Housing and Urban Development on the costs and benefits of removing lead paint from old houses.
     IV. Maybe reducing lead exposure could have an effect on violent crime too?
     V. A growing body of research had linked lead exposure in small children with a whole raft of complications later in life, including lower IQ and behavioral problems.
     The CORRECT answer is:
       A. I, III, V, II, IV   B. IV, I, II, V, III   C. I, III, V, IV, II   D. III, V, I, IV, II

12._____

13. I. Like Lord Byron a century earlier, he had learn to play himself, his own best hero, with superb conviction.
     II. Or maybe he was Tarzan Hemingway, crouching in the African bush with elephant gun at the ready.
     III. He was Hemingway of the rugged outdoor grin and the hairy chest posing beside the lion he had just shot.
     IV. But even without the legend, the chest-beating, wisecracking pose that was later to seem so absurd, his impact upon us was tremendous.
     V. By the time we were old enough to read Hemingway, he had become legendary.
     The CORRECT answer is:
       A. I, V, II, IV, III   B. II, I, III, IV, V   C. IV, II, V, III, I   D. V, I, III, II, IV

13._____

14. I. Why do the electrons that inhabit atoms jump around so strangely, from one bizarrely shaped orbital to another?
     II. And most importantly, why do protons, the bits that give atoms their heft and personality, stick together at all?
     III. Why are some atoms, like sodium, so hyperactive while others, like helium, are so aloof?
     IV. As any good contractor will tell you, a sound structure requires stable materials.
     V. But atoms, the building blocks of everything we know and love—brownies and butterflies and beyond—do not appear to be models of stability.
     The CORRECT answer is:
       A. IV, V, III, I, II   B. V, III, I, II, IV   C. I, IV, II, V, III   D. III, I, IV, II, V

14._____

15. I. Current atomic theory suggests that the strong nuclear force is most likely conveyed by massless particles called "gluons".
     II. According to quantum chromodynamics (QCD), protons and neutrons are composed of smaller particles called quarks, which are held together by the gluons.
     III. As a quantum theory, it conceives of space and time as tiny chunks that occasionally misbehave, rather than smooth predictable quantities.

15._____

IV. If you are hoping that QCD ties up atomic behavior with a tidy little bow, you will be disappointed.

V. This quark-binding force has "residue" that extends beyond protons and neutrons themselves to provide enough force to bind the protons and neutrons together.

The CORRECT answer is:

   A. III, IV, II, V, I   B. II, I, IV, III, V   C. I, II, V, IV, III   D. V, III, I, IV, II

16. I. I have seen him whip a woman, causing the blood to run half an hour at a time.

     II. Mr. Severe, the overseer, used to stand by the door of the quarter, armed with a large hickory stick, ready to whip anyone who was not ready to start at the sound of the horn.

     III. This was in the midst of her crying children, pleading for their mother's release.

     IV. He seemed to take pleasure in manifesting his fiendish barbarity.

     V. Mr. Severe was rightly named: he was a cruel man.

The CORRECT answer is:

   A. I, IV, III, II, I   B. II, V, I, III, IV   C. II, V, III, I, IV   D. IV, III, I, V, II

16.____

17. I. His death was recorded by the slaves as the result of a merciful providence.

     II. His career was cut short.

     III. He died very soon after I went to Colonel Lloyd's; and he died as he lived, uttering bitter curses and horrid oaths.

     IV. Mr. Severe's place was filled by a Mr. Hopkins.

     V. From the rising till the going down of the sun, he was cursing, raving, cutting, and slashing among the slaves in the field.

The CORRECT answer is:

   A. V, II, III, I, IV   B. IV, I, III, II, V   C. III, I, IV, V, II   D. I, II, V, III, IV

17.____

18. I. The primary reef-building organisms are invertebrate animals known as corals.

     II. They are located in warm, shallow, tropical marine waters with enough light to stimulate the growth of reef organisms.

     III. Coral reefs are highly diverse ecosystems, supporting greater numbers of fish species than any other marine ecosystem.

     IV. They belong to the class Anthozoa and are subdivided into stony corals, which have six tentacles.

     V. These corals are small colonial, marine invertebrates.

The CORRECT answer is:

   A. I, IV, V, II, III   B. V, I, III, IV, II   C. III, II, I, V, IV   D. IV, V, II, III, I

18.____

19. I. Jane Goodall, an English ethologist, is famous for her studies of the chimpanzees of the Gombe Stream Reserve in Tanzania.

     II. As a result of her studies, Goodall concluded that chimpanzees are an advanced species closely related to humans.

     III. Ultimately, Goodall's observations led her to write *The Chimpanzee Family Book*, which conveys a new, more humane view of wildlife.

19.____

IV. She is credited with the first recorded observation of chimps eating meat and using and making tools.

V. Her observations have forced scientists to redefine the characteristics once considered as solely human traits.

The CORRECT answer is:

A. V, II, IV, III, I   B. I, IV, II, V, III   C. I, II, V, IV, III   D. III, V, II, I, IV

20. I. Since then, research has demonstrated that the deposition of atmospheric chemicals is causing widespread acidification of lakes, streams, and soil.

II. "Acid rain" is a popularly used phrase that refers to the deposition of acidifying substances from the atmosphere.

III. This phenomenon became a prominent issue around 1970.

IV. Of the many chemicals that are deposited from the atmosphere, the most important in terms of causing acidity in soil and surface waters are dilute solutions of sulfuric and nitric acids.

V. These chemicals are deposited as acidic rain or snow and include sulfur dioxide, oxides of nitrogen, and tiny particulates such as ammonium sulfate.

The CORRECT answer is:

A. III, IV, I, II, V   B. IV, III, I, IV, V   C. V, I, IV, III, II   D. II, III, I, IV, V

20._____

21. I. Programmers wrote algorithmic software that precisely specified both the problem and how to solve it.

II. AI programmers, in contrast, have sought to program computers with flexible rules for seeking solutions to problems.

III. In the 1940 and 1950s, the first large, electronic, digital computers were designed to perform numerical calculations set up by a human programmer.

IV. The computers did so by completing a series of clearly defined steps, or algorithms.

V. An AI program may be designed to modify the rules it is given or to develop entirely new rules.

The CORRECT answer is:

A. I, III, II, V, IV   B. IV, I, III, V, II   C. III, IV, I, II, V   D. III, I, II, IV, V

21._____

22. I. Wildfire is a periodic ecological disturbance, associated with the rapid combustion of much of the biomass of an ecosystem.

II. Wildfires themselves are both routine and ecologically necessary.

III. It is where they encounter human habitation, of course, that dangers quickly escalate,

IV. Once ignited by lightning or by humans, the biomass oxidizes as an uncontrolled blaze.

V. This unfettered burning continues until the fire either runs out of fuel or is quenched.

The CORRECT answer is:

A. V, IV, I, II, III   B. I, II, V, III, IV   C. III, II, I, IV, V   D. IV, V, III, I, II

22._____

23.　I.　His arguments supported the positions advanced by the Democratic Party's southern wing and sharply challenged the constitutionality of the Republican Party's emerging political platform.

　　II.　Beginning in the mid-1840s as a simple freedom suit, the case ended with the Court's intervention in the central political issues of the 1850s and the intensification of the sectional crisis that ultimately led to civil war.

　　III.　During the Civil War, the decision quickly fell into disrepute, and its major rulings were overruled by ratification of the 13th and 14th Amendments.

　　IV.　*Dred Scott v. Sandford* ranks as one of the worst decisions in the Supreme Court's history.

　　V.　Chief Justice Roger Taney, speaking for a deeply divided Court, brought about this turn of events by ruling that no black American—whether free or enslaved—could be a U.S. citizen and that Congress possessed no legitimate authority to prohibit slavery's expansion into the federal territories.

The CORRECT answer is:

　A. II, IV, I, III, V　　B. V, I, III, IV, II　　C. I, V, II, V, III　　D. IV, II, V, I, III

23.____

24.　I.　Considered the last battle between the U.S. Army and American Indians, the Wounded Knee Massacre took place on the morning of 29 December 1890 beside Wounded Knee Creek on South Dakota's Pine Ridge Reservation.

　　II.　This was the culmination of the Ghost Dance religion that had started with a Paiute prophet from Nevada named Wovoka (1856-1932), who was also known as Jack Wilson.

　　III.　During the previous year, U.S. government officials had reduced Sioux lands and cut back rations so severely that the Sioux people were starving.

　　IV.　These conditions encouraged the desperate embrace of the Ghost Dance.

　　V.　This pan-tribal ritual had historical antecedents that go much further back than its actual founder.

The CORRECT answer is:

　A. I, II, III, IV, V　　B. V, IV, II, III, I　　C. IV, III, I, V, II　　D. III, I, V, II, IV

24.____

25.　I.　Their actions, which became known as the Boston Tea Party, set in motion events that led directly to the American Revolution.

　　II.　Urged on by a crowd of cheering townspeople, the disguised Bostonians destroyed 342 chests of tea estimated to be worth between $10,000 an $18,000.

　　III.　The Americans, who numbered around 70, shared a common aim: to destroy the ships' cargo of British East India Company tea.

　　IV.　Many years later, George Hewes, a 31-year-old shoemaker and participant, recalled "We then were ordered by our commander to open the hatches and take out all the chests of tea and throw them overboard. And we immediately proceeded to execute his orders, first cutting and splitting the chests with our tomahawks, so as thoroughly to expose them to the effects of the water.

25.____

V. At nine o'clock on the night of December 16, 1773, a band of Bostonians disguised as Native Americans boarded the British merchant ship Dartmouth and two companion vessels anchored at Griffin's Wharf in Boston harbor.

The CORRECT answer is:

A. V, III, IV, II, I   B. IV, II, III, I, V   C. III, IV, V, II, I   D. V, II, IV, III, I

_____

KEY (CORRECT ANSWERS)

1.	A		11.	A
2.	C		12.	D
3.	D		13.	D
4.	B		14.	A
5.	C		15.	C
6.	D		16.	B
7.	B		17.	A
8.	A		18.	C
9.	C		19.	B
10.	B		20.	D

21.	C
22.	B
23.	D
24.	A
25.	A

_____

TEST 2

DIRECTIONS: The sentences listed below are part of a meaningful paragraph, but they are not given in their proper order. You are to decide what would be the BEST order to put sentences to form a well-organized paragraph. Each sentence has a place in the paragraph; there are no extra sentences. *PRINT THE LETTER OF THE CORRECT ANSWER IN THE SPACE AT THE RIGHT.*

1. I.   Recently, some U.S. cities have added a new category: compost, organic matter such as food scraps and yard debris.
    II. For example, paper may go in one container, glass and aluminum in another, regular garbage in a third.
    III. Like paper or glass recycling, compositing demands a certain amount of effort from the public in order to be successful.
    IV. Over the past generation, people in many parts of the United States have become accustomed to dividing their household waste products into different categories for recycling.
    V.   But the inconveniences of composting are far outweighed by its benefits.
    The CORRECT answer is:
       A. V, II, III, IV, I   B. I, III, IV, V, II   C. IV, II, I, III, V   D. III, I, V, II, IV

1.____

2. I.   It also enhances soil texture, encouraging healthy roots and minimizing the need for chemical fertilizers.
    II. Most people think of banana peels, eggshells, and dead leaves as "waste," but compost is actually a valuable resource with multiple practical uses.
    III. When utilized as a garden fertilizer, compost provides nutrients to soil and improves plant growth while deterring or killing pests and preventing some plant diseases.
    IV. In large quantities, compost can be converted into a natural gas that can be used as fuel for transportation or heating and cooling systems.
    V.   Better than soil at holding moisture, compost minimizes water waste and storm runoff, increases savings on watering costs, and helps reduce erosion on embankments near bodies of water.
    The CORRECT answer is:
       A. II, III, I, V, IV   B. I, IV, V, III, II   C. V, II, IV, I,III   D. III, V, II, IV, I

2.____

3. I.   The street is a sea of red, the traditional Chinese color of luck and happiness.
    II. Buildings are draped with festive, red banners and garlands.
    III. Crowds gather then to celebrate Lunar New Year.
    IV. Lamp posts are strung with crimson paper lanterns, which bob in the crisp winter breeze.
    V.   At the beginning of February, thousands of people line H Street, the heart of Chinatown in Washington, D.C.
    The CORRECT answer is:
       A. I, V, II, III, IV   B. IV, II, V, I, III   C. III, I, II, IV, V   D. V, III, I, II, IV

3.____

4. I.   Experts agree that the lion dance originated in the Han dynasty; however, there is little agreement about the dance's original purpose.
    II. Another theory is that an emperor, upon waking from a dream about a lion, hired an artist to choreograph the dance.
    III. Dancers must be synchronized with the music accompanying the dance, as well as with each other, in order to fully realize the celebration.
    IV. Whatever the origins are, the current function of the dance is celebration.
    V.   Some evidence suggests that the earliest version of the dance was an attempt to ward off an evil spirt.
    The CORRECT answer is:
      A. V, II, IV, III, I   B. I, V, II, IV, III   C. II, I, III, V, IV   D. IV, III, V, I, II

4._____

5. I.   Half the population of New York, Toronto, and London do not own cars; instead they use public transport.
    II. Every day, subway systems carry 155 million passengers, thirty-four times the number carried by all the world's airplanes.
    III. Though there are 600 million cars on the planet, and counting, there are also seven billion people, which means most of us get around taking other modes of transportation.
    IV. All of that is to say that even a century and a half after the invention of the internal combustion engine, private car ownership is still an anomaly.
    V.   In other words, traveling to work, school, or the market means being a straphanger: someone who relies on public transport.
    The CORRECT answer is:
      A. I, II, IV, V, III   B. III, V, I, II, IV   C. III, I, II, IV, V   D. II, IV, V, III, I

5._____

6. I.   "They jumped up like popcorn," he said, describing how they would flap their half-formed wings and take short hops into the air.
    II. Dan settled on the Chukar Partridge as a model species, but he might not have made his discovery without the help of a local rancher that supplied him with the birds.
    III. At field sites around the world, Dan Kiel saw a pattern in how young ground birds ran along behind their parents.
    IV. So when a group of graduate students challenged him to come up with new data on the age-old ground-up-tree-down debate, he designed a project to see what clues might lie in how baby game birds learned to fly.
    V.   When the rancher stopped by to see how things were progressing, he yelled at Dan to give the birds something to climb on.
    The CORRECT answer is:
      A. IV, II, V, I, III   B. III, II, I, V, IV   C. III, I, IV, II, V   D. I, II, IV, V, III

6._____

7. I.   Honey bees are hosts to the pathogenic large ectoparasitic mite, *Varroa destructor*.
    II. These mites feed on bee hemolymph (blood) and can kill bees directly or by increasing their susceptibility to secondary infections.
    III. Little is known about the natural defenses that keep the mite infections under control.

7._____

IV. Pyrethrums are a group of flowering plants that produce potent insecticides with anti-mite activity.

V. In fact, the human mite infestation known as scabies is treated with a topical pyrethrum cream.

The CORRECT answer is:

   A. I, II, III, IV, V   B. V, IV, II, I, III   C. III, IV, V, I, II   D. II, IV, I, III, V

8.   I.   He hardly ever allowed me to pay for the books he placed in my hands, but when he wasn't looking I'd leave the coins I'd managed to collect on the counter.

   II.   My favorite place in the whole city was the Sempere & Sons bookshop on Calle Santa Ana.

   III.   It smelled of old paper and dust and it was my sanctuary, my refuge.

   IV.   The bookseller would let me sit on a chair in a corner and read any book I liked to my heart's content.

   V.   It was only small change—if I'd had to buy a book with that pittance, I would probably have been able to afford only a booklet of cigarette papers.

The CORRECT answer is:

   A. I, III, V, II, IV   B. II, IV, I, III, V   C. V, I, III, IV, II   D. II, III, IV, I, V

8.____

9.   I.   At school, I had learned to read and write long before the other children.

   II.   My father, however, did not see things the way I did; he did not like to see books in the house.

   III.   Where my school friends saw notches of ink on incomprehensible pages, I saw light, streets, and people.

   IV.   Back then my only friends were made of paper and ink.

   V.   Words and the mystery of their hidden science fascinated me, and I saw in them a key with which I could unlock a boundless world.

The CORRECT answer is:

   A. IV, I, III, V, II   B. I, V, III, IV, II   C. II, I, V, III, IV   D. V, IV, II, III, I

9.____

10.   I.   Gary King of Harvard University says that one main reason null results are not published is because there were many ways to produce them by messing up.

   II.   Oddly enough, there is little hard data on how often or why null results are squelched.

   III.   The various errors make the null reports almost impossible to predict, Mr. King believes.

   IV.   In recent years, the debate has spread to social and behavioral science, which help sway public and social policy.

   V.   The question of what to do with null results in research has long been hotly debated among those conducting medical trials.

The CORRECT answer is:

   A. I, III, IV, V, II   B. V, I, II, IV, III   C. III, II, I, V, IV   D. V, IV, II, I, III

10.____

11. I.   In a recent study, Stanford political economist Neil Malholtra and two of his graduate students examined all studies funded by TESS (Time-sharing Experiments for Social Sciences).
     II. Scientists of these experiments cited deeper problems within their studies but also believed many journalists wouldn't be interested in their findings.
     III. TESS allows scientists to order up internet-based surveys of a representative sample of U.S. adults to test a particular hypothesis.
     IV. One scientist went on record as saying, "The reality is that null effects do not tell a clear story."
     V.   Well, Malholtra's team tracked down working papers from most of the experiments that weren't published to find out what had happened to their results.
     The CORRECT answer is:
       A. IV, II, V, III, I   B. I, III, V, II, IV   C. III, V, I, IV, II   D. I, III, IV, II, V

11.____

12. I.   The work also suggests that these ultra-tiny salt wires may already exist in sea spray and large underground salt deposits.
     II. Scientists expect for metals such as gold or lead to stretch out at temperatures well below their melting points, but they never expected this superplasticity in a rigid, crystalline material like salt.
     III. Inflexible old salt becomes a softy in the nanoworld, stretching like taffy to more than twice its length, researchers report.
     IV. The findings may lead to new approaches for making nanowires that could end up in solar cells or electronic circuits.
     V.   According to Nathan Moore of Sandia National Laboratories, these nanowires are special and much more common than we may think.
     The CORRECT answer is:
       A. IV, III, V, II, I   B. I, V, III, IV, II   C. III, IV, I, V, II   D. V, II, III, I, IV

12.____

13. I.   The Venus flytrap (Dionaea muscipula) needs to know when an ideal meal is crawling across its leaves.
     II. The large black hairs on their lobes allow the Venus flytraps to literally feel their prey, and they act as triggers that spring the trap closed.
     III. To be clear, if an insect touches just one hair, the trap will not spring shut; but a large enough bug will likely touch two hairs within twenty seconds which is the signal the Venus flytrap waits for.
     IV. Closing its trap requires a huge expense of energy, and reopening can take several hours.
     V.   When the proper prey makes its way across the trap, the Dionaea launches into action.
     The CORRECT answer is:
       A. IV, I, V, II, III   B. II, V, I, III, IV   C. I, II, V, IV, III   D. I, IV, II, V, III

13.____

14. I. These books usually contain collections of stories, many of which are much older than the books themselves.
    II. Where other early European authors wrote their literary works in Latin, the Irish began writing down their stories in their own language as early as 6th century B.C.E.
    III. Ireland has the oldest vernacular literature in Europe.
    IV. One of the most famous of these collections is the epic cycle, *The Táin Bó Culainge*, which translates to "The Cattle Raid of Cooley."
    V. While much of the earliest Irish writing has been lost or destroyed, several manuscripts survive from the late medieval period.
    The CORRECT answer is:
    A. V, IV, I, II, III   B. III, II, V, I, IV   C. III, I, IV, V, II   D. IV, II, III, I, V

14.____

15. I. Obviously the plot is thin, but it works better as a thematic peace, exploring several great issues that plagued authors and people during that era.
    II. The story begins during a raid when Meb's forces are joined by Frederick and his men.
    III. In the end, many warriors on both sides perish, the prize is lost, and peace is somehow re-established between the opposing sides.
    IV. The middle of the story tells of how Chulu fends off Meb's army by herself while Concho's men struggle against witchcraft.
    V. The prize is defended by the current king, Concho, and the young warrior, Chulu.
    The CORRECT answer is:
    A. II, V, IV, III, I   B. V, I, IV, III, II   C. I, III, V, IV, II   D. III, II, I, V, IV

15.____

16. I. However, sometimes the flowers that are treated with the pesticides are not as vibrant as those that did not receive the treatment.
    II. The first phase featured no pesticides and the second featured a pesticide that varied in doses.
    III. In the cultivation of roses, certain pesticides are often applied when the presence of aphids is detected.
    IV. Recently, researchers conducted two phases of an experiment to study the effects of certain pesticides on rose bushes.
    V. To start, aphids are small plant-eating insects known to feed on rose bushes.
    The CORRECT answer is:
    A. IV, III, II, I, V   B. I, II, V, III, IV   C. V, III, I, IV, II   D. II, V, IV, I, III

16.____

17. I. My passion for it took hold many years ago when I happened to cross paths with a hiker in a national park.
    II. The wilderness has a way of cleansing the spirit.
    III. His excitement was infectious as he quoted various poetic verses pertaining to the wild; I was hooked.
    IV. For some, backpacking is the ultimate vacation.
    V. While it once felt tedious and tiring, backpacking is now an essential part of my summer recreation.
    The CORRECT answer is:
    A. IV, II, V, I, III   B. II, III, I, IV, V   C. I, IV, II, V, III   D. V, I, III, II, IV

17.____

18. I.   When I was preparing for my two-week vacation to southern Africa, I realized that the continent would be like nothing I have ever seen.
     II. I wanted to explore the continent's urban streets as well as the savannah; it's always been my dream to have "off the grid" experiences as well as touristy ones.
     III. The largest gap in understanding came from an unlikely source; it was the way I played with my host family's dog.
     IV. Upon my arrival to Africa, the people I met welcomed me with open arms.
     V.   Aside from the pleasant welcome, it was obvious that our cultural differences were stark, which led to plenty of laughter and confusion.
     The CORRECT answer is:
        A. IV, I, II, III, V   B. III, V, IV, II, I   C. I, IV, II, III, V   D. I, II, IV, V, III

18.____

19. I.   There, I signed up for a full-contact, downhill ice-skating race that looked like a bobsled run.
     II. It wasn't until I took a trip to Montreal that I realized how wrong I was.
     III. As an avid skier and inline skater, I figured I had cornered the market on downhill speeds.
     IV. After avoiding hip and body checks, both of which were perfectly legal, I was able to reach a top speed of forty-five miles per hour!
     V.   It was Carnaval season, the time when people from across the province flock to the city for two weeks of food, drink and winter sports.
     The CORRECT answer is:
        A. II, I, III, IV, V   B. III, II, V, I, IV   C. IV, V, I, III, II   D. I, IV, II, V, III

19.____

20. I.   It is a spell that sets upon one's soul and a sense of euphoria is felt by all who experience it.
     II. Pictures and postcards of the Caribbean do not lie; the water there shines with every shade of aquamarine, from pastel to emerald.
     III. As I imagine these sights, I recall one trip in particular that neatly captures the allure of the Caribbean.
     IV. The ocean hypnotizes with its glassy vastness.
     V.   On that beautiful day, I was incredibly happy to sail with my family and friends.
     The CORRECT answer is:
        A. I, V, IV, III, II   B. V, I, II, IV, III   C. II, IV, I, III, V   D. I, II, IV, III, V

20.____

21. I.   It wasn't until the early 1700s that it began to resemble the masterpiece museum it is today.
     II. The Louvre contains some of the most famous works of art in the history of the world including the *Mona Lisa* and the *Venus de Milo*.
     III. Before it was a world famous museum, The Louvre was a fort built by King Philip sometime around 1200 A.D.
     IV. The Louvre, in Paris, France, is one of the largest museums in the world.
     V.   It has almost 275,000 works of art, which are displayed in over 140 exhibition rooms.
     The CORRECT answer is:
        A. V, I, III, IV, II   B. II, IV, I, V, III   C. V, III, I, IV, II   D. IV, V, II, III, I

21.____

22. I. It danced on the glossy hair and bright eyes of two girls, who sat together hemming ruffles for a white muslin dress.
     II. The September sun was glinting cheerfully into a pretty bedroom furnished with blue.
     III. These girls were Clover and Elsie Carr, and it was Clover's first evening dress for which they were hemming ruffles.
     IV. The half-finished skirt of the dress lay on the bed, and as each crisp ruffle was completed, the girls added it to the snowy heap, which looked like a drift of transparent clouds.
     V. It was nearly two years since a certain visit made by Johnnie to Inches Mills and more than three since Clover and Katy had returned home from the boarding school at Hillsover.
     The CORRECT answer is:
        A. III, V, IV, I, II   B. II, I, IV, III, V   C. V, II, I, IV, III   D. II, IV, III, I, V

22.____

23. I. The "invisible hand" theory is harshly criticized by parties who argue that untampered self-interest is immoral and that charity is the superior vehicle for community improvement.
     II. Standing as a testament to his benevolence, Smith bequeathed much of his wealth to charity.
     III. Second, Smith was not arguing that all self-interest is positive for society; he simply did not agree that it was necessarily bad.
     IV. First, he was not declaring that people should adopt a pattern of overt self-interest, but rather that people already act in such a way.
     V. Some of these people, though, fail to recognize several important aspects of Adam Smith's the Scottish economist who championed this theory, concept.
     The CORRECT answer is:
        A. I, V, IV, III, II   B. III, IV, II, I, V   C. II, III, V, IV, I   D. IV, III, I, V, II

23.____

24. I. Though they rarely are awarded for their many accomplishments, composers and performers continue to innovate and represent a substantial reason for classical music's persistent popularity.
     II. It is often the subject of experimentation on the part of composers and performers.
     III. Even more restrictive is the mainstream definition of "classical," which only includes the music of generations past that has seemingly been pushed aside by such contemporary forms of music as jazz, rock, and rap.
     IV. In spite of its waning limelight, however, classical music occupies an enduring niche in Western culture.
     V. Many people take classical music to be the realm of the symphony orchestra or smaller ensembles of orchestral instruments.
     The CORRECT answer is:
        A. IV, I, III, II, V   B. II, IV, V, I, III   C. V, III, IV, II, I   D. I, V, III, IV, II

24.____

25. I. The Great Pyramid at Giza is arguably one of the most fascinating and
contentious pieces of architecture in the world.
II. Instead of clarifying or expunging older theories about its age, the results of
the study left the researchers mystified.
III. In the 1980s, researchers began focusing on studying the mortar from the
pyramid, hoping it would reveal important clues about the pyramid's age
and construction.
IV. This discovery was controversial because these dates claimed that the
structure was built over 400 years earlier than most archaeologists
originally believed it had been constructed.
V. Carbon dating revealed that the pyramid had been built between 3100 BCE
and 2850 BCE with an average date of 2977 BCE.
The CORRECT answer is:
   A. I, III, II, V, IV   B. II, III, IV, V, I   C. V, I, III, IV, II   D. III, IV, V, I, II

25.____

KEY (CORRECT ANSWERS)

1.	C	11.	B
2.	A	12.	C
3.	D	13.	D
4.	B	14.	B
5.	B	15.	A
6.	C	16.	C
7.	A	17.	A
8.	D	18.	D
9.	A	19.	B
10.	D	20.	C

21.	D
22.	B
23.	A
24.	C
25.	A

GRAPHS, MAPS, SKETCHES

EXAMINATION SECTION
TEST 1

DIRECTIONS: Each question or incomplete statement is followed by several suggested answers or completions. Select the one that BEST answers the question or completes the statement. *PRINT THE LETTER OF THE CORRECT ANSWER IN THE SPACE AT THE RIGHT.*

Questions 1-7.

DIRECTIONS: Questions 1 to 7, inclusive, are based on information contained on Chart A.

1. Puerto Ricans were the LARGEST number of people in   1.____

   A. 1975   B. 1973   C. 1979   D. 1971

2. At some time between 1974 and 1975, two groups had the same number of persons.   2.____
   These two groups were

   A. Puerto Rican and Black
   B. Caucasian and Black
   C. Oriental and Black
   D. Puerto Rican and Caucasian

3. In the same year that the Black population reached its GREATEST peak, the LOWEST   3.____
   number of people residing in Revere were of the following group or groups:

   A. Puerto Rican and Caucasian
   B. Oriental
   C. Puerto Rican
   D. Puerto Rican and Oriental

4. The group which showed the GREATEST increase in population from 1970 to 1979 is   4.____

   A. Puerto Rican
   B. Caucasian
   C. Oriental
   D. not determinable from the graph

5. In 1977, the Black population was higher by APPROXIMATELY 20% over   5.____

   A. 1972   B. 1976   C. 1974   D. 1978

6. The SMALLEST number of people in 1973 were   6.____

   A. Puerto Rican and Black
   B. Oriental and Black
   C. Puerto Rican and Caucasian
   D. Puerto Rican and Oriental

7. The percent increase in population of Puerto Ricans from 1971 to 1978 is *most nearly*   7.____

    A. 34%   B. 18%   C. 62%   D. 80%

CHART A

ETHNIC MAKEUP OF THE POPULATION OF REVERE

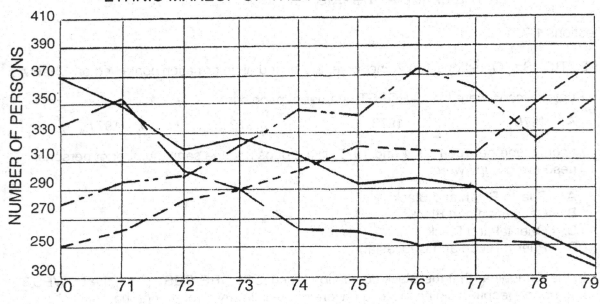

YEAR

PUERTO RICAN
CAUCASIAN
ORIENTAL
BLACK

KEY (CORRECT ANSWERS)

1. C
2. D
3. B
4. A
5. A
6. D
7. A

TEST 2

DIRECTIONS: Each question or incomplete statement is followed by several suggested answers or completions. Select the one that BEST answers the question or completes the statement. *PRINT THE LETTER OF THE CORRECT ANSWER IN THE SPACE AT THE RIGHT.*

Questions 1-2.

DIRECTIONS: Questions 1 and 2 are based on information contained on Chart B.

1. The percent of Black middle students attending overcrowded schools in the period 1967 to 1968 is *most nearly*   1.____

   A. 34.6   B. 37.6   C. 44.0   D. 47.5

2. The percent growth in total school enrollment between 1960-61 and 1967-68 is *most nearly*   2.____

   A. 37.6
   B. 45.7
   C. 35.8
   D. cannot be determined from data given

Summary: School Utilization and Enrollment

PRIMARY SCHOOLS	1960-61		1967-68	
NUMBER OF/ PERCENT				
SCHOOLS / UTILIZATION	20/105		20/102	
ENROLLMENT/CAPACITY	16685/15842		18204/17811	
UTILIZATION: OVER/UNDER	+1942/-1099		+2045/-1654	
	NET +843		NET +391	
	NO.	%	NO.	%
WHITE ENROLLMENT	3645	21.8	3146	17.2
NEGRO ENROLLMENT	12691	76.1	14304	78.5
PUERTO RICAN ENROLLMENT	349	2.1	754	4.1

MIDDLE SCHOOLS	1960-61		1967-68	
NUMBER OF / PERCENT				
SCHOOLS / UTILIZATION	3/101		5/96	
ENROLLMENT/CAPACITY	4869/4808		7502/7811	
UTILIZATION: OVER/UNDER	+235/-174		+276/-585	
	NET +61		NET -309	
	NO.	%	NO.	%
WHITE ENROLLMENT	1478	30.4	1717	22.8
NEGRO ENROLLMENT	3279	67.3	5228	69.6
PUERTO RICAN ENROLLMENT	112	2.3	557	7.4

HIGH SCHOOLS	1960-61		1967-68	
NUMBER OF/ PERCENT				
SCHOOLS / UTILIZATION	2/78		3/107	
ENROLLMENT/CAPACITY	1791/2300		6003/5847	
UTILIZATION: OVER/UNDER	+15/-509		+985/-829	
	NET -509		NET +156	
	NO.	%	NO.	%
WHITE ENROLLMENT	1106	61.8	3266	54.4
NEGRO ENROLLMENT	650	36.3	2561	42.6
PUERTO RICAN ENROLLMENT	35	2.0	176	2.9

Detail: School Utilization and Enrollment 1967-1968

PRIMARY SCHOOLS	CONSTRUCTION DATES AND TYPE*	GRADES	AVERAGE YRS OVER OR UNDER GRADE	SPECIAL PROGRMS	ENROLLMENT TOTAL	WHITE NO	%	NEGRO NO	%	PUERTO RICAN NO	%	CAPACITY TOTAL	AVAIL-SHORT*	% OF UTIL	# OF OTHER UTIL ROOMS
PS 15	1939	K-5	-.1	T,AS	565	2	.3	523	92.5	40	7.0	649	- 104	84.4	18 (NOTE M)
PS 3C	1965	K-5	+1.2	T,AS	1605	854	53.2	748	46.4	3		1099	+906	146.0	6 PORTABLES
PS 35	1931	K-5	+.6	AS	640	345	53.9	259	40.4	36	5.6	702	+ 62	91.1	6 PORTABLES
PS 36	1924,63	K-5	+.7	SS	703	9	1.2	684	97.2	10	1.4	509	-194	138.1	
PS 37	1928	K-5	+.8	MES,AS	615	61	9.9	544	88.4	10	1.6	419	+196	146.7	
PS 40	1912,42,64	K-5	+.8	SS,MES	1038	7	.7	994	93.4	55	5.1	869	-169	121.7	6 (NOTE N)
PS 45	1912,28,63	K-5	+.7	SS	986	7		949	96.2	30	3.0	856	-130	115.1	4 PORTABLES
PS 48	1936	K-5	-1.2	SP	495	10	2.0	482	97.2			632	+137	78.3	1 (NOTE O)
PS 5C	1922	K-5	+.7	SS	772	116	15.0	593	76.8	63	8.1	833	+ 61	92.6	
PS 80	1964	K-5	-.1	T,AS	1052	421	40.0	574	54.5	57	5.4	1197	+145	87.8	
PS 82	1906	K-5	-.1		440	375	85.2	21	4.7	44	10.0	378	- 62	116.4	2 (NOTE P)
PS 95	1915,25	K-5	-.1	SS	1274	489	38.3	647	50.7	138	10.8	1320	+ 46	96.5	
PS 116	1925,64	K-5	-.0	T	914	2	.2	902	98.4	10	1.0	1067	+153	85.6	
PS 118	1923,32	K-5	-1.2	SS	887	28	3.1	832	93.7	27	3.0	1089	+202	81.4	
PS 123	1928,32,64	K-5	-.3		1565	41	2.6	1448	92.5	27	4.8	1103	-462	141.8	12 PORTABLES
PS 134	1928,38	K-5	-.1	T	1067	42	3.9	959	89.8	66	6.1	761	-306	140.2	
PS 136	1928,37	K-5	+.8	T	987	10	1.0	950	96.2	27	2.7	1301	+314	75.8	1 (NOTE Q)
PS 140	1929,38,63	K-5	-.1	SS	1160	44	3.9	1098	94.6	16	1.3	1241	+ 61	93.4	
PS 160	1939	K-5	-.8	SS	1019	11	1.0	1006	98.7	14	1.3	1030	+ 11	98.9	
PS 178	1951	K-5	+1.8		400	268	67.0	91	22.7	41	10.2	738	-338	54.2	
TOTAL PRIMARY SCHOOLS— 20					18204	3146	17.2	14304	78.5	754	4.1	17811	+2045 -1654	102.1	

MIDDLE SCHOOLS															
IS 8	1963	6-8	-.5	SS,PI	1562	325	20.8	1124	71.9	113	7.2	1523	+ 39	102.5	
IS 59	1956	6-8	-.7	P,T,AS	1433	621	38.0	846	51.4	166	10.1	1394	-237	116.9	
IS 72	1964	6-7			1396	210	15.0	1111	83.8	15	1.0	1647	+251	84.7	
JS 142	1930,38	7-8	-1.5	T,AS	1096	21	1.9	1004	91.6	71	6.4	1333	+237	82.2	
JS 192	1963	7-8	-.8	SS	1815	540	29.7	1083	59.6	192	10.5	1912	- 97	94.9	
TOTAL MIDDLE SCHOOLS— 5					7502	1717	22.8	5228	69.6	557	7.4	7811	-309	96.0	

HIGH SCHOOLS															
SPRINGFLD GDNS	1965	9-12	-.3		4277	2758	64.4	1462	34.1	57	1.3	3292	-985	129.9	
JAMAICA VOC	1896-C	9-12	-2.9		644	382	59.3	235	36.4	27	4.1	895	+251	71.9	
W WILSON VOC	1942	9-12	-3.7		1082	126	11.6	864	79.8	92	6.5	1660	+578	65.1	
TOTAL HIGH SCHOOLS— 3					6003	3266	54.4	2561	42.6	176	2.9	5847	+985 -829	102.6	

CODE
T: TRANSITIONAL SCHOOL
AS: AFTER SCHOOL STUDY CENTER
SS: SPECIAL SERVICE SCHOOL
MES: MORE EFFECTIVE SCHOOL
SP: SPECIAL PRIMARY SCHOOL
PI: PILOT INTERMEDIATE SCHOOL

NOTES
1 INCLUDES ENROLLMENT AND CAPACITY AT ANNEX (PS 17O) IN QUEENS PLANNING DISTRICT 8
* EXCEPT AS NOTED ALL SCHOOLS ARE OF FIREPROOF CONSTRUCTION
C NOT FIREPROOF
N NOT AVAILABLE

M IN ROCHDALE VILLAGE
N 4 PORTABLES, 2 IN UNION METHODIST CHURCH
O IN BROOKS MEMORIAL METHODIST CHURCH
P AT 139-35 88TH STREET
Q IN GRACE METHODIST EPISCOPAL CHURCH

KEY (CORRECT ANSWERS)

1. B
2. C

TEST 3

Questions 1-4.

DIRECTIONS: Questions 1 to 4, inclusive, are based on the information contained on Chart C.

1. What percent of all households in 1960 are Puerto Rican households with incomes of $6,000 or more per year?

   A. 38%   B. 57%   C. 6%   D. 0.6%

1._____

2. The median income in all households in 1960 is in the range of

   A. $3,000 - $5,999
   B. $6,000 - $9,999
   C. $10,000 - $14,999
   D. cannot be determined from data given

2._____

3. The total number of white persons living in one or two person households in 1960 is

   A. 13,126   B. 28,884   C. 24,704   D. 46.5

3._____

4. Which of the following statements is MOST likely to be true?

   A. In 1970, the majority of the population in the above data is white.
   B. The majority of households in 1960 have incomes under $6,000.
   C. There are 8668 people in 1960 in households with incomes under $3,000.
   D. The majority of households in 1960 with incomes under $2,000 are white.

4._____

CHART C

Population and Housing Data

Housing Units

	TOTAL	1 ROOM	2 ROOMS	3 ROOMS	4 ROOMS	5 ROOMS	6+ ROOMS
TOTAL HOUSING UNITS – 1960	57611	1484	2492	10491	9074	8409	25661
TOTAL OCCUPIED HOUSING UNITS	56187						
RENTER OCCUPIED – TOTAL	23040						
PUBLIC	1048	–	46	240	553	199	12
PUBLICLY AIDED	–	–	–	–	–	–	–
OWNER OCCUPIED – TOTAL	33147						
PUBLICLY AIDED	–	–	–	–	–	–	–
PUBLIC HOUSING – 1970							
PUBLIC RENTER	1434	44	321	736	300	33	
PUBLICLY AIDED RENTER	65	–	22	26	17	–	
PUBLICLY AIDED OWNER	6075	–	3	2770	2214	568	520

Income 1960

	PERSONS IN HOUSEHOLD						TOTAL NUMBER OF HOUSEHOLDS
	1	2	3	4	5+		
WHITE HOUSEHOLDS							
UNDER $ 2000	1652	1153	276	143	122		3346
$ 2000 – $ 2999	459	717	176	67	58		1477
$ 3000 – $ 5999	1472	3018	1688	1290	944		8412
$ 6000 – $ 9999	501	3520	2649	1936	1900		10564
$10000 – $14999	79	1378	1255	1069	1144		4925
$15000 AND OVER	17	476	535	637	680		2345
NEGRO AND OTHER NON-WHITE HOUSEHOLDS							
UNDER $ 2000	454	664	366	303	444		2291
$ 2000 – $ 2999	237	453	315	192	280		1477
$ 3000 – $ 5999	587	2368	1721	1304	2313		8293
$ 6000 – $ 9999	98	1735	1984	1650	2465		7932
$10000 – $14999	13	370	567	679	1370		3025
$15000 AND OVER	–	23	82	116	435		656
PUERTO RICAN HOUSEHOLDS							
UNDER $ 2000	9	7	7	11	11		45
$ 2000 – $ 2999	4	17	14	14	12		32
$ 3000 – $ 5999	10	42	45	26	71		169
$ 6000 – $ 9999	–	8	5	30	112		219
$10000 – $14999	–	–	–	21	53		87
$15000 AND OVER	–	4	4	3	19		26
ALL HOUSEHOLDS							
UNDER $ 2000	2155	1824	648	457	577		5682
$ 2000 – $ 2999	700	1170	498	273	380		2986
$ 3000 – $ 5999	2069	5463	3454	2620	3328		16874
$ 6000 – $ 9999	599	5297	4660	3616	4477		16657
$10000 – $14999	92	1746	1857	1769	2567		8061
$15000 AND OVER	17	499	621	756	1134		3027

Population Growth

250,000
200,000
150,000
100,000
50,000
0

1950   1960   1970

Ethnic Make-up (in percent)

White ○

Black

Puerto Rican *

Households 1960 (in percent)

% OF ALL HOUSEHOLDS	PERSONS IN HOUSEHOLDS						
	1	2	3	4	5	6+	7
White	56	14	33	21	17	9	7
Black	43	7	23	20	19	13	18
Puerto Rican	1	4	13	17	18	21	27
All Households	100%	12	23	20	17	12	12

KEY (CORRECT ANSWERS)

1. D
2. B
3. C
4. D

TEST 4

DIRECTIONS: Each question or incomplete statement is followed by several suggested answers or completions. Select the one that BEST answers the question or completes the statement. *PRINT THE LETTER OF THE CORRECT ANSWER IN THE SPACE AT THE RIGHT.*

Questions 1-4.

DIRECTIONS: Questions 1 through 4, inclusive, are based on information contained on Chart D.

1. The percentage of households by ethnic make-up in 1960 was *most nearly*

    A. 16% white, 12% Black and other non-white, 16% Puerto Rican, and 56% not reported
    B. 39% white, 26% Black and other non-white, and 35% Puerto Rican
    C. 95% white, 3% Black and 2% Puerto Rican
    D. 99% white, 1% Black and other non-white, and 0% Puerto Rican

1.____

2. In 1960, the predominant age group was in the age range of

    A. 5-15   B. 25-44   C. 45-64   D. 0-15

2.____

3. In 1960, the LARGEST singular and discrete income group consisted of households with the following characteristics:

    A. Black and other non-white households of 3 persons with total earnings of between $6,000 and $9,999
    B. White households with 3 persons with total earnings from under $2,000 to $5,999
    C. White households of 2 persons with total earnings between $6,000 and $9,999
    D. White households with total earnings under $2,000

3.____

4. The percent population increase between 1950 and 1970 was most nearly

    A. 56%   B. 30%   C. 25%   D. 33%

4.____

CHART D

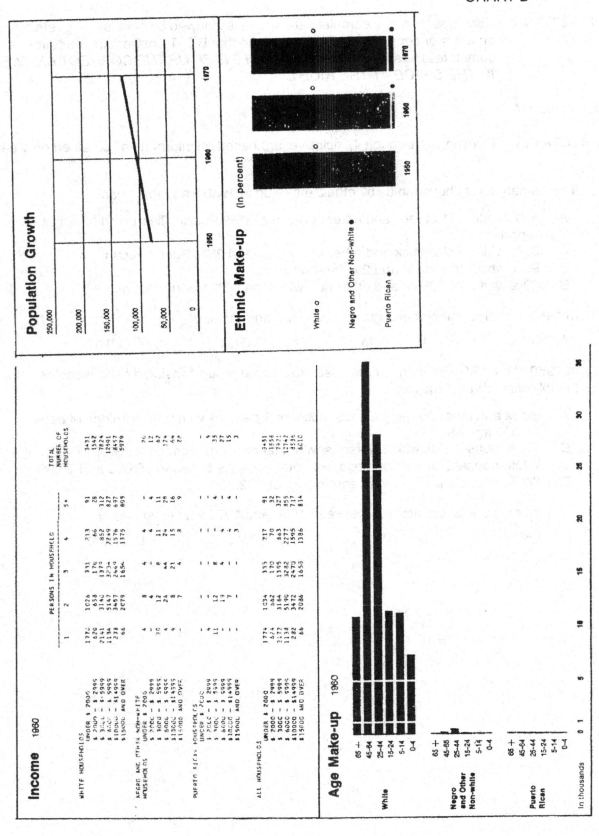

Population Growth

Ethnic Make-up (In percent)

White o

Negro and Other Non-white ●

Puerto Rican *

Income 1960

Age Make-up 1960

KEY (CORRECT ANSWERS)

1. D
2. C
3. C
4. A

TEST 5

DIRECTIONS: Each question or incomplete statement is followed by several suggested answers or completions. Select the one that BEST answers the question or completes the statement. *PRINT THE LETTER OF THE CORRECT ANSWER IN THE SPACE AT THE RIGHT.*

Questions 1-3.

DIRECTIONS: Questions 1 through 3, inclusive, are based on information contained on Zoning Map E. Zoning Map E is drawn to scale. Candidates are to scale off measurements.

1. One-third of Block A (shaded area) has already been developed as a public housing   1._____
   project. It is proposed that a second development be built on the remainder of the site.
   The approximate size of the proposed site, in acres, is *most nearly* (43,650 sq.ft. = 1
   acre)

   A. 5.9   B. 55   C. 1.8   D. 10.3

2. If Site B were developed for housing and 40% of the site was covered by buildings, the   2._____
   amount of open space would be *most nearly* _____ acres.

   A. 2.5   B. 6.3   C. 3.8   D. 2.7

3. A new elementary school will have to be built to accommodate the children from the two   3._____
   proposed projects at A and B.
   If the new school must be within 1/2 mile walk of any point in either project, which
   would be the *most likely* site?

   A. 1   B. 2   C. 3   D. 4

ZONING MAP E

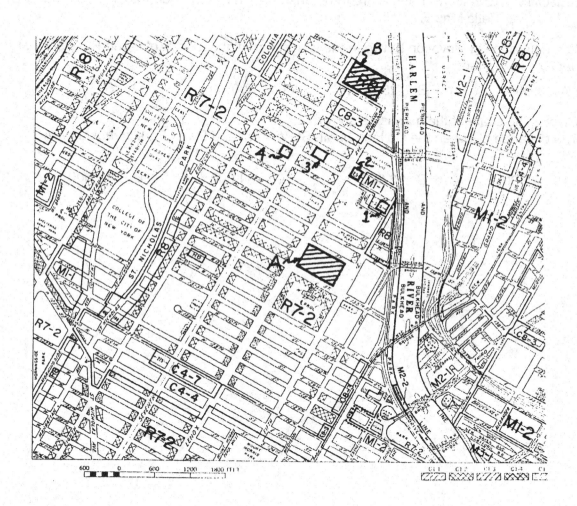

KEY (CORRECT ANSWERS)

1. A
2. C
3. B

TEST 6

Questions 1-2.

DIRECTIONS: Questions 1 and 2 are to be answered in accordance with the Coast and Geodetic Map F.

1. The difference in elevation between the lowest and highest point of Ewen Park is *most nearly* _____ feet.

    A. 100   B. 25   C. 200   D. 50

1.____

2. Given: The scale of the map is as shown.
    The distance between the College of Mt. St. Vincent and Ewen Park is *most nearly* _____ feet.

    A. 2,000   B. 6,000   C. 24,000   D. 12,000

2.____

COAST & GEODETIC MAP F

1000   0   1000   2000   3000   4000   5000   6000   7000 FEET

1   2   0   1 KILOMETER

CONTOUR INTERVAL 10 FEET

KEY (CORRECT ANSWERS)

1. A
2. D

TEST 7

DIRECTIONS: Each question or incomplete statement is followed by several suggested answers or completions. Select the one that BEST answers the question or completes the statement. *PRINT THE LETTER OF THE CORRECT ANSWER IN THE SPACE AT THE RIGHT.*

Questions 1-3.

DIRECTIONS: Questions 1 to 3, inclusive, are based on information contained on Sketch G, a birds-eye view of a proposed development.

NOTE: The attached single family homes in the periphery are one-story high and contain 1,000 square feet. They are square buildings.

1. The dimension A of this single family attached home is *most nearly* _____ feet.   1._____

    A. 20   B. 32   C. 50   D. 100

2. The dimension B of the road is *most nearly* _____ feet.   2._____

    A. 25   B. 48   C. 75   D. 100

3. The dimension C of the courtyard is *most nearly* _____ feet.   3._____

    A. 40   B. 85   C. 57   D. 150

SKETCH G

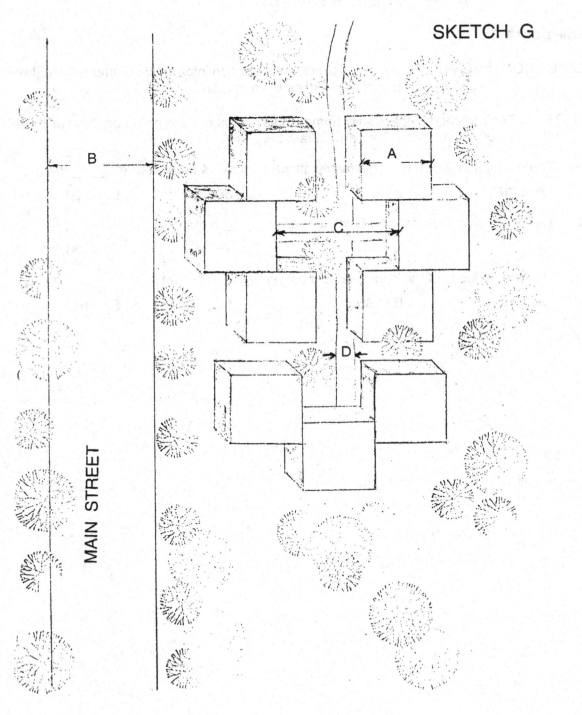

MAIN STREET

KEY (CORRECT ANSWERS)

1. B
2. B
3. C

———

EXAMINATION SECTION
TEST 1

DIRECTIONS: Each question or incomplete statement is followed by several suggested answers or completions. Select the one that BEST answers the question or completes the statement. *PRINT THE LETTER OF THE CORRECT ANSWER IN THE SPACE AT THE RIGHT.*

1. When using the cost depreciation approach, value equals   1.____

    A. the reconciled value of comparables
    B. income divided by the capitalization rate
    C. vacant land value plus depreciated building value
    D. gross income times the standard multiplier

2. Which of the following is CORRECT concerning appraisers?   2.____

    A. An appraiser's license is necessary
    B. They are compensated on a fee basis according to the difficulty of their assignment
    C. They search for market price
    D. All of the above

3. When the question of title arises, the broker should   3.____

    A. be sure to base any statement he makes upon his opinion only
    B. do nothing since brokers have no duty to the prospect because there is no fiduciary relationship
    C. advise the prospect to procure an abstract to be examined by a competent attorney or obtain title insurance
    D. tell the prospect to seek the seller's opinion

4. A broker may have a branch office   4.____

    A. near his main office
    C. in his home
    B. anywhere in the country
    D. all of the above

5. A broker has fiduciary duties because he   5.____

    A. is licensed
    B. adheres to a code of ethics
    C. is responsible to his principal
    D. is bound by contract

6. A broker has a listing for $10,000.00. He obtains an offer of $12,000.00. The broker buys   6.____
the property for $10,000.00 and resells it for $12,000.00.
This is a(n)

    A. conspiracy
    C. illegal commission
    B. overage
    D. lawful practice

7. A salesperson can have an escrow account   7.____

    A. in the normal course of business
    B. only with the approval of his employer

    C.   only with the approval of his employer and the licensing commission
    D.   under no circumstances

8.   Which of the following statements BEST describes the relationship between the broker and his prospect?   8._____

    A.   They are dealing at arm's length.
    B.   The broker must report any facts or rumors concerning the property.
    C.   They are governed by the rule *caveat emptor.*
    D.   The prospect can rely upon material statements.

9.   A salesperson selling his own property   9._____

    A.   must have the broker place the ad and need not state that he is a registered salesperson
    B.   can advertise in his own name and need not state that he is a registered salesperson
    C.   can avoid the rule about advertising in the broker's name and advertise as for sale by owner, indicating that he is a registered salesperson and giving his employer's telephone number
    D.   must have the broker place the ad and give the broker's and salesperson's names

10.   If a broker wishes to obtain a true option, he must   10._____

    A.   pay a definite, valuable consideration
    B.   divest himself of his identity as a broker
    C.   pay a definite valuable consideration and divest himself of his identity as a broker
    D.   do no more than any other purchaser

11.   Which of the following is(are) CORRECT?   11._____
      I.   A contract for sale of a homestead requires two witnesses.
     II.   An individual must file annually for homestead exemption.
The CORRECT answer is:

    A.   I *only*   B.   II *only*
    C.   Both I and II   D.   Neither I nor II

12.   Eminent domain is thought of in connection with   12._____

    A.   courts
    B.   the government
    C.   private enterprise
    D.   death intestate with no heirs

13.   An encumbrance affects   13._____

    A.   existing mortgages   B.   title
    C.   possession   D.   zoning

14.   The secret sale of more than one-half of a business's assets is prevented by the   14._____

    A.   Fictitious Names Act
    B.   State Real Estate License Law
    C.   Division of State Land Sales
    D.   Bulk Sales Act

15. Which of the following are proof of merchantable title?

    A. Abstract and survey
    B. Abstract and title insurance
    C. Title insurance and survey
    D. None of the above

15._____

16. Which of the following is(are) CORRECT?
    A(n)

    I. abstract is an assurance of clear title
    II. title search required for closing always takes place on the day of closing; therefore, the buyer is protected when he receives the deed

The CORRECT answer is:

    A. I *only*   B. II *only*
    C. Both I and II   D. Neither I nor II

16._____

17. The mortgage insurance premium for the insurance on FHA 203(b) loans is

    A. one-half of 1 percent of the remaining principal balance payable monthly
    B. paid with the annual casualty insurance premium
    C. one-half of 1 percent of the monthly payment
    D. paid with the discount at the closing

17._____

18. The PRIMARY concern of any real estate investment should be

    A. tax shelter aspects   B. depreciation deductions
    C. economic soundness   D. location

18._____

19. Which of the following are INCORRECT concerning mortgages?

    A. Signed by the mortgagee
    B. Signed by two witnesses
    C. Signed by the mortgagor
    D. Both A and B

19._____

20. Broker Brown receives three offers on a parcel of property he has listed. Two of the offers were oral.
In order to PROPERLY serve his employer, he must submit

    A. the offers in the order he received them
    B. only the written offer
    C. only those offers accompanied by a binder deposit
    D. all of the offers regardless of form, binder deposit, price, or order in which they were received

20._____

KEY (CORRECT ANSWERS)

1.	C		11.	D
2.	B		12.	B
3.	C		13.	B
4.	D		14.	D
5.	A		15.	D
6.	B		16.	D
7.	D		17.	D
8.	D		18.	C
9.	B		19.	D
10.	C		20.	D

TEST 2

DIRECTIONS: Each question or incomplete statement is followed by several suggested answers or completions. Select the one that BEST answers the question or completes the statement. *PRINT THE LETTER OF THE CORRECT ANSWER IN THE SPACE AT THE RIGHT.*

1. A contract with a promise of performance on one side is called a(n) _____ contract.   1.____

    A. implied   B. bilateral
    C. executed   D. unilateral

2. The passage or amendment of rules by the licensing commission is an exercise of which   2.____
    power?

    A. Executive   B. Quasi-legislative
    C. Ministerial   D. Quasi-judicial

3. Which of the following is probably NOT real estate?   3.____
    A

    A. tree   B. refrigerator
    C. lease   D. fence

4. Prior to acceptance of the offer, the earnest money deposit is under control of the   4.____

    A. broker
    B. seller
    C. broker and buyer-depositor
    D. buyer-depositor

5. A purchaser signs an offer stating that he wishes to offer $65,000 for a home listed for   5.____
    $67,000. His offer is accepted and signed by the offeree. Prior to being notified of the
    acceptance, the purchaser enters into an agreement to purchase another property.
    Which of the following applies?

    A. If the purchaser revokes the $65,000 offer prior to being notified of the acceptance
        of the offer, no breach of contract has occurred.
    B. The purchaser has breached the contract because offers must remain in effect for
        a reasonable length of time.
    C. The purchaser will be found guilty of fraud because this is a direct violation of the
        Statute of Frauds.
    D. Both B and C are correct.

6. If a seller of property did not receive all money due him and did not receive security for   6.____
    that unpaid money, he is eligible for a

    A. lis pendens   B. second mortgage
    C. mechanic's lien   D. vendor's lien

7. Which of the following business organizations can register as a broker?   7.____

    A. Corporation not for profit
    B. Corporation for profit
    C. Corporation sole
    D. Cooperative association

8. Broker A pays $50 for a 90-day option to owner Owen. The agreed-upon price is $100,000. On the 60th day, broker A finds a purchaser for the property at a sales price of $130,000. Broker A exercises his option and sells the property for $130,000. Which of the following applies?   8._____

    A. Broker A is entitled to a $30,000 profit
    B. Broker A has violated his fiduciary duties and is liable
    C. Broker A will have to share his profit
    D. None of the above

9. The right granted by a property owner to another to enter upon that owner's property is known as an   9._____

    A. encumbrance   B. easement
    C. encroachment   D. escheat

10. Real estate salesmen may be employed by   10._____

    A. owners *only*
    B. brokers *only*
    C. broker or owner-employer
    D. none of the above

11. A deed warranting title only against claims of the grantor, his heirs, assigns, executors, or administrators, and others claiming by or through him is called a _____ deed.   11._____

    A. general warranty   B. bargain and sale
    C. quit-claim   D. special warranty

12. Brokers A and B are partners in developing a parcel of land. C, a licensed salesperson, later purchases a share of the partnership. All proceeds from the sale of the developed land are divided according to ownership shares. Which of the following is CORRECT?   12._____

    A. C must be a broker to become a true partner.
    B. The salesperson must be inactive.
    C. No registration with the licensing commission is necessary.
    D. This partnership must register with the licensing commission.

13. In order to reduce the risk inherent in originating high loan-to-value ratio loans, lenders require   13._____

    A. increased interest rates   B. mortgage insurance
    C. discount   D. all of the above

14. Prior to the marriage, real estate owned by a husband or wife is presumed to be   14._____

    A. in a joint estate
    B. in a tenancy in common
    C. in an estate by the entireties
    D. separate property

15. The mortgagor's right to bring himself out of default by paying money owed to the lender is called   15._____

    A. the assumption of mortgage   B. the amortization of mortgage
    C. the equity of redemption   D. strict foreclosure

16. A mentally incompetent person may act as a grantor and deliver title to his own property by signing a _____ deed.

    A. guardian's   B. committee's
    C. quit-claim   D. none of the above

16._____

17. A member of the licensing commission may serve no more than _____ years.

    A. four   B. eight
    C. ten   D. none of the above

17._____

18. A written offer to purchase is submitted to a seller and he, in turn, changes the terms or conditions, initials the changes, signs the instrument, and sends it back to the offeror. In the law of contracts, this is a(n)

    A. offer   B. binding offer
    C. irrevocable offer   D. counteroffer

18._____

19. How many acres are contained in the N 1/2 of the SW 1/4 of the SE 1/4 of the NE 1/4 of Section 9?
    _____ acres.

    A. 10   B. 5   C. 2 1/2   D. 1 1/4

19._____

20. Negative taxable income is known as

    A. capital gain   B. cash flow
    C. debt service   D. tax shelter

20._____

KEY (CORRECT ANSWERS)

1.	D	11.	D
2.	B	12.	C
3.	B	13.	B
4.	D	14.	D
5.	A	15.	C
6.	D	16.	D
7.	B	17.	D
8.	B	18.	D
9.	B	19.	B
10.	C	20.	D

TEST 3

DIRECTIONS: Each question or incomplete statement is followed by several suggested answers or completions. Select the one that BEST answers the question or completes the statement. *PRINT THE LETTER OF THE CORRECT ANSWER IN THE SPACE AT THE RIGHT.*

1. During periods of disintermediation in the primary mortgage market, the mortgage money supply

    A. is unaffected
    B. decreases
    C. increases
    D. either increases or decreases, according to demand

1.____

2. Under the income approach to appraisal, value equals

    A. vacant land value plus depreciated building value
    B. rate times income
    C. rate divided by income
    D. income divided by rate

2.____

3. A and B form a business in which A is totally liable for any debts which are incurred, but B is only liable to the extent of his investment.
This is PROBABLY a

    A. corporation   B. general partnership
    C. joint venture   D. limited partnership

3.____

4. Brokers are permitted to draw leases

    A. in the normal course of their business
    B. if power of attorney is granted to the owner
    C. never
    D. only if the brokers divest

4.____

5. The license of a broker is revoked.
Licenses of salespeople employed by that broker are

    A. revoked   B. suspended
    C. reprimanded   D. canceled

5.____

6. Which of the following may involve the securities laws as well as the real estate laws?

    A. Condominiums
    B. Sales of real estate by transfer of stock of a corporation
    C. Group investment
    D. All of the above

6.____

7. Finders' fees paid to unlicensed individuals

    A. are illegal
    B. are simply poor business practices
    C. should be made to stimulate referrals
    D. are not illegal

7.____

8. Qualifying refers to

    A. lender analyzing borrower and property
    B. salesperson determining a prospect's needs and capabilities
    C. broker checking up on past clients
    D. both A and B

8.____

Questions 9-12.

DIRECTIONS: Questions 9 through 12 are to be answered on the basis of the following passage.

    John is a salesperson working for Ann, the broker. John obtains a written offer and a deposit on a property listed with the office. He deposits the money in his own account, indicating that it is to be held in escrow for the buyer. The seller accepts the offer, and John writes a check to his broker for the deposit. She deposits the check in her business account. The buyer defaults, and Ann divides the escrow deposit with John.

9. What should John have done with the deposit money?

    A. Exactly what he did since the problem is the action taken by Ann, the broker
    B. Left it in his own escrow account
    C. Immediately turned it over to his broker
    D. Held it until the offer was accepted, then turned it over to his broker

9.____

10. What should Ann have done when she received the deposit?

    A. Exactly what she did since the buyer and seller agreed to it
    B. Immediately deposited it in her escrow account
    C. Returned the money to the buyer
    D. Left the money in John's escrow account

10.____

11. Which of the following is(are) CORRECT?
    I. John is guilty of conversion.
    II. Ann is guilty of conversion.

The CORRECT answer is:

    A. I *only*
    C. Both I and II
    B. II *only*
    D. Neither I nor II

11.____

12. Assuming that the money had been handled properly up until the time of default by the buyer, what should Ann do upon the buyer's default?

    A. Return the deposit
    B. Exactly what she did
    C. Divide the money equally with John and the seller
    D. Divide the money with the seller according to their agreement and divide her share with John according to their agreement

12.____

13. A first-degree misdemeanor will be imposed by courts as a result of   13._____

    A. violations of advance fee accounting requirements or false advertising
    B. payment made from the Recovery Fund
    C. any violation of law
    D. B and C are correct

14. Owner A lists 1000 acres with broker B, and specifies the price and terms he will accept.   14._____
B discovers that by selling on the price and terms stated, A will be liable for a large
amount of income tax.
B should

    A. change the listing for the protection of the principal
    B. tell A nothing because he has nothing to do with income tax
    C. follow the instructions of the principal
    D. advise A of this and tell him to seek the advice of an income tax expert

15. Which of the following shares of real property will a widow with no children receive at her   15._____
husband's death in the absence of a will?

    A. One-third   B. All   C. One-half   D. None

16. An estate held by two or more parties in which each has equal or proportionate rights as   16._____
to possession, enjoyment, and the time and duration, having the same or different origin,
is being held as a(n)

    A. estate for years
    B. joint estate
    C. estate by the entireties
    D. tenancy in common

17. A seller agrees to deliver to a buyer a perfect record title. Examination of the abstract by   17._____
a competent attorney reveals breaks in the chain of title.
The seller would then do which of the following?

    A. Buy title insurance for the buyer
    B. File a suit to quiet title
    C. Get an affidavit from the Clerk of the Circuit Court attesting to his knowledge and
       belief that the seller's title is good
    D. Transfer title by quit-claim deed

18. A broker-salesperson employed by more than one owner should   18._____

    A. apply for a multiple license
    B. apply for a group license
    C. broker-salesperson may not be employed by an owner
    D. none of the above

19. If all rights under a lease are subrogated, the result is   19._____

    A. a sublease   B. an assignment
    C. a violation of law   D. either A or B

20. A broker may collect a commission when he has negotiated a sale of property with the   20.____
knowledge and consent of the owner even though no previous express listing was given
the broker on the basis that he had a(n)

    A. open listing
    B. true option
    C. implied listing
    D. option which should be treated as a listing

KEY (CORRECT ANSWERS)

1.	B		11.	C
2.	D		12.	D
3.	D		13.	A
4.	C		14.	D
5.	D		15.	B
6.	D		16.	D
7.	A		17.	B
8.	D		18.	D
9.	C		19.	B
10.	B		20.	C

TEST 4

DIRECTIONS: Each question or incomplete statement is followed by several suggested answers or completions. Select the one that BEST answers the question or completes the statement. *PRINT THE LETTER OF THE CORRECT ANSWER IN THE SPACE AT THE RIGHT.*

1. If a grantor in a deed is insolvent, a quit-claim deed is as desirable as a _____ deed.   1._____

   A. bargain and sale   B. special warranty
   C. general warranty   D. all of the above

2. What is the government survey method description of the property shown at the right?   2._____

   A. NE 1/4 of the NE 1/4 of the SW 1/4 of Section 8
   B. NW 1/4 of the NW 1/4 of the SW 1/4 of Section 8
   C. N 1/2 of the NE 1/4 of the SE 1/4 of Section 8
   D. SW 1/4 of the NE 1/4 of the NE 1/4 of Section 8

   Section B

3. A violation of law may result in   3._____

   A. imprisonment   B. injunction
   C. suspension   D. all of the above

4. The mortgage lien remains in effect until   4._____

   A. the note is paid in full
   B. defeasance clause is satisfied
   C. a satisfaction is signed and recorded
   D. all of the above

5. An exclusive listing   5._____

   A. guarantees the listing broker a commission if the property is sold through another broker
   B. must be in writing
   C. is given to only one broker
   D. all of the above

6. A broker sells a prospective tenant a rental list for $100. The prospective tenant inspected all the properties and found them to be occupied.   6._____
   The tenant then demanded a full refund; what action should the broker take?

   A. Refund $100   B. Refund $25
   C. Refund $75   D. No refund should be made

7. A license is   7._____

   A. prima facie evidence of licensure
   B. issued for a period not to exceed two years
   C. proof of residency
   D. both A and B

8. B wants a motel site, and salesperson A showed him a good location which was zoned for a motel. A then went on vacation. Upon A's return, B purchased the site with A's assistance. A did not know that while he was on vacation the zoning had been changed, and B was subsequently denied a building permit for his motel.
Which applies?

    A. A is guilty of nothing as there was no intent.
    B. A is guilty of negligence and may be disciplined.
    C. A and his broker are both guilty of fraud and may be disciplined.
    D. A is guilty of culpable negligence and subject to discipline.

8.____

9. When a broker represents two parties in a transaction,

    A. he must have the consent of both parties in order to collect a dual commission
    B. he must disclose his agency to both parties
    C. he may not represent two parties with adverse interests in a transaction
    D. both A and B are correct

9.____

10. When the license period is about to expire, the licensee should apply for a renewal. The effective date for that renewal will be the date

    A. the licensee makes the proper application to the department
    B. the department receives the application in proper form with proper fee attached
    C. following the expiration date of the original license
    D. the licensee receives the license

10.____

11. When a dispute arises concerning the disposition of escrowed funds and the broker is the escrow agent, the broker's FIRST action should be to

    A. ask the licensing commission for an Escrow Disbursement Order
    B. give the deposit to the seller
    C. collect his portion of the deposit as damages
    D. notify the licensing commission

11.____

12. Which of the following is(are) CORRECT?
    I. All officers and directors of real estate corporations must be brokers
    II. All partners in a real estate partnership must be brokers
The CORRECT answer is:

    A. I *only*   B. II *only*
    C. Both I and II   D. Neither I nor II

12.____

13. Paul, a service station owner, has been appointed by a court to appraise another service station. Paul has no real estate license.
Which of the following applies?

    A. He may apply to the licensing commission for a special exception.
    B. He may appraise the property only if he is knowledgeable as to its value.
    C. He must appraise the property while under the supervision of a licensed real estate broker.
    D. He may be compensated for appraising the property.

13.____

14. Using borrowed money to finance the purchase of real estate is known as   14.____

    A. larceny   B. conversion
    C. leverage   D. commingling

15. A licensee who appeals a decision by the real estate commission regarding a disciplin-   15.____
ary decision may have his license privileges restored by

    A. injunction   B. warrant
    C. the hearing officer   D. writ of mandamus

16. Concerning the collection of advance fees, the broker should place   16.____

    A. 75 percent in escrow to be used for the benefit of the principal
    B. 100 percent in escrow
    C. 25 percent in escrow to be used for the benefit of the principal
    D. 100 percent in escrow to be used for the benefit of the principal

17. In order for a salesperson to become a successful broker applicant, he must   17.____

    A. work for one active broker for one year as an active salesperson
    B. complete the required educational course for broker
    C. work for one active broker or an owner-employer for one year as an active sales-
person
    D. both A and B are correct

18. Which of the following is(are) CORRECT?   18.____
      I. If the first mortgage is paid off and satisfied, the second mortgage becomes
the first.
     II. Both husband and wife must execute a satisfaction of mortgage when the
mortgage is held in the husband's name only.
The CORRECT answer is:

    A. I *only*   B. II *only*
    C. Both I and II   D. Neither I nor II

19. Broker Alice and broker Bob formed a partnership to provide real estate services for oth-   19.____
ers. Broker Alice converts funds and has her license suspended.
Which applies?

    A. Listings held by the partnership have been terminated
    B. The partnership license has been canceled
    C. Salespeople working for the partnership should obtain a reissue of their license
under a new employer if they desire to continue operating
    D. All of the above

20. A real estate salesperson wishes to incorporate to buy, develop, and sell real estate.   20.____
Which of the following BEST applies?

    A. He must obtain a broker's license.
    B. He must register the corporation with the real estate commission.
    C. No license is necessary.
    D. Both A and B are correct.

KEY (CORRECT ANSWERS)

1.	D		11.	D
2.	A		12.	D
3.	D		13.	D
4.	C		14.	C
5.	C		15.	D
6.	A		16.	A
7.	D		17.	B
8.	D		18.	A
9.	C		19.	D
10.	C		20.	C

———

EXAMINATION SECTION
TEST 1

DIRECTIONS: Each question or incomplete statement is followed by several suggested answers or completions. Select the one that *BEST* answers the question or completes the statement. *PRINT THE LETTER OF THE CORRECT ANSWER IN THE SPACE AT THE RIGHT.*

1. It has been stated that in renting there is no substitute for accompanying a prospect to the space you are trying to rent. Of the following, the MOST important reason for this is that   1.____

    A. prospects are not likely to be willing to inspect space unless they are accompanied
    B. prospects are likely to see the least attractive points of the available space unless skillfully diverted from them
    C. the real estate manager is able to exhibit the good points of the space
    D. the presence of the real estate manager alerts the staff to the necessity for making a good impression

2. As real estate manager, you have commercial space for rent which contains a certain defect which is known to you. In showing the space to a prospective tenant it would be *ADVISABLE tor* you to   2.____

    A. attempt to ignore the defect and disparage its importance if it is mentioned by the prospect
    B. explain the defect in advance of showing the space to the prospect
    C. ignore the defect and immediately change the subject if it is mentioned by the prospect
    D. show the space at a time when the defect may not be apparent

3. The owner of a building containing commercial space has informed his renting agent of the rent he expects to receive for this commercial space. When shown the space and told of the rent, a prospective tenant, of good reputation, agrees immediately and without argument to rent the space. It would be *BEST* for the renting agent to   3.____

    A. indicate that he has made an error and ask for a somewhat higher rent which the prospect may be willing to pay
    B. make immediate arrangements to close the deal on the basis of the rent already discussed
    C. set conditions of leasing, other than rent, which are disadvantageous to the prospect, indicating that these conditions may be withdrawn if a higher rent is agreed upon
    D. make no binding commitment until he has an opportunity to look for other prospective tenants who might be willing to pay a higher rental

4. Assume that approximately 7% of the commercial rental space in a neighborhood is vacant and that this and other rental conditions are the same now as they were when certain commercial space, for which you are managing agent, was last rented. The lease is about to expire on the commercial space. Faced with the problem of renting the space to a new tenant or renewing the occupancy of the present tenant, it is *USUALLY* true that   4.____

A. new tenants are willing to pay higher rents than old tenants
B. new tenants make fewer demands than old tenants if the real estate agent is of good reputation
C. old tenants make fewer demands than new tenants if the real estate agent has properly handled their requests while under the old lease
D. it is more desirable to get a new tenant than retain an old one

5. The one of the following factors to which you should give *LEAST* consideration in determining the rental value of office space in a building under your management is   5.____

    A. accessibility of the building to means of transportation
    B. height of the ceilings in the office space
    C. prestige value of tenancy in the building
    D. rental value of office space in other buildings in the neighborhood

6. The *LEAST* accurate of the following statements concerning the determination of the rental value of office space within an office building is: 6.____

    A. Space along the side of the building is less valuable than space on a comer.
    B. The better the view from windows in the space, the more valuable is the space.
    C. Above the eighth floor, the higher the floor, the less valuable the space.
    D. The more accessible space is to the toilet facilities (of modern design), the more valuable it is.

7. One of the factors to be considered in renting apartments is the likelihood that the prospective tenant may later wish to renew his lease. In a building in a stable neighborhood, the one of the following types of families which a real estate manager should *LEAST* expect to want to remain after the expiration of the lease is a   7.____

    A. single person, age about 67 years
    B. young couple, age about 25 years
    C. couple, age about 40 years, with two children, age 7 and 9 years
    D. couple, age about 45 years, with four children age 7, 8, 9 and 12 years

8. Assume that a great deal of building is going on in a neighborhood where there is much unimproved land in order to take care of an increasing population. It is to be expected that real estate values in this neighborhood are   8.____

    A. decreasing
    B. increasing
    C. increasing for existing buildings while decreasing for unimproved land
    D. remaining relatively constant

9. In a neighborhood where there is a trend toward increasing population due to conversions of private dwellings into rooming houses, the value of neighborhood real estate will generally be   9.____

    A. decreasing
    B. increasing
    C. increasing for unimproved land but decreasing for land having residential buildings
    D. unaffected

10. An apartment consists of the following: a living room 12 ft. X 14 ft.; a bedroom 8 ft. X 8 ft.; a bathroom 6 ft. X 6 ft.; a bedroom 11 ft. X 12 ft.; a kitchen 6 ft. X 10 ft., at one end of which is a dining area 6 ft. X 6 ft. separated from the kitchen by room dividers in the form of 5 ft. high cabinets; a hallway 4 ft. X 15 ft.; two closets 2 1/2 ft. X 5 ft.; and a closet 4 ft. X 7 ft. The only windows in the apartment are in the bedrooms, living room, kitchen, and bathroom. According to the system of calculation generally used, the number of rooms in this apartment is   10._____

    A. 3 1/2   B. 4 1/2   C. 4 3/4   D. 5 1/4

11. The one of the following statements which is *NOT* a valid reason for demanding a security deposit of a month's rent as part of the lease agreement is: 11._____

    A. Ability to pay a security deposit as well as the first month's rent before taking occupancy tends to indicate that a tenant is solvent.
    B. Current expenses of the building may in part be defrayed by security deposits.
    C. If a tenant moves before the expiration of his lease, the security deposit reduces the loss due to vacancy that is likely to occur.
    D. Loss of income will be minimized in the event that action to evict a tenant for non-payment of rent becomes necessary.

12. At the expiration of a lease on commercial space where the tenant has installed sinks and toilets, it is the *USUAL* practice that ownership of these fixtures   12._____

    A. passes to the landlord
    B. passes to the landlord, with the tenant retaining the right of purchase at a price equal to the original cost less depreciation
    C. remains with the tenant
    D. remains with the tenant, unless otherwise specified in the lease

13. The term "percentage lease," when used in connection with leasing of a store, refers *USUALLY* to an agreement   13._____

    A. to assume the remaining portion of an existing lease and at its termination to renew the lease at an agreed percentage increase
    B. to lease a percentage portion of previously undivided premises and to erect suitable partitions
    C. to pay a fixed rent plus a percentage of the tenant's gross receipts above an agreed amount
    D. among several lessees of one premises, each to assume responsibility for a percentage portion of an undivided premises and a percentage portion of the lease

14. The term "title insurance" refers to insurance that protects a   14._____

    A. prospective purchaser with a preliminary purchase agreement against refusal of the owner to convey title of the property
    B. purchaser against any outstanding taxes or liens against the property prior to the transfer of title
    C. purchaser against damage to property between the time of the agreement to purchase and the final transfer of title
    D. purchaser against the discovery of a defect in the seller's title to the property

15. Where a store or commercial establishment which uses water is situated in a residential building, the *MAJORITY* of commercial lease agreements provide that

    A. a fixed amount be paid with the rent to the landlord to cover water use
    B. a fixed percentage of the water charge for the building be paid by the commercial tenant
    C. water charges be paid by the landlord
    D. water charges, dependent upon water use, be paid separately by the commercial tenant

15.____

16. The *LEAST* amount of time that it will take to have a tenant removed from an apartment for non-payment of rent, from the date that the owner decides to evict the tenant, who is already more than one month delinquent in the payment of his rent, is *GENERALLY*

    A. less than 7 days   B. between 13 and 19 days
    C. between 17 and 30 days   D. not less than 10 months

16.____

17. The one of the following which is *NOT* provided for by Workmen's Compensation Insurance is payment

    A. for hospitalization of the injured employee
    B. for medicines and crutches or other implements that may be necessary to restore the employee's health
    C. when an injury is due to the employee's being under the influence of alcohol
    D. when an injury is due to the employee's own negligence

17.____

18. Public liability insurance *GENERALLY* protects the insured, landlord when

    A. a tenant's property is damaged by water used to put out a fire in another tenant's apartment
    B. a visitor to one of the tenants is injured by falling over a worn and broken step at the entrance to the building
    C. an employee is injured while performing his assigned duties
    D. damage to the building has been caused by an airplane crash

18.____

19. Assuming that sufficient fire insurance is carried, the *MOST* important factor considered by fire insurance companies in making a settlement after a fire has destroyed a building is the _____ of the building.

    A. assessed valuation   B. most recent sale price
    C. original construction cost   D. replacement cost

19.____

20. In purchasing fire insurance in your State, it should be realized that

    A. all members of the Board of Fire Underwriters will charge the same rates, while non-member companies may have different rates
    B. insurance companies incorporated in your State all charge the rates which are fixed by law, while out-of-state companies are free to charge any rates that they deem appropriate
    C. insurance rates are determined by bargaining between the insurance broker and the prospective customer as in any free market
    D. no rate agreements exist, each insurance company individually determining its own rates based upon such factors as past experience, profit margins, and competitive position

20.____

21. The owner of a building in a city of over one million population proposes to carry one percent co-insurance to protect himself against loss by fire. It would generally be *BEST* for a real estate agent to recommend that

    A. a greater amount of insurance be purchased if the replacement cost of the building is greater than the original construction cost
    B. a lesser amount be purchased because total loss of a building in this city by fire is unlikely
    C. a lesser amount be purchased since insurance companies will not sell insurance for the full value of a building
    D. the insurance be purchased if the owner has the funds available to pay the premiums

    21.____

22. From the point of view of good real estate management, a tenant should *FIRST be* told of the necessity to pay his rent on time

    A. when he makes application for a lease
    B. whenever he is more than one week delinquent in the payment of his rent
    C. whenever he is more than three days delinquent in the payment of his rent
    D. within the first month after the lease becomes operative

    22.____

23. If a tenant refuses to pay his rent until the real estate manager has had an inexpensive but necessary repair made, it would be *BEST* for the real estate manager to

    A. refuse even to consider the repair until the rent is paid
    B. explain to the tenant that he has an obligation to pay rent but agree to investigate the need for the repair, insisting that rent be paid after the investigation is completed
    C. have the repair made and then insist on the payment of rent
    D. insist that the rent be paid, refusing to couple consideration of the need for the repair with the payment of rent

    23.____

24. Examination of the public hallways of a building containing tile floors reveals that a blackened and dirty area exists along the base of the walls, extending up the walls for a couple of inches. The *MOST* likely of the following explanations for this condition is that

    A. children have been scuffing their feet along the walls
    B. it is a normal development caused by the traffic of dirty feet in the halls, elimination of the dirty area being impractical because of the expense
    C. the floors have been cleaned with a mop which was not sufficiently clean
    D. there is a structural fault in the flooring or walls requiring immediate attention from an expert

    24.____

25. The charge for water supplied by cities of over one million population to an apartment house with no commercial tenants is *GENERALLY* made on the basis of

    A. assessed valuation of the building
    B. frontage and number of apartments
    C. frontage, number of stories, and number and type of water outlets
    D. water meter readings

    25.____

KEY (CORRECT ANSWERS)

1.	C	11.	B
2.	B	12.	A
3.	B	13.	C
4.	C	14.	D
5.	B	15.	D
6.	C	16.	B
7.	B	17.	C
8.	B	18.	B
9.	A	19.	D
10.	B	20.	A

21.	B
22.	A
23.	D
24.	C
25.	C

TEST 2

DIRECTIONS: Each question or incomplete statement is followed by several suggested answers or completions. Select the one that *BEST* answers the question or completes the statement. *PRINT THE LETTER OF THE CORRECT ANSWER IN THE SPACE AT THE RIGHT.*

1. The term *HATCH DOOR* is generally used to describe a door   1.____

    A. between the outdoors and the basement
    B. giving access from the boiler room to the fire tubes of a boiler
    C. giving access to the roof from the top of the stairway
    D. giving entrance from the hallway to the elevator shaft

2. A *PARAPET* is   2.____

    A. a device through which a fine spray of oil enters the firebox of an oil burner
    B. a hot water drain used mornings to bleed off cold water which has accumulated overnight
    C. a protective low wall at the edge of a roof
    D. the primary support of an arch

3. *2-4-D is* used to designate   3.____

    A. an oil moisture used to start an oil burner in operation
    B. a size of threaded pipe of the type used to carry waste water
    C. a type of weed killer for use on lawns
    D. a type of pre-mixed cement for patching walks

4. A *CONDENSER* is a part of a   4.____

    A. boiler where the oil is preheated
    B. fertilizer spreader where concentrated fertilizer is mixed with water
    C. radiator where the return water forms from steam
    D. refrigerator where the refrigerant takes liquid form

5. A *LOW WATER CUT-OFF* is usually a device to   5.____

    A. close the waste line opening when the waste has flushed out of the toilet bowl
    B. shut down the automatic lawn-watering system when the moisture level in the lawn reaches a predetermined level of saturation
    C. stop a sump pump when the water level is below floor level in the sump well
    D. stop an oil burner motor when the water level in the system falls below a predetermined level

6. The purpose of a *CHECK VALVE* is to   6.____

    A. interrupt the flow of electricity in an overloaded circuit
    B. limit the amount of electrical current which can fl flow from a main line into a branch circuit
    C. prevent water from flowing in a pipe system in a direction opposite to that desired
    D. stop the flow of water when the water in a system reaches a predetermined level

7. An investigation has been made of a broken window pane in an apartment on the third floor which the tenant claims was broken by children playing outside. The investigation disclosed that there were several small holes in the window pane. Each hole is approximately cone shaped and is about 3/16 inch in diameter on the inside of the glass (room side) and about 1/2 inch in diameter on the outside. Cracks connected some of these holes. On the basis of this information, the tenant should

   7._____

   A. be charged for the window pane since the damage is not normal wear and tear and it is not possible to substantiate the tenant's claim
   B. be charged for the window pane since the nature of the damage indicates that it was caused from inside
   C. not be charged for the window pane since it is not possible to determine the cause of the damage and the low floor involved does not tend to support the tenant's explanation
   D. not be charged for the window pane since the nature of the damage indicates that it was caused from outside

8. The one of the following which has come into common use for the extermination of roaches and silverfish is

   8._____

   A. 2-4 D   B. chlordane   C. paris green   D. red squill

9. When the building superintendent tells you that the transformer of one of the oil burners is defective, he is referring to the device which

   9._____

   A. atomizes the liquid oil prior to ignition
   B. changes low pressure steam to high pressure steam
   C. increases the voltage for oil ignition
   D. regulates oil temperature prior to atomization

10. When a building superintendent reports corroded flashings resulting in leakage, the part of the building he is referring to is the

   10._____

   A. basement piping   B. boiler room
   C. pavement adjoining building   D. roof

11. If an automatic elevator is not leveling properly at floor stops, the proper action to take is to

   11._____

   A. allow the car to remain in service only if the distance between the car floor and floor landing is 3 inches or less
   B. post signs to that effect in the elevator car to warn passengers
   C. station a maintenance man near the ground floor stop to warn passengers
   D. take the car out of service during slow periods to make necessary adjustments

12. Although rock salt is commonly used on the walks when they are iced or heavily packed with snow, the *CHIEF* disadvantage of its use is that it

   12._____

   A. creates a very slushy condition
   B. generally causes deterioration of concrete walks
   C. increases cleaning costs if used intensively
   D. is harmful to adjacent trees and shrubs

13. When instructing tenants how to clean enamel-painted woodwork, the tenant should be advised to wash the surfaces with   13._____

    A. ammonia water
    C. plain warm water
    B. mild soap and water solution
    D. strong soda solution

14. Of the following items included in the work schedule of porters, the one that should be assigned as a daily duty is   14._____

    A. cleaning incinerators
    B. cleaning stairhall windows and woodwork
    C. mopping all assigned stairhalls
    D. sweeping all stair landings

15. A building has a coal-fired steam boiler as the heating plant. While using the boiler, proper examination of the water gauge fails to reveal the presence of any water. Of the following, it would be best that   15._____

    A. a small amount of water be let into the boiler immediately, increasing the amount of water gradually until the proper level is reached
    B. the fire be put out immediately by covering with sand
    C. the fire be put out immediately by spraying with warm water
    D. the required amount of water be put into the boiler immediately

---

KEY (CORRECT ANSWERS)

1.	D		6.	C
2.	C		7.	B
3.	C		8.	B
4.	D		9.	C
5.	D		10.	D

11.	D
12.	D
13.	B
14.	D
15.	B

EXAMINATION SECTION
TEST 1

DIRECTIONS: Each question consists of a statement. You are to indicate whether the statement is TRUE (T) or FALSE (F). *PRINT THE LETTER OF THE CORRECT ANSWER IN THE SPACE AT THE RIGHT.*

1. All of the property of the Thirteen Colonies was described by metes and bounds.   1._____

2. This means that the legal description was by direction and measurement from some designated starting point called a *monument*.   2._____

3. After the unit of measurement became the township, a block of land six miles square, this was further divided into sections one mile square.   3._____

4. After a township has been surveyed, the sections are numbered beginning at the southeast corner and numbering east and then back until all of the 36 sections are numbered.   4._____

5. Each township is made up of 11 full sections and 25 fractional sections.   5._____

6. Since the numbering of the sections always begins at the northeast corner, this section is always numbered 36.   6._____

7. The rectangular system provides a comprehensive and complete system for the prompt location of any land in any area.   7._____

8. In a metes and bounds description, the piece of land is described by giving its boundaries.   8._____

9. If natural objects such as trees, streams, or stone monuments are used to form the boundary, no attempt is made at an accurate measurement as to distance and angles. This is called a formal description.   9._____

10. The first requisite of a metes and bounds description is a definite and stable starting point, e.g., the intersection of the center lines of two streets.   10._____

11. A metes and bounds description which encloses a tract of land is fatally defective.   11._____

12. The bearing of a line is its angular deviation measured in degrees, minutes, and seconds from a true north and south line.   12._____

13. Land is unlike any other commodity in that it is lacking in segmentation or natural divisions.   13._____

14. The accuracy and sufficiency of the description will barely affect the success or failure of a real estate transaction.   14._____

15. If it is necessary to use a street address, the dimensions of the tract should be specified.   15._____

16. The use of the tax lot number is a sure way to identify the parcel.   16._____

17. A reference to an earnest money receipt is an infallible method of identifying land.   17._____

18. A reference to a recorded document such as a deed or mortgage which contains a correct legal description is an accept able method of describing a particular parcel.   18.____

19. Land development quite generally means the creation of a subdivision.   19.____

20. A plat is a temporary map, diagram, drawing, replat or other writing containing all the descriptions, locations, specifications, dedications, provisions, and information concerning a subdivision.   20.____

21. The initial point of all plats must be marked with a monument.   21.____

22. No name of a plat of a town or an addition to a town may have a name the same as, similar to, or pronounced the same as any other town or addition in the same county.   22.____

23. A typical description in a plat might be, *Lot Seven (7), Block Eleven (11), Smith Addition to the city of Ann Arbor, Washtenaw County, Michigan.*   23.____

24. It is illegal to divide any lot of any recorded plat for the purpose of sale or building development if the resulting parcels do not conform to the requirements of the state, the municipality where they are located, and other governmental units.   24.____

25. When the transaction involves only a portion of the land owned by a party at a particular location, a description based on reference to outside facts is especially invulnerable to attack.   25.____

KEY (CORRECT ANSWERS)

1.	T	11.	F
2.	T	12.	T
3.	T	13.	T
4.	F	14.	F
5.	F	15.	T
6.	F	16.	F
7.	T	17.	F
8.	T	18.	T
9.	F	19.	T
10.	T	20.	F

21.	T
22.	T
23.	T
24.	T
25.	F

TEST 2

DIRECTIONS: Each question consists of a statement. You are to indicate whether the statement is TRUE (T) or FALSE (F). *PRINT THE LETTER OF THE CORRECT
ANSWER IN THE SPACE AT THE RIGHT.*

1. Unless one is able through the description to locate the property on the ground, the
   whole contract fails to meet the requirements of the statute of frauds.

   1._____

2. Where the description describes lots and blocks of an unrecorded plot, or a street number, or *My farm on Whirlpool Ridge,* oral testimony is not admitted to clarify the intention of the parties, but oral testimony as to the terms of the contract itself is admitted.

   2._____

3. Contracts should always describe the property with references, to recorded instru-
   ments or plots, or by metes and bounds, referable to some well-established point or line.

   3._____

4. The writing of metes and bounds descriptions in a deed can safely and surely be done
   by any licensed, experienced real estate broker.

   4._____

5. Describing lands according to regular government surveys is easy.

   5._____

6. Fundamentally, the government survey consists, in part, of certain lines in an East and
   West direction, called PRINCIPAL MERIDIANS, and other lines in a North and South
   direction called BASE LINES, to which all descriptions within several hundred miles are
   referred.

   6._____

7. The spherical shape of the earth causes all North and South lines to converge as they
   run toward the Poles, so that a township, if accurately laid down on the ground, must
   necessarily be narrower on the North line than on the South line; and the East and West
   line, when laid down on the earth's surface, must be a curved line having a radius equal
   to the distance from the North Pole, in this latitude.

   7._____

8. The effects of the spherical shape of the earth have resulted in fractional sections along
   the North and West sides of a township.

   8._____

9. The ranges and townships are numbered consecutively East and West, and North and
   South, of the base line and principle meridian, respectively.

   9._____

10. In every description under the government survey system, the concluding words are
    Township .... South, Range .... East, or, as customarily abbreviated, *T .... S, R .... E.* (Of
    course, if the area is North of the base line or West of the principal meridian, those words
    or symbols are used.)

    10._____

11. The sections were numbered from 1 to 36, beginning in the North East corner of a town-
    ship.

    11._____

12. Section 1 was in the North East Corner, section 6 in the South East corner, section 31 in
    the North West corner, and section 36 in the South West Corner.

    12._____

13. The numbering proceeds South from sections 1 to 6, West to section 7, South to section
    12, East to section 13, South to section 18, West to section 19, South to section 24, East
    to section 25, South to section 30, West to section 31, and East to section 36.

    13._____

14. The boundaries of the sections are rarely exactly North, South, East, and West in direction, rarely one mile square and rarely contain exactly 640 acres.   14._____

15. If less than a section is to be conveyed, it is divided first (using the usual abbreviations) into N.E. 1/4, a N.W. 1/4, a S.W. 1/4. and a S.E. 1/4, each containing approximately 160 acres.   15._____

16. Next, if one of these quarters is, in turn, divided into sixteenths, on *forties*, it may be correctly described as, for example, the N.E. 1/4 of the N.E. 1/4, the N.W. 1/4 of the N.E. 1/4, the S.W. 1/4 of the N.E. 1/4, and the S.E. 1/4 of the N.E. 1/4.   16._____

17. If one half of one of the subdivisions described in the preceding question is to be conveyed, that is, the 20 acre tract having its longer dimension East and West, and bounded on the North by the North line of the section, and on the East by the East line of the section, it MAY be correctly described as *the N 1/2 of the N.E. 1/4 of the N.E. 1/4* of the section, followed by *of Sec. ... T, ... N., R. ... E.,* or the like.   17._____

18. An adequate or good land description is one which describes a general class of property.   18._____

19. The metes and bounds description should be used as a first resort due to its many advantages.   19._____

20. Surveyors drafting descriptions today always give distances in chains, links, rods, or furlongs.   20._____

21. The public domain is divided into north and south lines, six miles apart, called *township* lines, and into east and west lines, also six miles apart, called *ranges.*   21._____

22. The intersection of the base line and meridian is the starting point of calculations east or west, north or south, to locate a definite township.   22._____

23. Ranges are numbered east or west from a principal meridian, while townships are numbered north or south from the principal base line.   23._____

24. Deed descriptions, in order to eliminate error, usually spell out directions and the fractional part of the section, followed by the abbreviation in parentheses, or vice versa.   24._____

25. The abbreviations for a deed description of *the southwest quarter of the northeast quarter of Section 6, Township 7 South, Range 14 East, Mt. Diablo Base and Meridian,* are to be correctly written as *the SW 1/4 of the NE 1/4 of Sec. 6, T7S, R14E, M.D.B.& M.*   25._____

KEY (CORRECT ANSWERS)

1.	T	11.	T
2.	F	12.	F
3.	T	13.	F
4.	F	14.	T
5.	T	15.	T
6.	F	16.	T
7.	T	17.	T
8.	T	18.	F
9.	T	19.	F
10.	T	20.	F

21.	F
22.	T
23.	T
24.	T
25.	T

TEST 3

DIRECTIONS: Each question consists of a statement. You are to indicate whether the statement is TRUE (T) or FALSE (F). *PRINT THE LETTER OF THE CORRECT ANSWER IN THE SPACE AT THE RIGHT.*

1. An insufficient description in a listing agreement may result in a denial of an agent's commission when he sells the property.   1.____

2. An insufficient description in an offer to purchase may serve as the basis of an action by either buyer or seller to break the contract.   2.____

3. An insufficient description in an offer to purchase may serve as the basis of an action by the buyer for damages for misrepresentation.   3.____

4. The governmental survey responsible for the checkerboard pattern of real estate in the western United States uses the northern boundary of the state as its baseline.   4.____

5. Parallels to the baseline are spaced 8 miles apart.   5.____

6. Townships drawn as the result of the government survey are always 6-mile squares.   6.____

7. Townships are numbered north from the base line.   7.____

8. The measurement east or west of the principal meridian is referred to as township.   8.____

9. The distance north of the base line is referred to as range.   9.____

10. T 3 N, R 4 E means Township 3 North, Range 4 East.   10.____

11. Townships are divided into sections, each 1 mile square.   11.____

12. Sections are always numbered starting in the northeast corner of the township.   12.____

13. Sections are always rigidly uniform.   13.____

14. If a township included a lake or river, there were parcels of land along the shore which were not large enough to be considered sections; these partial sections were called government lots and were USUALLY identified by number.   14.____

15. A metes-and-bounds description is any description which describes a parcel of land by starting from a known point and following the outside boundaries of the parcel, giving the direction and length of each side.   15.____

16. The typical known points in metes-and-bounds descriptions of rural land are section corners or quarter corners.   16.____

17. The typical known points in metes-and-bounds descriptions of platted land are lot corners.   17.____

18. Street or road intersections are never used as known points in metes-and-bounds descriptions.   18.____

19. Metes-and-bounds descriptions can not be used when a parcel has irregular or curved boundaries.   19.____

20. Today, drafting descriptions will always be given in chains, links, rods, or furlongs. 20._____

21. One mile is equal in length to 8 furlongs. 21._____

22. Eighty chains is equal in length to 320 rods. 22._____

23. When a parcel of land is platted, it is surveyed and divided into lots and blocks, each of which is given a number. 23._____

24. After property is divided into lots and blocks, the lot and block numbers are a sufficient description of the land. 24._____

25. A parcel of land can never be described by its street address. 25._____

KEY (CORRECT ANSWERS)

1.	T	11.	T
2.	T	12.	T
3.	T	13.	F
4.	F	14.	T
5.	F	15.	T
6.	T	16.	T
7.	T	17.	T
8.	F	18.	F
9.	F	19.	F
10.	T	20.	F

21.	T
22.	T
23.	T
24.	T
25.	F

EXAMINATION SECTION
TEST 1

DIRECTIONS: Each question or incomplete statement is followed by several suggested answers or completions. Select the one that BEST answers the question or completes the statement. *PRINT THE LETTER OF THE CORRECT ANSWER IN THE SPACE AT THE RIGHT.*

1. Real property, as legally defined, includes

    A. gas ranges   B. refrigerators
    C. furniture   D. heating systems

1.____

2. Ownership of real estate includes the exclusive right, in every instance, to

    A. take minerals from the sub-surface portions
    B. receive unobstructed light and air from adjacent parcels
    C. use adjacent parcels for access if the property is land-locked
    D. perpetuate a non-conforming use

2.____

3. The *Bundle of Rights* refers to the

    A. constitutional authority to appropriate property
    B. various rights attached to ownership of real estate
    C. rights of tenants under net lease arrangements
    D. sheaf of papers in a real estate transaction

3.____

4. Cost equals value when

    A. construction cost indices are stable
    B. national conditions are normal
    C. a new building improves a site most profitably
    D. depreciation is not excessive

4.____

5. Market value is BEST defined as the

    A. highest price, expressed in dollars, that a property would sell for under the most favorable market conditions
    B. difference between the Cost Approach and Income Approach
    C. average of the three approaches to Value
    D. highest price, expressed in dollars, that a willing, well-informed buyer would pay and a willing, well-informed seller would accept

5.____

6. In order for an object to have value in an economic sense, it MUST have

    A. an attractive appearance   B. practical utility
    C. a clear title   D. tangible materials

6.____

7. *Highest and Best Use* means

    A. most profitable use
    B. most intensive use
    C. the use which produces the largest dollar income
    D. the largest structure

7.____

8. The PROPER point in the appraisal process at which the highest and best use analysis should be made is   8.____

    A. correlation of the three approaches
    B. definition of the appraisal problem
    C. final valuation estimate
    D. preliminary survey of the appraisal task

9. The *principle of change* is evidenced in   9.____

    A. restrictive covenants running with the land
    B. the evolutionary stages in the life of a neighborhood
    C. the land residual technique
    D. the Sheridan-Karkow formula

10. The *principle of balance* is exhibited in the   10.____

    A. process of making adjustments in a market data analysis
    B. refining of the capitalization rate through the utilization of quality considerations on a relative basis
    C. agents in production in a property existing in such relative proportions that they produce the maximum residual net income to land
    D. number of apartments and rooms in an apartment house

11. The *principle of contribution states* that   11.____

    A. all three approaches to value contribute equally to the final valuation estimate
    B. land and buildings contribute to the creation of economic rents
    C. the value of an agent in production depends upon how much it adds to net income
    D. only business enterprise makes a real contribution

12. In the cost approach to value, under ideal conditions, land value is estimated by the   12.____

    A. analysis of market data on a comparative basis
    B. analysis of local tax assessment records
    C. land residual technique
    D. property residual technique

13. In estimating Replacement Cost, the majority of appraisers use the   13.____

    A. quantity survey method
    B. unit cost in place method
    C. ENGINEERING NEWS RECORD
    D. unit cost per cubic or square foot method

14. In the Cost Approach of an appraisal of a parcel of real property, the Replacement Cost estimate should include cost of   14.____

    A. wall-to-wall carpeting
    B. insurance during construction of improvements
    C. agent's management fees
    D. washing machines

15. *Accrued Depreciation* is BEST defined as the   15.____

    A. provision for recapture of capital invested in improvements on the land
    B. measures taken to guard against excessive decay and physical deterioration
    C. difference between the cost of replacement, new, and the present appraised market value
    D. loss in value resulting from any and all causes

16. In estimating accrued depreciation, it is considered the BEST practice to use   16.____

    A. the *observed condition* technique
    B. Age-Life tables
    C. Bureau of Internal Revenue tables
    D. Real Estate Board statistics

17. Only one of the three major components of accrued depreciation is said to result from   17.____
causes extrinsic to the property being appraised.
This component is

    A. curable functional obsolescence
    B. physical deterioration
    C. economic obsolescence
    D. incurable functional obsolescence

18. The test to determine whether an item of functional obsolescence is curable or incurable   18.____
is

    A. the consensus of opinion among real estate brokers
    B. the expenditure required to cure it, an item requiring an expenditure of more than $100,000 being incurable
    C. whether the cost of effecting the cure can be recouped in equivalent or greater value
    D. whether the item is mechanical or structural, the former being curable, the latter incurable

19. A cause of economic obsolescence is   19.____

    A. utilization of sub-standard specifications in construction of improvements under appraisal
    B. inadequate electric wiring
    C. poor architectural planning for improvements under appraisal
    D. rent control legislation

20. For purposes of capitalization, net income is USUALLY computed before the expense of   20.____

    A. debt service charges   B. property taxes
    C. replacement reserve   D. management

21. Capitalization may be described as   21.____

    A. establishing the income to be received
    B. converting the net income into value
    C. computing the amortization on the investment
    D. taking an interest and depreciation return on the building value

22. The estimate of economic life is based PRIMARILY on the _____ of the improvement.   22.____

    A. physical durability
    B. age
    C. size
    D. relative competitive utility

23. Net income imputable to land is capitalized in perpetuity because   23.____

    A. the entire investment is amortized out of the building income
    B. the land returns are presumed to last forever since urban land does not physically depreciate and land may thus be successively utilized
    C. investors capitalize land income in this manner since they cannot take depreciation on the land for tax purposes
    D. land represents a reversionary interest

24. The capitalization process must provide for recovery of the building investment over the economic life of the building because   24.____

    A. the investment should be recovered at the same approximate rate as the building is anticipated to decline in value from depreciation
    B. it is customary to recover every asset out of income, regardless of whether it is depreciable or not
    C. the investor always believes the amortization on the mortgage is designed to achieve the recovery of his capital for him
    D. amortization may not be equal to depreciation

25. The capitalization process referred to as *direct capitalization plus straight line depreciation* is based on an assumption that the   25.____

    A. income stream will remain level
    B. building has suffered a substantial amount of functional obsolescence
    C. income stream will decline over the years
    D. curing of most accrued depreciation is possible

26. In capitalization techniques, the method of providing for future depreciation that generally permits highest valuation is the   26.____

    A. annuity system   B. quantity survey
    C. sinking fund   D. straight line method

27. The building residual technique is applicable when   27.____

    A. accurate building cost data is available
    B. the building improves the site to its highest and best use
    C. land is in short supply in the market
    D. there is an abundance of market data relating to comparable sites

28. A capitalization rate is the   28.____

    A. amount of taxes levied upon a capital gain
    B. equalization rate for property taxes
    C. rate of return necessary to attract capital
    D. rate of capital depreciation

29. The *Band of Investment* method of selecting a capitalization rate is   29._____

    A. built up on the *safe rate*
    B. applicable only when land residual technique will be used
    C. based on analysis of sales
    D. based on weighted average of mortgage and equity rates

30. Since the use of the Inwood (annuity) factor provides for complete depreciation of a real   30._____
estate investment over its assumed economic life, the use of such technique in the
appraisal of improved real property necessitates

    A. provision for substantial tax levies
    B. an estimate of the value of the land reversion
    C. an especially careful neighborhood analysis
    D. a very thorough inspection of improvements

31. In the land residual technique, the appraiser   31._____

    A. bases his opinion on careful analysis of market data
    B. need not inspect the building unless there are building violations on it
    C. sometimes bases his estimates on a hypothetical structure representing highest
       and best use
    D. is concerned only with raw land costs

32. The so-called *overall* capitalization rate is BEST arrived at by   32._____

    A. obtaining the ratio of net income to selling price of comparable properties
    B. consulting the Dow Service for the standard capitalization rates most frequently
       used
    C. examination of Census Statistics
    D. employing the summation or *build-up* technique

33. In real estate appraisal work, the market data approach should particularly be used   33._____

    A. when the sales market has experienced substantial activity
    B. when cost information is too difficult to obtain
    C. when the subject property is new
    D. only when a residential property is being appraised

34. The market data approach is used for direct valuation of properties and it is also useful in   34._____

    A. making quantity surveys
    B. making insurance appraisals
    C. establishing capitalization rates
    D. controlling depreciation

35. The heart of the market data approach is   35._____

    A. thorough checking of deed registration
    B. careful averaging of sales statistics
    C. thorough-going analysis of the records of the Building Department
    D. careful comparisons between comparables and property being appraised

KEY (CORRECT ANSWERS)

1.	D		16.	A
2.	A		17.	C
3.	B		18.	C
4.	C		19.	D
5.	D		20.	A
6.	B		21.	B
7.	A		22.	D
8.	D		23.	B
9.	B		24.	A
10.	C		25.	C
11.	C		26.	A
12.	A		27.	D
13.	D		28.	C
14.	B		29.	D
15.	C		30.	B

31.	C
32.	A
33.	A
34.	C
35.	D

TEST 2

DIRECTIONS: Each question or incomplete statement is followed by several suggested answers or completions. Select the one that BEST answers the question or completes the statement. *PRINT THE LETTER OF THE CORRECT ANSWER IN THE SPACE AT THE RIGHT.*

1. Appraisals for any purpose in the real estate field, in an economic sense, are required because

    A. a high unit cost is involved
    B. realty is a non-standardized commodity
    C. it is a customary practice
    D. brokers are usually uninformed

    1.____

2. The legal basis for the estimation of full value in real estate tax assessment appraisals is

    A. stabilized market value, without regard to cyclical extremes
    B. a combination of the market comparison and income approaches
    C. cost for improvements, less any depreciation, plus land value estimated by comparison
    D. capitalized value of the residual net income

    2.____

3. In a purely objective sense, no matter what the purpose of the appraisal may be, the market value of the real estate at a given moment is ALWAYS

    A. identical   B. varied
    C. mixed   D. dependent on the approach

    3.____

4. Certiorari appraisals are unique in technique because

    A. they frequently result in court actions
    B. the tax rate is incorporated in the capitalization rate
    C. all three value approaches are used
    D. they are used in no other state except New York

    4.____

5. There is an effective limitation on the height of reinforced concrete structures because

    A. the large columns required take up too much floor space and impair floor layouts
    B. the structural framework is too rigid for climatic changes
    C. the building code limits the height of reinforced concrete structures
    D. it is expensive to haul concrete to excessive heights

    5.____

6. Aside from zoning restrictions, the height of a steel skeleton frame building is limited by the

    A. cost of the steel framing
    B. labor cost involved at great heights resulting from labor scarcity
    C. cost of utility installations
    D. adequacy of the net rent received on the construction cost of the last floor

    6.____

7. A typical semi-fireproof apartment house has

    A. all wood floors but masonry walls
    B. concrete first floor arch, wood upper floors, load bearing masonry walls
    C. light steel bar joists, 2" poured concrete floors, load bearing masonry walls
    D. all concrete floors and load bearing masonry walls

    7.____

8. Continual flaking of paint on the inner surface of an outer masonry wall PROBABLY indicates   8._____
cates

    A. a poor paint job caused by adulterating the paint with a chemical
    B. shoddy construction permissible under an inadequate building code
    C. driving rains from the east
    D. a need for pointing up the loose and dislodged mortar in the joints

9. The appraiser makes an inspection of the realty under appraisal because   9._____

    A. it keeps him informed on building construction
    B. he must be an engineer to be qualified
    C. the results of the inspection have a direct bearing on the value
    D. a very detailed description of the realty is expected of him

10. The LEAST costly heating system to install and service, which takes the least amount of   10._____
space and costs the most for fuel, is

    A. coal stoker   B. oil burner
    C. gas-fired hot water   D. utility steam

11. The type of material used for plumbing risers, branches, and crotons has a direct bearing   11._____
on value because

    A. the better the quality and the more durable the material, the higher the anticipated
       net income
    B. superintendents are prohibited by union rules from making repairs to the plumbing
       system
    C. the mechanical equipment depreciates in the same manner as the building shell
    D. some types of material become functionally obsolete faster than others

12. An inspection of the rentable space is as important as an inspection of the building shell   12._____
and equipment because

    A. the appraiser can determine if there are any furnished units
    B. it establishes the basis for a comparable rent analysis
    C. the occupancy must be checked against the leases
    D. it makes the report look more impressive

13. Which one of the following is GENERALLY found in an unaltered old law tenement?   13._____

    A. Combination washtub and bathtub
    B. Dumbwaiters
    C. Central heat
    D. Off-foyer layouts

14. Which one of the following is MOST generally found in a new law tenement?   14._____

    A. A standpipe system   B. Dumbwaiters
    C. Colored tile baths   D. Windowless rooms

15. If an inspection revealed that an apartment house was dangerously underwired, the appraiser should PRIMARILY solve this in his appraisal report by   15.____

    A. advising the owner to correct the condition forthwith
    B. advising the client to notify the Building Department immediately
    C. subtracting the capital cost of re-wiring from the market value, after reflecting the rent increases permitted by the Rent Commission in the net income
    D. ignoring the condition on the assumption that the owner will eventually replace the wiring

16. If a building is of competitive, that is, average construction quality, and if it has been well maintained to the date of the appraisal, the LEAST significant type of depreciation is probably   16.____

    A. super session   B. physical deterioration
    C. functional obsolescence   D. inadequacy

17. The type of air conditioning system installed in most new apartment houses is   17.____

    A. air-cooled central system with adequate ducts
    B. peripheral system circulating chilled water
    C. heavy duty fan system
    D. unit in wall sleeve

18. Land use is usually the MOST intensive in _____ districts.   18.____

    A. apartment   B. hotel   C. loft   D. office

19. A significant decline in employment in a city may affect real estate market values through   19.____

    A. economic obsolescence
    B. neighborhood decay
    C. removal of middle class to the suburbs
    D. the aging process

20. The removal of some of the middle income class from the core of the city to the suburbs has resulted in a(n)   20.____

    A. increase in the available supply of dwelling units
    B. decline in controlled rents
    C. acceleration of physical deterioration and economic obsolescence in those central residential neighborhoods
    D. opportunity to modernize controlled rent apartments

21. Downtown major retail sections have been adversely affected PRIMARILY by   21.____

    A. obsolete buildings
    B. too many taxicabs and too few buses
    C. poor planning of merchant associations
    D. outlying shopping center competition

22. If published material were not available, the BEST source for obtaining the net annual addition to the housing stock would be   22.____

    A. condemnation records

B. tax and assessment records
C. the Register's Office
D. building and demolition permits

23. The trend referred to as *decentralization* is caused LARGELY by 　　　　　23._____

    A. encroachment of industry into residential areas in outlying cities throughout the country
    B. rent control legislation
    C. removal of commerce, industry, and people from the heart of the city to outlying cities or to the periphery
    D. inequitable tax assessment policies

24. The cubical content of an office building was 2,100,000 cubic feet. The Dow Service Val-　24._____
uation Calculator gave $1.10 as the net field reproduction cost. The appraiser added
20% to cover all miscellaneous costs and excavation. Depreciation was estimated at 2 1/2%
per annum. The building was 25 years old on the appraisal date. Land value was estimated at $15,000 a front foot for the 200' x 100' plot.
The total value by the cost approach is MOST NEARLY

    A. $4,039,500　　　　　　　　　　B. $4,762,000
    C. $5,191,300　　　　　　　　　　D. $6,244,000

25. The quantity survey method of cost estimation is not used by most market value apprais-　25._____
ers because

    A. appraisal groups oppose it
    B. they are not qualified to use it
    C. cost has no importance in valuation
    D. the unit-in-place method is better

26. An over-calculation or over-estimation of building cost, assuming a particular level of rent　26._____
is obtainable, will

    A. influence lenders on the mortgage to require less amortization
    B. penalize the land value by the approximate amount of the over-calculation of the building cost
    C. result in a faulty depreciation allowance for income tax purposes
    D. make necessary the engagement of a cost expert on a sub-contract basis

27. The construction cost of a six-story semi-fireproof apartment house is less than that of a　27._____
fireproof reinforced concrete apartment house of similar size by APPROXIMATELY

    A. 40%　　　　　B. 30%　　　　　C. 15%　　　　　D. 10%

28. The cost approach can ALWAYS be used in any appraisal because 　　　　　28._____

    A. it can be used as a ceiling of possible market value for the real estate
    B. no appraisal can be made without it
    C. the physical components of realty are the primary bases for market value
    D. it makes the appraisal report more convincing as a result of the cost figures

29. The assessor was assigned to re-appraise for property tax purposes a 60-year-old loft-   29.____
type structure that was 50% vacant. Many similar structures in the same district had
been demolished, and the plots improved with new commercial buildings.
Under the circumstances, which appraisal approach, of the following, would BEST be
utilized?

    A. Reproduction cost, less depreciation, plus land value
    B. Replacement cost, plus land value
    C. Market comparison, treating the improvement as almost fully depreciated
    D. the building residual method of capitalization

30. The assessor was assigned to re-appraise for property tax purposes a privately-owned,   30.____
specially designed and constructed art gallery with high ceilings and ornate construction,
for which there was no market in its present use. He concluded that it would not be practical to convert the structure to another use should the art gallery use terminate. He
decided to use the cost approach and worked out a reproduction cost for the structure.
In the absence of a market for similar structures, the depreciation computation should
MOST probably be based on

    A. May's quantity survey method of computing depreciation
    B. a sinking fund technique
    C. an age-life method based on a straight-line depreciation allowance
    D. an observation derived from personal experience

31. In comparing the results of the cost approach and the income approach when assessing   31.____
a new building on a given plot, the assessor noted that the income approach yielded a
greater total value, despite the use of a high capitalization rate.
Assuming the assessor's cost calculations to be accurate, the differential can BEST be
attributed to the fact that

    A. there is always a higher total value when the income approach is used rather than
the cost approach
    B. there is usually an increment in value attributable to the land over its acquisition
cost, underlying a successfully rented and completed building in a market of equi-
librium
    C. the cost approach never reflects the value obtained from the income approach
because the former is independent of the rents obtained in the property
    D. the law does not permit equipment in the realty to be treated as real fixtures sub-
ject to real estate taxation

32. The assessor was asked to estimate the market land value underlying a one-story store   32.____
building. The property had recently sold for $1,200,000. The land assessment was
$400,000, and the total assessment was $800,000.
Using the assessment ratio extraction process, the assessor should estimate the land
value at

    A. $300,000   B. $500,000   C. $600,000   D. $800,000

33. The assessor's unit lot value for a typical side street had been established at $500,000. A   33.____
vacant corner plot 100' x 75' on the same street sold for $3,000,000. The Hoffman-Neill
rule depth factor for 75 feet was 84.49. Assuming standard corner and key lot incre-
ments, the unit lot value indicated by the sale is MOST NEARLY

    A. $625,000   B. $700,000   C. $800,000   D. $890,000

34. One of the BEST means of finding the appropriate overall capitalization rate for income   34.____
    property on a market comparison basis is the

    A. earnings price ratio of similar properties
    B. long-term government bond rate in the money market
    C. risk rates in the market
    D. mortgage interest rates

35. You are asked to assess a six-story apartment house on a 100' x 100' plot. You find   35.____
    records of four sales of similar properties.
    Which one has no applicability?

    A. R.S. $.55 mortgage $125,000
    B. R.S. $77. mortgage $80,000 P.M.M. $30,000
    C. R.S. $110. mortgage $65,000
    D. Stated consideration: $1,800,000

KEY (CORRECT ANSWERS)

1.	B		16.	B
2.	C		17.	A
3.	A		18.	D
4.	B		19.	A
5.	A		20.	C
6.	D		21.	D
7.	B		22.	B
8.	D		23.	C
9.	C		24.	A
10.	C		25.	B
11.	A		26.	B
12.	B		27.	C
13.	A		28.	A
14.	B		29.	C
15.	C		30.	C

31.	B
32.	C
33.	B
34.	A
35.	A

TEST 3

DIRECTIONS: Each question or incomplete statement is followed several suggested answers or completions. Select one that BEST answers the question or completes the statement. *PRINT THE LETTER OF THE CORRECT ANSWER IN THE SPACE AT THE RIGHT.*

1. Which one of the following is an INCORRECT technique for analyzing comparable sales?   1.____

    A. Ratio of selling price to assessed valuation
    B. Applying locational differential rating factor
    C. Selling price per unit of measurement
    D. Going back fifteen years in checking sales

2. The appraiser employed in a certiorari proceeding submitted twenty-five sales, eighteen of which were made prior to the appraisal date, three within six months after the appraisal date, and the balance two and one-half years after the appraisal date. The MAXIMUM number of sales which the trial justice could admit as evidence of value was   2.____

    A. 23   B. 21   C. 19   D. 17

3. The market comparison approach is frequently considered the primary or best approach, provided the   3.____

    A. income approach is used as a check
    B. subject property is a standardized type and recent comparable market sales are numerous
    C. reproduction cost, less age-life depreciation, plus land value, yields the same result
    D. appraiser subscribes to a sales service

4. The assessor was appraising a newly completed apartment house which, in his judgement, was worth less than its replacement cost because of some serious deficiencies in design, layout, and equipment.
In capitalizing the net income, the CORRECT capitalization method to apply to this new building is the _____ method.   4.____

    A. building residual   B. land residual
    C. property residual   D. land reversion

5. You wish to establish a capitalization rate for the capitalization of net income, before any deduction for depreciation. You decide the Band of Investment Theory is best for this purpose. Debt service charges for similar property is running 8% on a 60% mortgage. Equity returns currently are 10%.
The MOST appropriate capitalization rate is   5.____

    A. 7.60%   B. 8.80%   C. 8.90%   D. 9.10%

6. Of the following, the BEST mathematical means of capitalizing a net rental from property occupied by an AAA-1 tenant under a thirty year net lease is   6.____

    A. annuity table, as Inwood's Premise
    B. interest plus sinking fund
    C. interest plus straight-line depreciation
    D. interest rate, after subtracting depreciation

7. The land residual method of capitalization must be used with great caution, particularly   7.____
when the building has not yet been constructed, because

    A.   it requires exceptional technical competence
    B.   the leverage factor can produce gross distortions in the residual land return
    C.   construction costs are difficult to estimate
    D.   it is unethical to capitalize income attributable to a building not yet constructed

8. The method of capitalization which recognizes the valuation principle that land value   8.____
should never be penalized or discounted merely because of the inadequacy of a depreciated structure is the _____ method.

    A.   gross multiplier   B.   net multiplier
    C.   building residual   D.   Kniskern-Schmutz

9. Land value under a rent-controlled apartment house was estimated by comparison at   9.____
$1,000,000. Net income after all expenses except debt service charges was $120,000.
The building's economic life was estimated at 25 years and the interest rate at 6%. The
annuity factor for 25 years at 6% was 12.78.
The total value of land and improvements was

    A. $1,766,800   B. $1,873,600
    C. $2,056,530   D. $2,593,600

10. The equity return was $4,000. Debt service charges were $6,000. The property sold for   10.____
$150,000.
The overall rate of return, free of mortgage debt, was MOST NEARLY

    A. 5.8%   B. 6.2%   C. 6.7%   D. 7.5%

11. The assessor was asked to appraise, for property tax purposes by the property residual   11.____
method, a department store property under a 40-year lease at $1,000,000 a year. Build-
ing life and the lease term are considered coincident. Land value at lease expiration was
estimated at $10,000,000. The annuity factor for 40 years at 7% interest was 13.3. The
deferment factor for 40 years at 7% interest was .07.
The present value is MOST NEARLY

    A. $9,800,000   B. $12,500,000
    C. $13,300,000   D. $14,000,000

12. A new retail shopping center was considered to represent the highest utilization of the   12.____
site. It produced a total net income of $1,000,000. The building cost was $8,000,000.
Economic life was 40 years. Interest rate was 7%. Assuming straight-line depreciation
and employing the most appropriate capitalization methods, the total value
is MOST NEARLY

    A. $32,650,000   B. $26,300,000
    C. $21,250,000   D. $11,430,000

13. For the property in the preceding question, the ratio of land to total appraised value is   13.____
MOST NEARLY

    A. 20%   B. 30 %   C. 40%   D. 50%

14. You are appraising a vacant lot 25' x 75', 25' from the corner.   14._____
   Which of the following would you consider in estimating the size of the unit lot?

    A. Corner influence, plus Hoffman-Neill factor
    B. Corner and key influence
    C. Key influence, plus Hoffman-Neill factor
    D. Key influence

15. The RECORD AND GUIDE reported the following sale: Park Ave., 908-910 (5:149-37   15._____
   swc, 80th (Nos. 70-76) 81.2 x 80.6, 14 sty. apt; Harry and Jane Fischel Foundation
   (Albert Wald, v.pres.) 960 Park Ave. to 910 Park Ave., Inc. 910 Park Ave.; B&S; 1st mtg.
   $165,734.19; PM mtge. $489,151.08; Apr. 30; May 2 '57; A $235,000. $470,000 (RS
   $725.45).
   What is the selling price and cash payment, respectively?

    A. $825,234.19; $170,348.12
    B. $1,413,583.72; $569,250.00
    C. $319,681.41; $320,281.00
    D. $975,432.00; $251,684.44

16. Using the sales figures given in the preceding question and assuming the depth factor for   16._____
   80' is 87.73, the number of unit lots and the unit lot value, respectively, are MOST
   NEARLY _____ unit lots and _____.

    A. 3.27; $78,904.00   B. 3.69; $91,283.00
    C. 3.92; $69,524.00   D. 3.72; $111,130.00

17. According to the Tax Department, the assessor's field book must contain   17._____

    A. notations on national real estate conditions for each tax year
    B. annuity tables pasted on the inside fold
    C. the actual condition of all buildings in course of construction as of taxable status
       date
    D. the telephone numbers of taxpayers

18. The CHIEF function of the Tax Department's Research Bureau is to   18._____

    A. engage in primary research in real estate, economics, and valuation techniques
    B. prepare research reports for the City Planning Commission
    C. tabulate the ratio of selling prices to assessed values in various cities throughout
       the country
    D. act as an adjunct of the Certiorari Bureau

19. The property cards furnished each assessor do NOT contain   19._____

    A. sales and leases
    B. court decisions
    C. construction costs
    D. national real estate market index

20. Which one of the following is NOT entitled to partial or complete tax exemption?   20._____

    A. Medical society   B. Parsonages
    C. Trade association   D. Veterans' organization

21. In New York City, exempt property is MOST NEARLY what percent of the total of all prop-   21._____
erty?

    A. 15%   B. 25%   C. 30%   D. 35%

22. The *Assessor's Report for Certiorari Hearing,* in addition to providing a detailed physical   22._____
description, also computes

    A. the capitalization of the income
    B. the percent of net on the assessed value
    C. the operating costs per cubic foot
    D. a quantity survey cost estimate

23. An example of a typical expense usually listed under Item 9, OTHER EXPENSES, in an   23._____
Application for Correction of Assessed Valuation of Real Estate is

    A. hall and corridor painting
    B. plumbing repairs
    C. liability insurance
    D. management fees

24. In connection with an Application for Additional Veteran Exemption, the item of informa-   24._____
tion which the assessor must obtain is the

    A. cost of capital improvements to property since purchase
    B. quantity survey cost estimates from reliable contractors
    C. type of veteran's discharge
    D. date on which the veteran purchased the property

25. A remission of real estate from taxation occasionally occurs when   25._____

    A. a corporation has a foreign charter
    B. taxes have been in arrears for three or more years
    C. an *in rem* proceeding is pending
    D. a corporation qualifies for tax exemption

———

KEY (CORRECT ANSWERS)

1.	D		11.	D
2.	B		12.	D
3.	B		13.	B
4.	A		14.	C
5.	B		15.	A
6.	A		16.	D
7.	B		17.	C
8.	C		18.	A
9.	A		19.	D
10.	C		20.	C

21.	C
22.	B
23.	D
24.	A
25.	D

———

EXAMINATION SECTION
TEST 1

DIRECTIONS: Each question or incomplete statement is followed by several suggested answers or completions. Select the one that BEST answers the question or completes the statement. *PRINT THE LETTER OF THE CORRECT ANSWER IN THE SPACE AT THE RIGHT.*

1. In the assessment of a single-family attached home, seven sales of similar property at the following prices are noted: $231,000, $234,000, $232,000, $232,500, $228,700, $230,500, and $228,000.
   The MEDIAN sales price of these properties is

   A. $231,500   B. $230,750   C. $239,951   D. $231,000   1.____

2. A study of sales trends in a neighborhood indicates the following data on average prices (2010 - base year):   2.____

Year	Price Index
2010	1.00
2011	1.10
2012	1.32
2013	1.20
2014	1.15

   All other things being equal, if a parcel sold for $100,000 in 2011, it would have an EQUIVALENT price in 2014 of
   A. $115,000   B. $104,545   C. $104,498   D. $101,500

3. For an object to have value in an economic sense, it must   3.____

   A. be visually attractive
   B. have utility and relative scarcity
   C. have a clear title
   D. be scarce and be transferrable

4. The *principle of change* is evidenced in the   4.____

   A. use of one interest rate for mortgage and a different one for equity
   B. building residual technique
   C. various forms of land ownership
   D. evolutionary stages in the life of a neighborhood

5. In determining whether property is personal rather than real, the one of the following factors which is NOT pertinent is the   5.____

   A. relative cost of the property as compared to value of land on which it is located
   B. use and occupancy of the premises
   C. manner in which the property is attached to the land
   D. intention of the party who installed the property in the premises

6. The one of the following statements about the *principle of substitution* which is MOST   6.____
   accurate is that it

   A. has application to the three approaches to value
   B. is no longer accepted by the courts
   C. affirms that when a builder cannot get specified material, he may substitute other
      material reasonably similar
   D. relates to the alternate choices in capitalization rate selection

7. The one of the following statements which is MOST valid about the *principle of anticipa-*   7.____
   tion in its application to the appraisal of real property is that it

   A. affirms that change is ever present, especially with regard to rental projections
   B. states that excess profits breed ruinous competition
   C. affirms that value is the present worth of future benefits
   D. provides the basis for the use of escalator clauses in leases

8. Sales assessment ratios, compiled from a statistical analysis of sales data, are LEAST   8.____
   likely to reveal the validity of the

   A. level or levels of assessed valuations
   B. equality of assessments in various areas of the assessing district
   C. sales data itself to sale/purchase motivations
   D. cost and depreciation factors used in assessing property

9. The *purpose* of an appraisal should be included as a section in the final report CHIEFLY   9.____
   to

   A. give a short summary of the approach used to determine value
   B. provide the basis for fixing the appraiser's compensation
   C. indicate the destination of the report
   D. set forth the reason for making the appraisal

10. The income capitalization evaluation approach is MOST valid when applied to a   10.____

    A. taxpayer   B. townhouse
    C. two-family dwelling   D. condominium unit

11. Which of the following is the BEST source of demographic data?   11.____

    A. Chamber of Commerce reports
    B. F.H.A. Rental Surveys
    C. U.S. Census Tract Studies
    D. Real Estate Board Tracts

12. In general, the one of the following statements about rental conditions in city neighbor-   12.____
    hoods which is MOST valid is that they

    A. follow national trends
    B. may indicate trends which do not necessarily correspond to regional and national
       trends
    C. may lag behind national trends but will eventually coincide with them
    D. do not always follow national trends but follow regional trends

13. *Highest and best use* of land can be defined as the

    A.   most intensive use under urban renewal plans
    B.   use which produces the largest gross income
    C.   use which permits the largest building compatible with zoning provisions
    D.   most profitable use

13.____

14. The *Bundle of Rights* relates to

    A.   rights of tenants under rent laws
    B.   constitutional authority to appropriate real property
    C.   various rights attached to ownership of real estate
    D.   four rights which state governments possess with regard to real estate

14.____

15. *Plottage* is GENERALLY considered an incremental influence in the appraisal of

    A.   a 40-by-100-foot parcel in a single-family home area
    B.   a 30-foot corner parcel at the intersection of two major retail streets
    C.   two or more contiguous lots held under single ownership and utility
    D.   a corner lot with a depth of 118 feet

15.____

16. If an independent appraiser in need of sales information does not have access to the published sales data, he can BEST obtain the information he needs by

    A.   securing sales data from assessors' cards in the finance administration
    B.   consulting sales data in the county clerk's register's office
    C.   reviewing the newspaper accounts of sales
    D.   examining the city sales tax records

16.____

17. *Appraisal area,* as used in local courts, might BEST be defined as the actual area

    A.   computed by the appraiser
    B.   adjusted for various increments and depth factors
    C.   adjusted for locational amenities
    D.   stipulated by both sides in litigation

17.____

18. The term *trending* means adjusting sales data for the

    A.   time of sale
    B.   physical characteristics of the building
    C.   locational factors involved
    D.   shape and depth of the lot

18.____

19. When sales data is exchanged prior to a trial on assessment appeal, it MUST include

    A.   name of the grantor's attorney
    B.   date sale was confirmed
    C.   appraiser's rating of *comparable* as compared to *subject*
    D.   date and page of recorded instrument

19.____

20. Confirmation of sales information as evidence of value is accomplished when

    A.   a copy of the closing statement is obtained
    B.   title actually passes

20.____

C. ownership changes appear on the assessment roll
D. revenue stamps affixed to the deed agree with *reported* price

21. The *vesting* date in condemnation cases is the date on which   21.____

    A. a case goes to trial
    B. the owner first makes a claim for his money
    C. the payment of the award is designated by the court
    D. the taking order is signed by the court

22. Depreciation, as the term is used in appraisal literature, USUALLY means a loss in value   22.____

    A. from all causes
    B. from physical deterioration only
    C. from physical deterioration and economic factors only
    D. as certified by a qualified insurance adjuster

23. *Economic Tent* is that rental which is   23.____

    A. reserved in a lease agreement
    B. derived from market data
    C. the average of yearly rentals received during past years
    D. the projected rental expectancy

24. *Effective* rental refers to the   24.____

    A. annualized montly rental now being collected
    B. gross rental expectancy less vacancy allowance
    C. rental stipulated in a lease
    D. base rental plus *overage*

25. The amount of rental income expected to be collected over economic rental is designated as   25.____

    A. overage   B. percentage rental
    C. reserve rental   D. excess rental

26. Office building operational costs are USUALLY expressed in terms of cost per _____ foot.   26.____

    A. gross square   B. cubic
    C. net usable   D. net rentable square

27. The LARGEST single item of operating expense in a modern office building is, generally,   27.____

    A. contractual cleaning
    B. wages (exclusive of cleaning)
    C. oil for heating and cooling
    D. electricity for tenants and buildings

28. The present worth of a net income stream for a period of 15 years deferred five years is the net income multiplied by the _____ factor.   28.____

    A. 20-year   B. 15-year
    C. 20-year factor less the 15-year   D. 20-year factor less the 5-year

29. The following formula can be used to develop overall capitalization rate:

    R = Y - MC + Depreciation X sinking fund factor

    In this formula, the symbol M stands for

    A. money
    C. mortgage ratio
    B. mortgage amount
    D. mortgage rate

29.____

30. The leased fee position is valued by

    A. discounting reserved rentals and adding value of reversion
    B. discounting the contract rental stream and adding the present worth of reversion
    C. subtracting the present worth of the rental stream from the free-and-clear value of property
    D. adding the future value of property to the future value of rental income

30.____

31. A title of the administrative code imposes a tax on each deed at the time of delivery of the deed from the grantor to the grantee when the consideration exceeds $250,000. The LEAST valid of the following statements regarding the payment of this transfer tax is that

    A. the tax shall be at one-half of one percent of the net consideration
    B. a return must be filed either by the grantor or grantee
    C. the tax is paid by the grantor but the grantee is liable if the grantor does not pay
    D. the grantee, if not otherwise exempt, must pay the tax, if the grantor is exempt

31.____

32. Real property owned by senior citizens may be eligible for partial exemption from real estate taxation pursuant to the state real property tax law and the city charter. The one of the following situations which will preclude the granting of the exemption is that the

    A. property is owned by husband and wife who are aged 66 and 60 years, respectively
    B. combined income of the owners is $24,000 per annum
    C. property consists of an owner-occupied legal residence above a grocery store
    D. property was acquired less than ten years prior to the date of making application for exemption

32.____

33. Pursuant to a section of the real property tax law, new construction deemed eligible for tax exemption benefits by the city during construction and the following four years shall be _____ exempt during the period of construction, followed by _____ of the full assessed valuation.

    A. *fully,* two years of exemption at 100% and then two years of exemption at 80%
    B. *partially;* two years of exemption at 80% of the full assessed valuation, and an additional two years at 60%
    C. *fully;* exemptions of one year at 80%, one year at 60%, one year at 40%, and one year at 20%
    D. *fully;* exemptions of one year at 90%, one year at 80%, and two years at 60%

33.____

34. An honorably discharged Army Chaplain who is currently ministering to a congregation   34.____
    has applied for a clergyman's exemption and a veteran's exemption on his home. Accord-
    ing to the state tax law, this chaplain

    A. cannot get both exemptions on a single piece of property
    B. may be able to get both exemptions but the total exemption is limited to $60,000
    C. may obtain both exemptions if he proves that he resides at the property for which
        he is claiming exemption
    D. may get both exemptions only if his equity in the house is greater than 30% of its
        market value

35. The one of the following statements that is VALID with respect to the tax commission is   35.____
    that

    A. the tax commission may place upon the books of the annual record of assessed
        valuations any omitted parcels prior to the date for public inspection thereof
    B. at least three of the members of the commission must be of a political party differ-
        ent from that of the president of the commission
    C. members of the tax commission have the right of entry upon real property at all
        reasonable times to ascertain the character of the property
    D. the tax commission may remit or reduce a tax is such tax is found excessive or
        erroneous within two years after delivery of the assessment rolls to the finance
        administration for the collection of such tax

36. After a certiorari report has been prepared by an assessor and submitted to the certiorari   36.____
    bureau, he learns that the property has been refinanced.
    The one of the following which is the PROPER course of action for an assessor to take
    in this situation is to

    A. notify the certiorari bureau immediately
    B. note the fact in the field book for future consideration
    C. notify the assessor-in-charge of the county in which the property is located
    D. ignore it as properties are assessed on a free-and-clear basis

37. In order to equalize the tax roll, the finance administrator decides to decrease the   37.____
    assessed value of a parcel of real estate on March 1. The owner has never filed for cor-
    rection of the valuation.
    The finance administrator

    A. must direct the owner to file an application prior to March 15
    B. may make the change on the assessment rolls immediately without notice to the
        owner
    C. may make the change on the assessment rolls immediately but must give the
        owner notice prior to March 15
    D. must give the owner ten days' notice prior to making the change

38. An assessor is required to enter certain relevant appraisal data in his field book.   38.____
    Of the following types of data, the one which he is NOT required to enter in the field
    book is

    A. zoning designations for each block
    B. gross square foot area and, where appropriate, the cubic content of each building

C.   information contained in permits issued by the department of marine and aviation concerning physical improvements to city-owned properties
D.   information contained in the city planning commission calendars

39.   The one of the following statements that is LEAST valid with regard to property exempted from real property taxes is that   39.____

A.   assessors, upon finding a change in either ownership or use for which the exemption was granted, may restore the property to the assessable tax rolls
B.   assessors, upon finding a new improvement on exempt property, must report this fact on a query sheet for referral to the tax commission
C.   if construction has not started on vacant land previously granted tax exemption because of an expressed intention to build upon or develop, the assessor must submit a query sheet for each year that the property remains unimproved
D.   exempt properties of any nature, if wholly exempt, must be assessed on the same basis as taxable realty

40.   The landlord's information return, filed with the finance administration, is a(n)   40.____

A.   certification of the actual consideration paid for the property by the grantee
B.   valuable source for rental data for commercial properties
C.   statement by the owner of a commercial property that he is not using the structure in violation of zoning use
D.   an architectural computation of the gross square foot area and, where appropriate, the cubic content of a building other than one-family dwellings

---

KEY (CORRECT ANSWERS)

1.	D	11.	C	21.	D	31.	B
2.	B	12.	B	22.	A	32.	C
3.	B	13.	D	23.	B	33.	A
4.	D	14.	C	24.	B	34.	C
5.	A	15.	C	25.	D	35.	C
6.	A	16.	B	26.	D	36.	C
7.	C	17.	B	27.	A	37.	B
8.	C	18.	A	28.	D	38.	D
9.	D	19.	B	29.	C	39.	A
10.	A	20.	A	30.	B	40.	B

PHILOSOPHY, PRINCIPLES, PRACTICES AND TECHNICS
OF
SUPERVISION, ADMINISTRATION, MANAGEMENT AND ORGANIZATION

TABLE OF CONTENTS

PHILOSOPHY, PRINCIPLES, PRACTICES, AND TECHNICS
OF
SUPERVISION, ADMINISTRATION, MANAGEMENT AND ORGANIZATION

I. MEANING OF SUPERVISION

The extension of the democratic philosophy has been accompanied by an extension in the scope of supervision. Modern leaders and supervisors no longer think of supervision in the narrow sense of being confined chiefly to visiting employees, supplying materials, or rating the staff. They regard supervision as being intimately related to all the concerned agencies of society, they speak of the supervisor's function in terms of "growth", rather than the "improvement," of employees.

This modern concept of supervision may be defined as follows:

Supervision is leadership and the development of leadership within groups which are cooperatively engaged in inspection, research, training, guidance and evaluation.

II. THE OLD AND THE NEW SUPERVISION

TRADITIONAL
1. Inspection
2. Focused on the employee
3. Visitation
4. Random and haphazard
5. Imposed and authoritarian
6. One person usually

MODERN
1. Study and analysis
2. Focused on aims, materials, methods, supervisors, employees, environment
3. Demonstrations, intervisitation, workshops, directed reading, bulletins, etc.
4. Definitely organized and planned (scientific)
5. Cooperative and democratic
6. Many persons involved (creative)

III THE EIGHT (8) BASIC PRINCIPLES OF THE NEW SUPERVISION

1. *PRINCIPLE OF RESPONSIBILITY*
Authority to act and responsibility for acting must be joined.
   a. If you give responsibility, give authority.
   b. Define employee duties clearly.
   c. Protect employees from criticism by others.
   d. Recognize the rights as well as obligations of employees.
   e. Achieve the aims of a democratic society insofar as it is possible within the area of your work.
   f. Establish a situation favorable to training and learning.
   g. Accept ultimate responsibility for everything done in your section, unit, office, division, department.
   h. Good administration and good supervision are inseparable.

2. PRINCIPLE OF AUTHORITY
The success of the supervisor is measured by the extent to which the power of authority is not used.
- a. Exercise simplicity and informality in supervision.
- b. Use the simplest machinery of supervision.
- c. If it is good for the organization as a whole, it is probably justified.
- d. Seldom be arbitrary or authoritative.
- e. Do not base your work on the power of position or of personality.
- f. Permit and encourage the free expression of opinions.

3. PRINCIPLE OF SELF-GROWTH
The success of the supervisor is measured by the extent to which, and the speed with which, he is no longer needed.
- a. Base criticism on principles, not on specifics.
- b. Point out higher activities to employees.
- c. Train for self-thinking by employees, to meet new situations.
- d. Stimulate initiative, self-reliance and individual responsibility.
- e. Concentrate on stimulating the growth of employees rather than on removing defects.

4. PRINCIPLE OF INDIVIDUAL WORTH
Respect for the individual is a paramount consideration in supervision.
- a. Be human and sympathetic in dealing with employees.
- b. Don't nag about things to be done.
- c. Recognize the individual differences among employees and seek opportunities to permit best expression of each personality.

5. PRINCIPLE OF CREATIVE LEADERSHIP
The best supervision is that which is not apparent to the employee.
- a. Stimulate, don't drive employees to creative action.
- b. Emphasize doing good things.
- c. Encourage employees to do what they do best.
- d. Do not be too greatly concerned with details of subject or method.
- e. Do not be concerned exclusively with immediate problems and activities.
- f. Reveal higher activities and make them both desired and maximally possible.
- g. Determine procedures in the light of each situation but see that these are derived from a sound basic philosophy.
- h. Aid, inspire and lead so as to liberate the creative spirit latent in all good employees.

6. PRINCIPLE OF SUCCESS AND FAILURE
There are no unsuccessful employees, only unsuccessful supervisors who have failed to give proper leadership.
- a. Adapt suggestions to the capacities, attitudes, and prejudices of employees.
- b. Be gradual, be progressive, be persistent.
- c. Help the employee find the general principle; have the employee apply his own problem to the general principle.
- d. Give adequate appreciation for good work and honest effort.
- e. Anticipate employee difficulties and help to prevent them.
- f. Encourage employees to do the desirable things they will do anyway.
- g. Judge your supervision by the results it secures.

7. PRINCIPLE OF SCIENCE

Successful supervision is scientific, objective, and experimental. It is based on facts, not on prejudices.

   a. Be cumulative in results.
   b. Never divorce your suggestions from the goals of training.
   c. Don't be impatient of results.
   d. Keep all matters on a professional, not a personal level.
   e. Do not be concerned exclusively with immediate problems and activities.
   f. Use objective means of determining achievement and rating where possible.

8. PRINCIPLE OF COOPERATION

Supervision is a cooperative enterprise between supervisor and employee.

   a. Begin with conditions as they are.
   b. Ask opinions of all involved when formulating policies.
   c. Organization is as good as its weakest link.
   d. Let employees help to determine policies and department programs.
   e. Be approachable and accessible - physically and mentally.
   f. Develop pleasant social relationships.

IV. WHAT IS ADMINISTRATION?

Administration is concerned with providing the environment, the material facilities, and the operational procedures that will promote the maximum growth and development of supervisors and employees. (Organization is an aspect, and a concomitant, of administration.)

There is no sharp line of demarcation between supervision and administration; these functions are intimately interrelated and, often, overlapping. They are complementary activities.

1. PRACTICES COMMONLY CLASSED AS "SUPERVISORY"

   a. Conducting employees conferences
   b. Visiting sections, units, offices, divisions, departments
   c. Arranging for demonstrations
   d. Examining plans
   e. Suggesting professional reading
   f. Interpreting bulletins
   g. Recommending in-service training courses
   h. Encouraging experimentation
   i. Appraising employee morale
   j. Providing for intervisitation

2. PRACTICES COMMONLY CLASSIFIED AS "ADMINISTRATIVE"

   a. Management of the office
   b. Arrangement of schedules for extra duties
   c. Assignment of rooms or areas
   d. Distribution of supplies
   e. Keeping records and reports
   f. Care of audio-visual materials
   g. Keeping inventory records
   h. Checking record cards and books
   i. Programming special activities
   j. Checking on the attendance and punctuality of employees

3. *PRACTICES COMMONLY CLASSIFIED AS BOTH "SUPERVISORY" AND "ADMINISTRATIVE"*
    a. Program construction
    b. Testing or evaluating outcomes
    c. Personnel accounting
    d. Ordering instructional materials

V. RESPONSIBILITIES OF THE SUPERVISOR

A person employed in a supervisory capacity must constantly be able to improve his own efficiency and ability. He represents the employer to the employees and only continuous self-examination can make him a capable supervisor.

Leadership and training are the supervisor's responsibility. An efficient working unit is one in which the employees work with the supervisor. It is his job to bring out the best in his employees. He must always be relaxed, courteous and calm in his association with his employees. Their feelings are important, and a harsh attitude does not develop the most efficient employees.

VI. COMPETENCIES OF THE SUPERVISOR

1. Complete knowledge of the duties and responsibilities of his position.
2. To be able to organize a job, plan ahead and carry through.
3. To have self-confidence and initiative.
4. To be able to handle the unexpected situation and make quick decisions.
5. To be able to properly train subordinates in the positions they are best suited for.
6. To be able to keep good human relations among his subordinates.
7. To be able to keep good human relations between his subordinates and himself and to earn their respect and trust.

VII. THE PROFESSIONAL SUPERVISOR-EMPLOYEE RELATIONSHIP

There are two kinds of efficiency: one kind is only apparent and is produced in organizations through the exercise of mere discipline; this is but a simulation of the second, or true, efficiency which springs from spontaneous cooperation. If you are a manager, no matter how great or small your responsibility, it is your job, in the final analysis, to create and develop this involuntary cooperation among the people whom you supervise. For, no matter how powerful a combination of money, machines, and materials a company may have, this is a dead and sterile thing without a team of willing, thinking and articulate people to guide it.

The following 21 points are presented as indicative of the exemplary basic relationship that should exist between supervisor and employee:

1. Each person wants to be liked and respected by his fellow employee and wants to be treated with consideration and respect by his superior.
2. The most competent employee will make an error. However, in a unit where good relations exist between the supervisor and his employees, tenseness and fear do not exist. Thus, errors are not hidden or covered up and the efficiency of a unit is not impaired.
3. Subordinates resent rules, regulations, or orders that are unreasonable or unexplained.
4. Subordinates are quick to resent unfairness, harshness, injustices and favoritism.
5. An employee will accept responsibility if he knows that he will be complimented for a job well done, and not too harshly chastised for failure; that his supervisor will check the cause of the failure, and, if it was the supervisor's fault, he will assume the blame therefore. If it was the employee's fault, his supervisor will explain the correct method or means of handling the responsibility.

6. An employee wants to receive credit for a suggestion he has made, that is used. If a suggestion cannot be used, the employee is entitled to an explanation. The supervisor should not say "no" and close the subject.

7. Fear and worry slow up a worker's ability. Poor working environment can impair his physical and mental health. A good supervisor avoids forceful methods, threats and arguments to get a job done.

8. A forceful supervisor is able to train his employees individually and as a team, and is able to motivate them in the proper channels.

9. A mature supervisor is able to properly evaluate his subordinates and to keep them happy and satisfied.

10. A sensitive supervisor will never patronize his subordinates.

11. A worthy supervisor will respect his employees' confidences.

12. Definite and clear-cut responsibilities should be assigned to each executive.

13. Responsibility should always be coupled with corresponding authority.

14. No change should be made in the scope or responsibilities of a position without a definite understanding to that effect on the part of all persons concerned.

15. No executive or employee, occupying a single position in the organization, should be subject to definite orders from more than one source.

16. Orders should never be given to subordinates over the head of a responsible executive. Rather than do this, the officer in question should be supplanted.

17. Criticisms of subordinates should, whoever possible, be made privately, and in no case should a subordinate be criticized in the presence of executives or employees of equal or lower rank.

18. No dispute or difference between executives or employees as to authority or responsibilities should be considered too trivial for prompt and careful adjudication.

19. Promotions, wage changes, and disciplinary action should always be approved by the executive immediately superior to the one directly responsible.

20. No executive or employee should ever be required, or expected, to be at the same time an assistant to, and critic of, another.

21. Any executive whose work is subject to regular inspection should, whever practicable, be given the assistance and facilities necessary to enable him to maintain an independent check of the quality of his work.

VIII. MINI-TEXT IN SUPERVISION, ADMINISTRATION, MANAGEMENT, AND ORGANIZATION

A. BRIEF HIGHLIGHTS

Listed concisely and sequentially are major headings and important data in the field for quick recall and review.

1. LEVELS OF MANAGEMENT

Any organization of some size has several levels of management. In terms of a ladder the levels are:

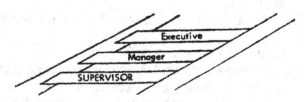

The first level is very important because it is the beginning point of management leadership.

2. WHAT THE SUPERVISOR MUST LEARN

A supervisor must learn to:

(1) Deal with people and their differences
(2) Get the job done through people
(3) Recognize the problems when they exist
(4) Overcome obstacles to good performance
(5) Evaluate the performance of people
(6) Check his own performance in terms of accomplishment

3. A DEFINITION OF SUPERVISOR

The term supervisor means any individual having authority, in the interests of the employer, to hire, transfer, suspend, lay-off, recall, promote, discharge, assign, reward, or discipline other employees or responsibility to direct them, or to adjust their grievances, or effectively to recommend such action, if, in connection with the foregoing, exercise of such authority is not of a merely routine or clerical nature but requires the use of independent judgment.

4. ELEMENTS OF THE TEAM CONCEPT

What is involved in teamwork? The component parts are:

(1) Members   (3) Goals   (5) Cooperation
(2) A leader   (4) Plans   (6) Spirit

5. PRINCIPLES OF ORGANIZATION

(1) A team member must know what his job is.
(2) Be sure that the nature and scope of a job are understood.
(3) Authority and responsibility should be carefully spelled out.
(4) A supervisor should be permitted to make the maximum number of decisions affecting his employees.
(5) Employees should report to only one supervisor.
(6) A supervisor should direct only as many employees as he can handle effectively.
(7) An organization plan should be flexible.
(8) Inspection and performance of work should be separate.
(9) Organizational problems should receive immediate attention.
(10) Assign work in line with ability and experience.

6. THE FOUR IMPORTANT PARTS OF EVERY JOB

(1) Inherent in every job is the *accountability* for results.
(2) A second set of factors in every job is *responsibilities*.
(3) Along with duties and responsibilities one must have the *authority* to act within certain limits without obtaining permission to proceed.
(4) No job exists in a vacuum. The supervisor is surrounded by key *relationships*.

7. PRINCIPLES OF DELEGATION

Where work is delegated for the first time, the supervisor should think in terms of these questions:

(1) Who is best qualified to do this?
(2) Can an employee improve his abilities by doing this?
(3) How long should an employee spend on this?
(4) Are there any special problems for which he will need guidance?
(5) How broad a delegation can I make?

8. PRINCIPLES OF EFFECTIVE COMMUNICATIONS
(1) Determine the media
(2) To whom directed?
(3) Identification and source authority
(4) Is communication understood?

9. PRINCIPLES OF WORK IMPROVEMENT
(1) Most people usually do only the work which is assigned to them
(2) Workers are likely to fit assigned work into the time available to perform it
(3) A good workload usually stimulates output
(4) People usually do their best work when they know that results will be reviewed or inspected
(5) Employees usually feel that someone else is responsible for conditions of work, workplace layout, job methods, type of tools/equipment, and other such factors
(6) Employees are usually defensive about their job security
(7) Employees have natural resistance to change
(8) Employees can support or destroy a supervisor
(9) A supervisor usually earns the respect of his people through his personal example of diligence and efficiency

10. AREAS OF JOB IMPROVEMENT
The areas of job improvement are quite numerous, but the most common ones which a supervisor can identify and utilize are:

(1) Departmental layout
(2) Flow of work
(3) Workplace layout
(4) Utilization of manpower
(5) Work methods
(6) Materials handling
(7) Utilization
(8) Motion economy

11. SEVEN KEY POINTS IN MAKING IMPROVEMENTS
(1) Select the job to be improved
(2) Study how it is being done now
(3) Question the present method
(4) Determine actions to be taken
(5) Chart proposed method
(6) Get approval and apply
(7) Solicit worker participation

12. CORRECTIVE TECHNIQUES OF JOB IMPROVEMENT

Specific Problems	General Improvement	Corrective Techniques
(1) Size of workload	(1) Departmental layout	(1) Study with scale model
(2) Inability to meet schedules	(2) Flow of work	(2) Flow chart study
(3) Strain and fatigue	(3) Work plan layout	(3) Motion analysis
(4) Improper use of men and skills	(4) Utilization of manpower	(4) Comparison of units produced to standard allowance
(5) Waste, poor quality, unsafe conditions	(5) Work methods	(5) Methods analysis
(6) Bottleneck conditions that hinder output	(6) Materials handling	(6) Flow chart & equipment study
(7) Poor utilization of equipment and machine	(7) Utilization of equipment	(7) Down time vs. running time
(8) Efficiency and productivity of labor	(8) Motion economy	(8) Motion analysis

13. A *PLANNING CHECKLIST*

(1) Objectives
(2) Controls
(3) Delegations
(4) Communications
(5) Resources

(6) Resources
(7) Manpower
(8) Equipment
(9) Supplies and materials
(10) Utilization of time

(11) Safety
(12) Money
(13) Work
(14) Timing of improvements

14. *FIVE CHARACTERISTICS OF GOOD DIRECTIONS*

In order to get results, directions must be:

(1) Possible of accomplishment
(2) Agreeable with worker interests

(3) Related to mission
(4) Planned and complete

(5) Unmistakably clear

15. *TYPES OF DIRECTIONS*

(1) Demands or direct orders
(2) Requests

(3) Suggestion or implication
(4) Volunteering

16. *CONTROLS*

A typical listing of the overall areas in which the supervisor should establish controls might be:

(1) Manpower
(2) Materials

(3) Quality of work
(4) Quantity of work

(5) Time
(6) Space

(7) Money
(8) Methods

17. *ORIENTING THE NEW EMPLOYEE*

(1) Prepare for him
(2) Welcome the new employee

(3) Orientation for the job
(4) Follow-up

18. *CHECKLIST FOR ORIENTING NEW EMPLOYEES*

	Yes	No
(1) Do your appreciate the feelings of new employees when they first report for work?	___	___
(2) Are you aware of the fact that the new employee must make a big adjustment to his job?	___	___
(3) Have you given him good reasons for liking the job and the organization?	___	___
(4) Have you prepared for his first day on the job?		
(5) Did you welcome him cordially and make him feel needed?		
(6) Did you establish rapport with him so that he feels free to talk and discuss matters with you?	___	___
(7) Did you explain his job to him and his relationship to you?	___	___
(8) Does he know that his work will be evaluated periodically on a basis that is fair and objective?	___	___
(9) Did you introduce him to his fellow workers in such a way that they are likely to accept him?	___	___
(10) Does he know what employee benefits he will receive?		
(11) Does he understand the importance of being on the job and what to do if he must leave his duty station?	___	___
(12) Has he been impressed with the importance of accident prevention and safe practice?	___	___
(13) Does he generally know his way around the department?	___	___
(14) Is he under the guidance of a sponsor who will teach the right ways of doing things?	___	___
(15) Do you plan to follow-up so that he will continue to adjust successfully to his job?	___	___

19. *PRINCIPLES OF LEARNING*
        (1) Motivation   (2) Demonstration or explanation   (3) Practice

20. *CAUSES OF POOR PERFORMANCE*
        (1) Improper training for job
        (2) Wrong tools
        (3) Inadequate directions
        (4) Lack of supervisory follow-up
        (5) Poor communications
        (6) Lack of standards of performance
        (7) Wrong work habits
        (8) Low morale
        (9) Other

21. *FOUR MAJOR STEPS IN ON-THE-JOB INSTRUCTION*
        (1) Prepare the worker
        (2) Present the operation
        (3) Tryout performance
        (4) Follow-up

22. *EMPLOYEES WANT FIVE THINGS*
        (1) Security (2) Opportunity (3) Recognition (4) Inclusion (5) Expression

23. *SOME DON'TS IN REGARD TO PRAISE*
        (1) Don't praise a person for something he hasn't done
        (2) Don't praise a person unless you can be sincere
        (3) Don't be sparing in praise just because your superior withholds it from you
        (4) Don't let too much time elapse between good performance and recognition of it

24. *HOW TO GAIN YOUR WORKERS' CONFIDENCE*
    Methods of developing confidence include such things as:
        (1) Knowing the interests, habits, hobbies of employees
        (2) Admitting your own inadequacies
        (3) Sharing and telling of confidence in others
        (4) Supporting people when they are in trouble
        (5) Delegating matters that can be well handled
        (6) Being frank and straightforward about problems and working conditions
        (7) Encouraging others to bring their problems to you
        (8) Taking action on problems which impede worker progress

25. *SOURCES OF EMPLOYEE PROBLEMS*
    On-the-job causes might be such things as:
        (1) A feeling that favoritism is exercised in assignments
        (2) Assignment of overtime
        (3) An undue amount of supervision
        (4) Changing methods or systems
        (5) Stealing of ideas or trade secrets
        (6) Lack of interest in job
        (7) Threat of reduction in force
        (8) Ignorance or lack of communications
        (9) Poor equipment
      (10) Lack of knowing how supervisor feels toward employee
      (11) Shift assignments

    Off-the-job problems might have to do with:
        (1) Health   (2) Finances   (3) Housing   (4) Family

26. THE SUPERVISOR'S KEY TO DISCIPLINE

There are several key points about discipline which the supervisor should keep in mind:

(1) Job discipline is one of the disciplines of life and is directed by the supervisor.
(2) It is more important to correct an employee fault than to fix blame for it.
(3) Employee performance is affected by problems both on the job and off.
(4) Sudden or abrupt changes in behavior can be indications of important employee problems.
(5) Problems should be dealt with as soon as possible after they are identified.
(6) The attitude of the supervisor may have more to do with solving problems than the techniques of problem solving.
(7) Correction of employee behavior should be resorted to only after the supervisor is sure that training or counseling will not be helpful.
(8) Be sure to document your disciplinary actions.
(9) Make sure that you are disciplining on the basis of facts rather than personal feelings.
(10) Take each disciplinary step in order, being careful not to make snap judgments, or decisions based on impatience.

27. FIVE IMPORTANT PROCESSES OF MANAGEMENT

(1) Planning   (2) Organizing   (3) Scheduling
(4) Controlling   (5) Motivating

28. WHEN THE SUPERVISOR FAILS TO PLAN

(1) Supervisor creates impression of not knowing his job
(2) May lead to excessive overtime
(3) Job runs itself -- supervisor lacks control
(4) Deadlines and appointments missed
(5) Parts of the work go undone
(6) Work interrupted by emergencies
(7) Sets a bad example
(8) Uneven workload creates peaks and valleys
(9) Too much time on minor details at expense of more important tasks

29. FOURTEEN GENERAL PRINCIPLES OF MANAGEMENT

(1) Division of work
(2) Authority and responsibility
(3) Discipline
(4) Unity of command
(5) Unity of direction
(6) Subordination of individual interest to general interest
(7) Remuneration of personnel
(8) Centralization
(9) Scalar chain
(10) Order
(11) Equity
(12) Stability of tenure of personnel
(13) Initiative
(14) Esprit de corps

30. CHANGE

Bringing about change is perhaps attempted more often, and yet less well understood, than anything else the supervisor does. How do people generally react to change? (People tend to resist change that is imposed upon them by other individuals or circumstances.

Change is characteristic of every situation. It is a part of every real endeavor where the efforts of people are concerned.

A. Why do people resist change?

People may resist change because of:
   (1) Fear of the unknown
   (2) Implied criticism
   (3) Unpleasant experiences in the past
   (4) Fear of loss of status
   (5) Threat to the ego
   (6) Fear of loss of economic stability

B. How can we best overcome the resistance to change?

In initiating change, take these steps:
   (1) Get ready to sell
   (2) Identify sources of help
   (3) Anticipate objections
   (4) Sell benefits
   (5) Listen in depth
   (6) Follow up

B. BRIEF TOPICAL SUMMARIES

I. WHO/WHAT IS THE SUPERVISOR?

1. The supervisor is often called the "highest level employee and the lowest level manager."
2. A supervisor is a member of both management and the work group. He acts as a bridge between the two.
3. Most problems in supervision are in the area of human relations, or people problems.
4. Employees expect: Respect, opportunity to learn and to advance, and a sense of belonging, and so forth.
5. Supervisors are responsible for directing people and organizing work. Planning is of paramount importance.
6. A position description is a set of duties and responsibilities inherent to a given position.
7. It is important to keep the position description up-to-date and to provide each employee with his own copy.

II. THE SOCIOLOGY OF WORK

1. People are alike in many ways; however, each individual is unique.
2. The supervisor is challenged in getting to know employee differences. Acquiring skills in evaluating individuals is an asset.
3. Maintaining meaningful working relationships in the organization is of great importance.
4. The supervisor has an obligation to help individuals to develop to their fullest potential.
5. Job rotation on a planned basis helps to build versatility and to maintain interest and enthusiasm in work groups.
6. Cross training (job rotation) provides backup skills.
7. The supervisor can help reduce tension by maintaining a sense of humor, providing guidance to employees, and by making reasonable and timely decisions. Employees respond favorably to working under reasonably predictable circumstances.
8. Change is characteristic of all managerial behavior. The supervisor must adjust to changes in procedures, new methods, technological changes, and to a number of new and sometimes challenging situations.
9. To overcome the natural tendency for people to resist change, the supervisor should become more skillful in initiating change.

III. PRINCIPLES AND PRACTICES OF SUPERVISION

1. Employees should be required to answer to only one superior.
2. A supervisor can effectively direct only a limited number of employees, depending upon the complexity, variety, and proximity of the jobs involved.
3. The organizational chart presents the organization in graphic form. It reflects lines of authority and responsibility as well as interrelationships of units within the organization.
4. Distribution of work can be improved through an analysis using the "Work Distribution Chart."
5. The "Work Distribution Chart" reflects the division of work within a unit in understandable form.
6. When related tasks are given to an employee, he has a better chance of increasing his skills through training.
7. The individual who is given the responsibility for tasks must also be given the appropriate authority to insure adequate results.
8. The supervisor should delegate repetitive, routine work. Preparation of recurring reports, maintaining leave and attendance records are some examples.
9. Good discipline is essential to good task performance. Discipline is reflected in the actions of employees on the job in the absence of supervision.
10. Disciplinary action may have to be taken when the positive aspects of discipline have failed. Reprimand, warning, and suspension are examples of disciplinary action.
11. If a situation calls for a reprimand, be sure it is deserved and remember it is to be done in private.

IV. DYNAMIC LEADERSHIP

1. A style is a personal method or manner of exerting influence.
2. Authoritarian leaders often see themselves as the source of power and authority.
3. The democratic leader often perceives the group as the source of authority and power.
4. Supervisors tend to do better when using the pattern of leadership that is most natural for them.
5. Social scientists suggest that the effective supervisor use the leadership style that best fits the problem or circumstances involved.
6. All four styles -- telling, selling, consulting, joining -- have their place. Using one does not preclude using the other at another time.
7. The theory X point of view assumes that the average person dislikes work, will avoid it whenever possible, and must be coerced to achieve organizational objectives.
8. The theory Y point of view assumes that the average person considers work to be as natural as play, and, when the individual is committed, he requires little supervision or direction to accomplish desired objectives.
9. The leader's basic assumptions concerning human behavior and human nature affect his actions, decisions, and other managerial practices.
10. Dissatisfaction among employees is often present, but difficult to isolate. The supervisor should seek to weaken dissatisfaction by keeping promises, being sincere and considerate, keeping employees informed, and so forth.
11. Constructive suggestions should be encouraged during the natural progress of the work.

V. PROCESSES FOR SOLVING PROBLEMS

1. People find their daily tasks more meaningful and satisfying when they can improve them.
2. The causes of problems, or the key factors, are often hidden in the background. Ability to solve problems often involves the ability to isolate them from their backgrounds. There is some substance to the cliché that some persons "can't see the forest for the trees."
3. New procedures are often developed from old ones. Problems should be broken down into manageable parts. New ideas can be adapted from old ones.

4. People think differently in problem-solving situations. Using a logical, patterned approach is often useful. One approach found to be useful includes these steps:

(a) Define the problem	(d) Weigh and decide
(b) Establish objectives	(e) Take action
(c) Get the facts	(f) Evaluate action

VI. TRAINING FOR RESULTS

1. Participants respond best when they feel training is important to them.
2. The supervisor has responsibility for the training and development of those who report to him.
3. When training is delegated to others, great care must be exercised to insure the trainer has knowledge, aptitude, and interest for his work as a trainer.
4. Training (learning) of some type goes on continually. The most successful supervisor makes certain the learning contributes in a productive manner to operational goals.
5. New employees are particularly susceptible to training. Older employees facing new job situations require specific training, as well as having need for development and growth opportunities.
6. Training needs require continuous monitoring.
7. The training officer of an agency is a professional with a responsibility to assist supervisors in solving training problems.
8. Many of the self-development steps important to the supervisor's own growth are equally important to the development of peers and subordinates. Knowledge of these is important when the supervisor consults with others on development and growth opportunities.

VII. HEALTH, SAFETY, AND ACCIDENT PREVENTION

1. Management-minded supervisors take appropriate measures to assist employees in maintaining health and in assuring safe practices in the work environment.
2. Effective safety training and practices help to avoid injury and accidents.
3. Safety should be a management goal. All infractions of safety which are observed should be corrected without exception.
4. Employees' safety attitude, training and instruction, provision of safe tools and equipment, supervision, and leadership are considered highly important factors which contribute to safety and which can be influenced directly by supervisors.
5. When accidents do occur they should be investigated promptly for very important reasons, including the fact that information which is gained can be used to prevent accidents in the future.

VIII. EQUAL EMPLOYMENT OPPORTUNITY

1. The supervisor should endeavor to treat all employees fairly, without regard to religion, race, sex, or national origin.
2. Groups tend to reflect the attitude of the leader. Prejudice can be detected even in very subtle form. Supervisors must strive to create a feeling of mutual respect and confidence in every employee.
3. Complete utilization of all human resources is a national goal. Equitable consideration should be accorded women in the work force, minority-group members, the physically and mentally handicapped, and the older employee. The important question is: "Who can do the job?"
4. Training opportunities, recognition for performance, overtime assignments, promotional opportunities, and all other personnel actions are to be handled on an equitable basis.

IX. IMPROVING COMMUNICATIONS

1. Communications is achieving understanding between the sender and the receiver of a message. It also means sharing information -- the creation of understanding.
2. Communication is basic to all human activity. Words are means of conveying meanings; however, real meanings are in people.
3. There are very practical differences in the effectiveness of one-way, impersonal, and two-way communications. Words spoken face-to-face are better understood. Telephone conversations are effective, but lack the rapport of person-to-person exchanges. The whole person communicates.
4. Cooperation and communication in an organization go hand in hand. When there is a mutual respect between people, spelling out rules and procedures for communicating is unnecessary.
5. There are several barriers to effective communications. These include failure to listen with respect and understanding, lack of skill in feedback, and misinterpreting the meanings of words used by the speaker. It is also common practice to listen to what we want to hear, and tune out things we do not want to hear.
6. Communication is management's chief problem. The supervisor should accept the challenge to communicate more effectively and to improve interagency and intra-agency communications.
7. The supervisor may often plan for and conduct meetings. The planning phase is critical and may determine the success or the failure of a meeting.
8. Speaking before groups usually requires extra effort. Stage fright may never disappear completely, but it can be controlled.

X. SELF-DEVELOPMENT

1. Every employee is responsible for his own self-development.
2. Toastmaster and toastmistress clubs offer opportunities to improve skills in oral communications.
3. Planning for one's own self-development is of vital importance. Supervisors know their own strengths and limitations better than anyone else.
4. Many opportunities are open to aid the supervisor in his developmental efforts, including job assignments; training opportunities, both governmental and non-governmental -- to include universities and professional conferences and seminars.
5. Programmed instruction offers a means of studying at one's own rate.
6. Where difficulties may arise from a supervisor's being away from his work for training, he may participate in televised home study or correspondence courses to meet his self-develop- ment needs.

XI. TEACHING AND TRAINING

A. The Teaching Process

Teaching is encouraging and guiding the learning activities of students toward established goals. In most cases this process consists in five steps: preparation, presentation, summarization, evaluation, and application.

1. Preparation

Preparation is twofold in nature; that of the supervisor and the employee.

Preparation by the supervisor is absolutely essential to success. He must know what, when, where, how, and whom he will teach. Some of the factors that should be considered are:

(1) The objectives
(2) The materials needed
(3) The methods to be used
(4) Employee participation
(5) Employee interest
(6) Training aids
(7) Evaluation
(8) Summarization

Employee preparation consists in preparing the employee to receive the material. Probably the most important single factor in the preparation of the employee is arousing and maintaining his interest. He must know the objectives of the training, why he is there, how the material can be used, and its importance to him.

2. Presentation

In presentation, have a carefully designed plan and follow it.
The plan should be accurate and complete, yet flexible enough to meet situations as they arise. The method of presentation will be determined by the particular situation and objectives.

3. Summary

A summary should be made at the end of every training unit and program. In addition, there may be internal summaries depending on the nature of the material being taught. The important thing is that the trainee must always be able to understand how each part of the new material relates to the whole.

4. Application

The supervisor must arrange work so the employee will be given a chance to apply new knowledge or skills while the material is still clear in his mind and interest is high. The trainee does not really know whether he has learned the material until he has been given a chance to apply it. If the material is not applied, it loses most of its value.

5. Evaluation

The purpose of all training is to promote learning. To determine whether the training has been a success or failure, the supervisor must evaluate this learning.
In the broadest sense evaluation includes all the devices, methods, skills, and techniques used by the supervisor to keep him self and the employees informed as to their progress toward the objectives they are pursuing. The extent to which the employee has mastered the knowledge, skills, and abilities, or changed his attitudes, as determined by the program objectives, is the extent to which instruction has succeeded or failed.
Evaluation should not be confined to the end of the lesson, day, or program but should be used continuously. We shall note later the way this relates to the rest of the teaching process.

B. Teaching Methods

A teaching method is a pattern of identifiable student and instructor activity used in presenting training material.
All supervisors are faced with the problem of deciding which method should be used at a given time.
As with all methods, there are certain advantages and disadvantages to each method.

1. Lecture

The lecture is direct oral presentation of material by the supervisor. The present trend is to place less emphasis on the trainer's activity and more on that of the trainee.

2. Discussion

Teaching by discussion or conference involves using questions and other techniques to arouse interest and focus attention upon certain areas, and by doing so creating a learning situation. This can be one of the most valuable methods because it gives the employees 'an opportunity to express their ideas and pool their knowledge.

3. Demonstration

The demonstration is used to teach how something works or how to do something. It can be used to show a principle or what the results of a series of actions will be. A well-staged demonstration is particularly effective because it shows proper methods of performance in a realistic manner.

4. Performance

Performance is one of the most fundamental of all learning techniques or teaching methods. The trainee may be able to tell how a specific operation should be performed but he cannot be sure he knows how to perform the operation until he has done so.

5. Which Method to Use

Moreover, there are other methods and techniques of teaching. It is difficult to use any method without other methods entering into it. In any learning situation a combination of methods is usually more effective than anyone method alone.

Finally, evaluation must be integrated into the other aspects of the teaching-learning process.

It must be used in the motivation of the trainees; it must be used to assist in developing understanding during the training; and it must be related to employee application of the results of training.

This is distinctly the role of the supervisor.

AN HISTORIC LOOK AT
REAL PROPERTY TAX ASSESSMENTS IN NEW YORK

CONTENTS

AN HISTORIC LOOK AT
REAL PROPERTY TAX ASSESSMENTS IN NEW YORK

The property tax bill—its amount and the fairness with which it is shared—has been a public issue for apparently as long as we have had such a tax. Its history in New York goes back to early colonial times.

A combination of events in the late 70s has pushed the issue forward again as an important public question that is likely to be debated for at least the next few years. Among the events are recent New York court decisions that appear to require a major overhaul of property assessment practices and may substantially alter the distribution of property taxes among taxpayers.

The real property tax remains the most important and continuing source of revenues raised by local governments. It has come to be exceeded in New York by the totals of state and federal aid received by these local governments. Federal and state taxes, which do not include the property tax, have become several times larger than local collections. The property tax thus plays a much less important part in the total tax picture—federal, state, and local—than it did earlier in the century. Real property tax collections in New York State have long been rising, however, and still exceed those of either the state personal income tax or state and local sales taxes.[1]

A thorough study of why property taxes have increased is beyond the scope of this discussion, but a few reasons may be mentioned. Local governmental expenditures have expanded even more than revenues from these taxes. Wages, salaries, and fringe benefits of employees, and the prices of materials and supplies have increased. Payments to aid the needy and sick have moved up as the cost of living and of medical care have risen. The introduction of new functions and the expansion of existing ones in response to public demand have added to local tax requirements. These changes have taken place against an economic background of growing incomes for most individuals and families and of rising market values for most real estate.

As property taxes have increased and property values have risen, issues relating to assessment or valuation of property for tax purposes have become more acute. Assessment changes tend to lag behind changes in the market. All properties or types of property have not shared in rising market values to the same degree. As a result, assessed values, which probably never have reflected real values accurately in most communities, have become more and more remotely related to current conditions. Even if properties once were assessed with reasonable equity in relation to one another, a long lag in adjusting assessments to changing values usually produces substantial inequities among property taxpayers.

HOW THE PROPERTY TAX BILL IS DETERMINED

Three factors influence the amount of property taxes that a property owner pays. They are:
1. The total amount of taxes levied by local authorities.
2. The assessed value placed on the property as compared with all other taxable properties in a town (or other assessing district).
3. The equalization rates fixed by the state and the county.

---

[1] For 1975, revenues from the property tax were $6.7 billion; from income tax, $5.4 billion; and from sales tax, $3.5 billion. In 2017 they were, respectively: $2.4 billion; $51.5 billion; and from sales tax plus excise and user taxes, $15.7 billion.

Total Tax Levies

Three "layers" of local government cover New York State and are supported in part by the property tax. In addition, other local governments may be supported, depending upon where the property is located.

The state outside of New York City is divided into 57 counties. Each county is divided into towns, or towns and cities. The state is also divided into school districts. Property is therefore located in (1) a county, (2) a town or city, and (3) a school district.

One or more incorporated villages may be in a town. Special taxing or improvement districts also are laid out in many towns for fire protection, water supply, street lighting, and the like. Property in villages or districts helps to support the services provided.

Generally, property taxes are included in budgets that the local governments prepare. The amount of tax is usually determined by the difference between estimated expenditures for the coming year and estimated receipts from sources other than the property tax.

Passing judgment upon budgets and levying property taxes usually are the responsibility of local governing bodies, with the important qualification that they must abide by the requirements of state laws and the State Constitution. The more important governing bodies in rural areas are the town board, the county board (variously named county legislature board of supervisors, or board of representatives), the school board and annual school district meeting, and the village board of trustees.

These governing bodies, not the assessors, determine the total amount of property taxes needed.

Assessed Value

The work of the assessors is essentially concerned with dividing among individual property owners the total amounts of taxes that are levied by other authorities. The assessors do this by placing a value upon each property in their assessing district (in rural areas, principally the town).

Let us use a greatly simplified example. Suppose a town needs $300 of property taxes to help meet expenses for the coming year. There are three properties in the town. The assessor has assessed or valued each one at $10,000. The total assessed value is then $30,000. The rate required to yield the $300 is $10 per $1,000 of assessed value or 10 mills per dollar ($300 divided by $30,000). A $10 per $1,000 tax rate on property assessed at $10,000 yields $100. The $300 tax levy for town purposes is divided equally among the three properties because each is assessed at the same figure.

If one property were assessed at $15,000, another at $5,000, and the third at $10,000 the total assessed value would be the same, and so would the tax rate, but the taxes payable on the first property would be $150; on the second, $50; and on the third, $100. The taxes have been divided differently by changing the relationship between the assessed value on two properties as compared with the total assessed value.

We may, therefore, conclude that once the total amount of the town tax levy is determined the share of the tax that is payable on a piece of property depends on the assessed value placed on that property compared with the total valuation in the town.

Note that the tax payable does not depend on the assessed value of the property alone, but also upon the total valuation in the town. The assessed value on a piece of property may be changed without changing the amount of tax if the total assessed value in the town is changed to the same degree. To illustrate, let us return to the example above where the three properties in a town are assessed at $10,000 each. Suppose the assessor doubles the $10,000 assessment on one of the properties and changes the assessment on the others so that the total assessed valuation in the town is also doubled. The total value is then $60,000. The tax rate required to yield $300 is then cut in half to $5 per $1,000 of assessed value ($300 divided by $60,000). A $5 tax rate on the new assessment of $20,000 yields the same tax as before, or $100.

Often this important fact is not understood. The assessor of a town may attempt to raise the general level of assessments in order to bring them more nearly into line with realistic levels of value. Protests often follow, partly because of the apparently widespread belief that raising the assessed value on a property necessarily involves increased taxes.

Increased taxes on a property result only if the total levy is increased or if the assessed value of the property is aided by a greater percentage than the total valuation. Assume that the assessed values of $10,000 each for the three properties in the example are changed to $30,000, $20,000, and $10,000. The total assessed value has been doubled, from $30,000 to $60,000. The tax rate needed to raise $300 has been halved from $10 to $5 per $1,000 of assessed value. The original tax of $100 payable on each property has been changed to $150 for the first, $100 for the second, and $50 for the third. Taxes against the first property have increased because its assessed value was tripled while the total was doubled. Taxes payable on the second property remain unchanged because its assessed value was increased at the same rate as the total assessed value. Taxes due on the third property are reduced because its assessed value was not changed while the total assessed value for the town was doubled.

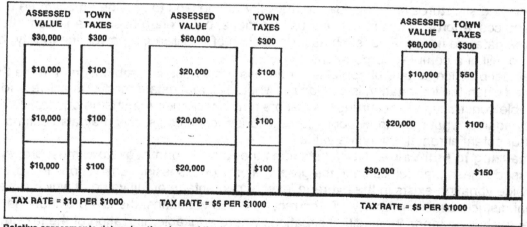

Relative assessments determine the share of the total property tax bill each individual pays.
The assessor's work essentially is to divide tax levies among taxpayers. Increased assessments do not necessarily mean increased taxes.

Equalization Rates

The Real Property Tax Law of New York (Section 306) requires that property be assessed at its full value. A common concept of full value in court decisions is the price at which a property would change hands under ordinary circumstances between a buyer who is willing but not compelled to buy and a seller who is willing but not compelled to sell. Full value thus is market value. Such a definition of full value cannot apply in all cases such as those involving highly specialized industrial properties which do not ordinarily change hands in the market. It is, however, applicable for more common types of property for which there is a market.

Property Appraisal. Placing a value on a property ultimately involves a subjective judgment by the appraiser. Well-established procedures are available, however, to make this decision as objective as possible. The three generally accepted methods of appraisal include not only the market approach, but also the income approach, but also the income approach and the cost approach.[2]

In the market approach, value is estimated by comparing the property with similar properties that have been sold recently (known by appraisers as "comparable sales"). The market approach approximates a value based on the amount a willing buyer would pay and a willing seller would take, neither being under undue pressure ("arm's-length sale"). Adjustments must be made for important differences between the property being appraised and the "comparable sales." This approach is useful and generally accurate when the market is active enough to make meaningful comparisons, and properties are fairly similar in nature, such as single family residences. A major limitation is the availability of comparable sales.

The income approach estimates values by treating the income earned or rental value of a property as a return on its capital value. Several methods are used to estimate property values through income capitalization. The reliability of this approach depends on the accuracy of income and rent as an indication of value and the extent to which the capitalization process actually exists in the market place. The value of a dairy farm, for example, may be estimated partly by the number of cows it will carry, and the income thereby yielded.

The third method of appraisal is the cost approach. The value of land must be estimated separately, using either the market or income approach. The replacement cost for new structures is estimated and then depreciated for loss in value over time. The depreciated value of buildings and structures is then added to the value of the land to provide an estimate for the parcel. The cost approach has many serious limitations, but is often used when adequate sales and income data are unavailable, such as for a section of a railroad, a power line facility, or a steel rolling mill of a complex corporation.

In actual practice, a careful appraiser or assessor may use a combination of these three approaches when the information is available. Where the real estate market is active and considerable construction is occurring, assessors may check their judgments on market value of a property against what they know about current construction costs, and may also estimate on the basis of potential rental or income value.

Equalizing to Full Value. Notwithstanding the Real Property Tax Law, most properties are assessed at less than full value in the great majority of assessing jurisdictions in New York. Further, wide variation exists in the average level or percentage of full value at which assessors in different districts assess property. To correct for these variations, the law provides that adjustments shall be made in specified situations where equitable allocation of the tax burden is affected. The adjustments are made by means of an equalization rate. The rate is simply a percentage figure that is expected to represent the average percentage of full value at which the assessor in an assessing district, such as a town, values properties.

The same law (Section 202 and Article 12) requires that the State Board of Equalization and Assessment establish sate equalization rates for each county, town, city, and village. To establish these rates, the Board regularly conducts market-value surveys on a sample of properties in each district and obtains information concerning valid, "arm's-length" sales of real estate.

The apportionment or allocation of taxes for county purposes among the towns and cities of a county is one situation where equalization rates are important. Town and city assessors assess property for county as well as town and city tax purposes. Typically, substantial differences exist among these local governments in a county in the average percentage of full value at which properties are assessed. To apportion taxes for county purposes among towns

---

[2] Hollis A. Swett, "Real Estate Value and the Property Tax, Some Basic Concepts," paper presented at the Association of Towns Annual Meeting, New York, New York, February 1976.

and cities in proportion to total assessed values in each town and city would be manifestly unfair. Equalization rates, therefore, are used to make adjustment.

Let us illustrate by a greatly simplified example. Suppose a county needs $900 of property taxes to help meet expenses for the coming, year. There are only two towns (and no cities) in the county, each with its own assessor. In Town A there are only three properties, each assessed at its full value of $30,000, $20,000, and $10,000. Total assessed value in Town A is, therefore, $60,000. The equalization rate, or average percentage of full value, at which properties are assessed is, therefore, the same as assessed value, $60,000.

In Town B, there are also three properties, each identical in full value to those in Town A. The assessor, however, has assessed each one at $10,000, making a total assessed value of $30,000, or one-half the total in Town A. The equalization rate for Town B should, therefore, be 50 percent. The $30,000 divided by 50 percent yields a full value of $60,000.

Let us further suppose that the tax levy of $900 for county purposes were to be apportioned between the two towns in proportion to their assessed values of $60,000 and $30,000. Taxpayers in Town A would bear two-thirds of the levy, or $600, since assessed value in Town A is two-thirds of the county total of $90,000. Taxpayers in Town B would bear one-third of the levy, or $300. Taxpayers in Town A would be paying double the amount of county tax compared with those in Town B although the full value of taxable property is identical in the two towns. The assessor for Town A, in conscientiously appraising each property at full value, would have penalized the taxpayers of the town. In Town B, the assessor has not only assessed all but one property at less than full value, but has failed to assess the three properties at a reasonably uniform percentage of their full value.

The law, therefore, provides for equalizing or adjusting assessed values of towns and cities in allocating county taxes. The equalization rate is the major factor in this adjustment. Essentially, taxes for county purposes are apportioned in proportion to full value of taxable property in each town or city.

To return to the example above, the assessed value of $60,000 in Town A divided by the equalization rate of 100 percent yields a full value of $60,000. The $30,000 assessed value in Town B divided by the 50 percent equalization rate yields a full value of $60,000. If the $900 of county taxes are apportioned in proportion to full value, the taxpayers of each town bear one-half the levy, or $450. Each town shares equally in the levy because the total full valuation in each town is the same.

The equalization rates correct for differences in average levels of assessment between the two towns. Note, however, that they do not correct for inequitable assessments on individual properties within a town. In Town B, for example, the three properties are assessed at $10,000 each although their value is $30,000, $20,000, and $10,000, respectively. Each property owner would have to pay one-third of the $450 county tax apportioned to the town although the full value of the first property is three times that of the third. In Town A, on the other hand, the three properties identical in value to those in Town B, have been assessed at full value, totaling $60,000. The tax rate of $7.50 per $1,000 required to raise $450 for county purposes in Town A would result in taxes of $225 against the $30,000 property, $150 against the $20,000 property, and #$75 against the $10,000 property. The assessor of Town B can correct inequitable assessments among individual properties in that town. An equalization rate cannot do this.

The assessor of Town B could correct the inequities by raising all assessments to full value as in Town A, by assessing each property at the current equalization rate level of 50 percent of full value, or by assessing each property at some other uniform percentage of full value. Instead of assessing the three properties at $10,000 each, the assessor could value the $30,000 property at $15,000, the $20,000 property at $10,000, and the $10,000 property at $5,000. Total assessed value would remain at $30,000, the equalization rate at 50 percent, and full value at $60,000. A tax rate of $15 per $1,000 assessed value would then be required to raise $450 of county taxes. Then, as in Town A, there would be taxes of $225 against the $30,000 property (assessed at $15,000), $150 against the $20,000 property (assessed at $10,000), and $75 against the $10,000 property (assessed at $5,000).

Importance of Accurate Equalization Rates. Although equalization rates do not correct for inequitable assessments on individual properties within a town, they can, as illustrated, effectively adjust for variations among towns (and cities) in average levels of value at which properties are assessed. They can do this to the degree that they are accurate.

Grossly inaccurate rates may be worse than none at all. For example, if the equalization rates in the illustration above were fixed at 100 percent for both Towns A and B, assessed value would be the same as full value in each town, and Town A would be penalized for its full value assessments. In effect, there would be no equalization rates or equalization of the tax levy for county purposes. If the equalization rates of both towns were fixed at 50 percent, the effect would be the same. If the rate for Town A were made lower than for Town B, Town A would be better off if the process were abolished. In any of these cases, Town A's assessor would have strong incentive to cut assessments on properties, and both towns could embark upon competitive undervaluation with chaotic results.

Two kinds of authorities are required to establish equalization rates annually: the state and the county. The state fixes rates for towns, cities, and villages. The county governing board, or a county equalization commission in a few counties, fixes rates for each town and city in that county. Appeal procedures are provided by state law for local jurisdictions that believe the state or county rates are unfair.

The county rates are used in apportioning taxes for county purposes among the towns and cities in the county. A county may adopt the state rates, and many do.

The state rates serve a variety of purposes. One of them, for example, is in distributing certain forms of state aid, especially state aid to school districts. A major part of state aid for education is distributed according to formulas that include as one factor the full valuation of taxable property in a school district. Full valuation is obtained by dividing assessed valuation by the state equalization rate, as in the illustrations above. School districts with a low full value of taxable property per pupil generally receive more state aid per pupil than their opposites.

The belief sometimes gains currency that raising the levels of assessed values in a community will curtail state aid for schools. As the examples above illustrate, this is not true so long as the state equalization rates reflect levels of assessment with reasonable accuracy, and the state uses the rates to calculate state aid.

In the present system of property taxation in New York, reasonably accurate equalization rates are essential for equitable allocation of property taxes and state aid, and for other purposes. They also help to assure those assessors who conscientiously try to readjust assessed values of properties in their communities that their efforts will not be penalized through apportionment of taxes and state aid.

PROPERTY SUBJECT TO TAX

Only real estate or real property (as defined in the Real Property Tax Law) is subject to the property tax in New York State, contrary to practice in many other states where all or part of personal property is also supposed to be included. All real property in the state is taxable unless exempt by law or other provision.

Exemptions, however, are substantial. In some assessing jurisdictions, they comprise the lion's share of all real estate. The more the exemptions, of course, the less the taxable property that remains to bear tax levies.

Exempt property includes not only that of governments (federal, state, and local) with certain exceptions, but also a variety of kinds of real estate held by various kinds of private organizations and individuals for various purposes. For example, property of churches, colleges, hospitals and charitable organizations used exclusively for nonprofit purposes is exempt. Certain railroad real property is entitled to partial exemption, as are certain agricultural and forest lands and business investments in real estate improvement. Property of war veterans and certain near relatives is entitled to exemption of up to $5,000, if purchased wi6th funds obtained from pensions and other sources provided by the federal or New York governments. Persons over 65 years old with limited incomes may be eligible for partial exemption of their homes. These examples are by no means comprehensive.

Generally, the kinds of exemptions have been growing in scope and complexity over a long period. The intended effect of state (and local) legislation of exemptions is, of course, to aid worthy causes, organizations, or individuals. A side effect is gradual erosion of the tax base as the list of exempt properties lengthens.

FULL VALUE ASSESSMENT

In no New York assessing jurisdiction—town, city, village or county—are all properties assessed precisely at full value. In very few does even the average level of assessment approximate 100 percent of full value.

These deficiencies in the statutory standard of perfection have a variety of causes. One is that property appraisal is not a precise science. Another is the lag between changing real estate values and the capacity of the governmental assessment machinery to keep up with them. Still another over the sweep of the long history of the state has been the absence of substantial support among local and state officials and other citizens for assessments uniformly approximating full value, except for occasional upsurges of revivalistic fervor in some localities, and even more rarely in the state capitol.

The Governor's Advisory Panel of Consultants reported in 1976 on an analysis of a sample of residential properties drawn from the 1973 state equalization survey.[3] The average ratio of assessment to sales was calculated, and then the average deviation of the assessment-to-sales ratio of each property from the sample average was determined (the coefficient of variation). In only 68 of 991 towns and cities in the state (excluding New York City) was the average deviation within 20 percent of the average assessment-sales ratio for that municipality. The average deviation was over 60 percent in 91 cities and towns. Said the panel, "[In] all but a handful of assessing units in New York State, assessments of residential property are scattered with appalling randomness over a wide range of deviation from the simple mean."[4] This comment was inspired, not simply by the failure to assess residences at full value, but by the failure to assess with reasonable consistency at any ratio of full value.

The panel chose to study residences probably partly because there are many more of them than other kinds of property and they are easier to appraise with some consistency. Other information shows wide variation in assessment of other properties and in average assessments of different classes of property.

As for overall average levels of assessment within assessing units, the state equalization rates for assessment rolls completed in 1975, the latest available year, are revealing. In only 60 of the 991 towns and cities were the rates within 10 percent of the full value standard (100

[3] Governor Hugh L. Carey, Educational Finance and the New York State Real Property Tax—*The Inescapable Relationship*, May 1976, Education Study Unit, N.Y. State Division of the Budget, State Capitol, Albany, New York 12224, 32 pp.
[4] Ibid., p. 7.

percent).[5] The rates themselves reflect market values at the January 1, 1973 price level, indicating that the State Board of Equalization and Assessment, like the local assessing units, has problems keeping up with changing real estate values.

The extreme range in equalization rates among towns and cities was from 1.16 percent in the town of Highland, Sullivan County to 136.36 percent in the Town of Manlius, Onondaga County. Within some counties the range was similarly very great. Within Ulster County, for example, the rates were 131.86 and 3.55 percent, respectively, in the Towns of Denning and Hardenburgh. In Westchester County, the Town of Cortlandt had a rate of 17.18 percent, and North Salem, 105.94 percent. In New York City, which is a single assessing district, the range among its five counties was from 36.57 percent in Richmond to 70.29 percent in New York.

Equalization rates were below 30 percent in 616 of the 991 towns and cities, and below 50 percent in 778. They exceeded 100 percent in 43 municipalities. In recent years, the rates have tended rapidly downward as the rise in real estate prices has accelerated faster than the great majority of assessors have reappraised their assessment rolls. One indication of the trend is that the State Board of Equalization and Assessment decided to add two decimals to the equalization rates beginning with 1974 assessment rolls; some are so low (for instance, the Town of Highland cited above) that a change of one whole percentage point would raise full value by a very large proportion.

In this situation of "appalling randomness" of assessment of individual properties, and declining equalization rates in a rising real estate market, the New York Court of Appeals, the highest state court, decided that the New York Real Property Tax Law requires assessment at full (market) value. On June 5, 1975, the court ordered that the Town of Islip in Suffolk County assess all real property within the Town at full value by December 31, 1976 (a deadline that was later delayed).[6] Although the "Hellerstein" decision was directed only to the Town of Islip, it binds the lower courts to uphold a similar challenge in any other assessing district. As of April 1977, at least 36 "Hellerstein-type" actions had been filed in courts throughout the state, and more undoubtedly will follow.

One of the taxpayer suits was against the Nassau County Board of Assessors, which a lower state court ordered in May 1977 to complete new assessment rolls at full value by May 1, 1980. The chairman of the board was quoted as saying, "Our present rolls date back to 1938...Since then the value of residential property has climbed sharply while commercial property has not risen as much."[7] The 1975 equalization rate for the county was 17.12 percent.

These developments are stimulating widespread interest in bringing assessments to full value and maintaining them from year to year at that changing level. These are difficult goals not attained statewide over the nearly 200 years that the state law has required assessment at full value or its equivalent. They had not been attained in other states with comparable assessment standards although the high courts of several states have rendered similar decisions—among them New Jersey, 1975; Connecticut, 1957; and Massachusetts, 1961.

The potential benefits of full value assessments are substantial. First, taxes on similar properties in the same tax districts would be equalized. (The same result would of course follow from consistent assessment at some fraction of full value.) Second, taxpayers are more likely to have some knowledge of the accuracy of their properties' assessed values in comparison to their market values, as opposed to some (often unknown) average fractional assessment in the district. Finally, taxpayers are more likely to challenge an excessive assessment if it exceeds their estimate of true value; a fractional assessment at far less than full value is less likely to

---

[5] N.Y. State Board of Equalization and Assessment, *State Equalization Rates for 1975 Assessment Rolls for Cities, Towns and Villages*, October 1976, 23 pp.

[6] Pauline Hellerstein v. The Assessor of the Town of Islip.

[7] *New York Times*, May 24, 1977.

create taxpayer concern, even if it is excessive in relation to assessments of comparable properties.

Full value assessment (or for that matter, consistent assessment at a percentage of full value) would inevitably cause a shift of taxes among individual properties and among different classes of property. This is an inevitable outcome of equalizing assessments of properties having equal full or market value. The studies done for the governor's panel (cited above) by the State Board of Equalization and Assessment and the Education Unit of the State Division of the Budget indicate that the shifts in taxes within the residential property class from one property to another would total far more than the shift from other property classes to the residential category.[8] Among classes, however, estimated statewide totals indicate a probable net tax shift to residential, vacant land, and farm property classes from the commercial, apartment, industrial, and utility classes.

It is hazardous to generalize from these statewide totals to a specific local situation because there is so much variation among assessing units. For example, these analyses indicate that, on the average over the state, commercial properties are over-assessed compared with residential and farm properties, but in a specific town this average relationship may not hold and the reverse situation can even be true. The average relationship is still less likely to prevail in comparing individual properties in a town, because the variation in ratios of assessment to full value within a property class such as residences is extreme in many towns and cities.

Once a number of revaluation programs have been completed in many assessing units, it will be possible to determine whether particular classes of taxpayers are unduly burdened. If such a burden results, some sort of relief could be granted by the State Legislature. Among many alternatives is legislating that certain types of property be assessed at a specified percentage of full value. If fractional assessment is authorized, however, it will still be necessary to determine the full values upon which the fractions can be based in a consistent manner. Other alternatives, such as partial exemption of single family residences, are also likely to require determining full values as a yardstick for exemptions.

COMPUTER-ASSISTED ASSESSMENTS

In trying to make assessment rolls conform more nearly to the statutory standard of full value or some uniform percentage of full value in a thorough-going, professional and equitable way, the assessors have commonly reappraised or revalued all properties. Alternatively, local governments have contracted with appraisal firms to do the work with the resulting values subject to acceptance by their assessors. Counties have often contracted for revaluation for their constituent towns and cities in anticipation of greater countywide uniformity in assessment.

A major limitation of this procedure has been the difficulty of keeping the information and values up-to-date once they have been compiled. Massive amounts of data must be accumulated and analyzed on a continuing basis. This is usually much beyond the capacity of the assessing office with the resources commonly available. Revaluations have quickly become outdated because of rapidly changing real estate values and changes in existing properties, such as new construction, demolition, or other destruction of property.

Attempts to apply computer technology in recent years to these mass appraisal procedures offer promise of making it possible for the first time to keep assessment roll listings and valuations reasonably current. Computers may well make it practical for assessing districts to implement the Hellerstein decision by revaluing properties and keeping abreast of changing market values thereafter.

---

[8] Governor Hugh L. Carey, op. cit., p. 17.

The New York State Board of Equalization and Assessment over the past few years has been developing what it terms the Real Property Information System, which includes computer assistance for property valuation. The system has been implemented by assessors of several local governments beginning with the Town of Ramapo (Rockland County). It provides assessors with the means of processing and updating market value information for all properties on assessment rolls.

Basically, the computer-assisted assessment procedure involves tabulating and recording all recent property sales in a jurisdiction. When a single-family residence is subjected to value estimating, this process is carried out:

1. The computer selects the five properties from the sales file that most closely resemble the one being appraised.
2. The computer calculates a predicted value for the subject residence. These calculations are based on the procedures customarily used by appraisers in judging value.
3. Once the computer estimates are generated, each one is reviewed by a professional appraisal at the property. If errors are found, appropriate information is fed back into the computer.

Computer-assisted assessments are most accurate for single-family residences, primarily because accurate comparable sales data for them are more readily available than for other kinds of property. Approximately 70 percent of the properties in the State (not including New York City) are in the residential class.[9] More than half the remainder, or almost a fifth of the total, is in the "vacant lands" class. The next most numerous properties are in the "commercial" and "farm" classes.

There are nearly 1,000 town, city, and county assessing districts in the state with approximately 3.5 million parcels outside New York City to be assessed. At best, full-scale implementation of computerized assessments will be a lengthy process. Current budgetary and staff restrictions, and attrition of the State Board of Equalization and Assessment's experienced professional personnel, will make it even more protracted. Historically, the state and the public have shown only desultory interest in matching assessment performance with statutory standards and these cutbacks are consistent with that record.[10]

ASSESSORS

Assessing units in New York include almost all towns and cities, some villages, two counties, and the state itself. The State Board of Equalization and Assessment is responsible for assessing some properties, principally special franchises and railroad property in connection with fixing ceilings for partial exemptions. Special franchise property is generally property of public utilities located in public lands, for example, a power or telephone line in a highway right of way.

Two counties—Nassau and Tompkins—are assessing units.[11] Elsewhere in the state, the 918 towns and 59 cities are assessing units; and their assessment rolls are used for town and city, special district, county and school taxation. The village board of trustees can also elect to

[9] Governor Hugh L. Carey, op. cit., p. 23.
[10] See Postscript at end of this bulletin. Recent legislation may speed implementation of computer-assisted assessments.
[11] In Nassau, the two cities (Glen Cove and Long Beach) and the 65 villages may assess for city and village tax purposes, respectively.

have town assessments used for village taxation, rather than to have separate village assessments.

The "Assessment Improvement Law" of 1970, how officially Article 15-A of the Real Property Tax Law, made substantial changes in the assessment organization affecting local assessors, except in the villages and New York City.

One such change required the appointment of one assessor in each district meeting minimum qualification standards who was to undergo training determined by the State Board of Equalization and Assessment. This assessor is appointed by the local legislative body (or chief executive in some cases) for a six-year term, unless the position has an indefinite term in the competitive civil service. The appointee may be removed, but only for just cause. Exceptions to this appointive single assessor requirement were made for Nassau County and cities of 100,000 or more population (New York, Buffalo, Rochester, Yonkers, Syracuse, Albany). Another important exception is that over half the towns and a few smaller cities opted before the prescribed deadline in 1971 to retain their traditional practice of electing a single assessor, or, as in most towns, a three-person board (two elected at each biennial town election, one for a two-year and the other for a four-year term). The only qualification the law requires of a candidate for election as an assessor has been that he or she be a voter of the town. Municipalities that exercised the option of electing their assessors, nevertheless, must conform with the assessor training and other requirements of the Assessment Improvement Law. These municipalities may also opt to shift to appointing a single assessor, and some have since 1971. It should be said that a number of cities and towns had appointed professional assessors and assessment staffs long before this law was passed.

A second change required by Article 15-A for cities and towns is appointment of a board of assessment review composed of persons who are not assessors and a majority of whom are not officers or employees of the local government. The board hears taxpayer complaints on grievance day. Prior to the new law, the assessors of most local governments sat as a board of review. The intent of the change was to meet criticism of long standing that the assessors sat as judges of their own work, to hear and make decisions on taxpayer appeals from their own work.

The governing body of the local government must appoint from three to five review board members who have knowledge of property values in the locality. Membership could include, for example, individuals engaged in banking, insurance, real estate, professional appraising and similar occupations, and persons formerly assessors. Appointments are for five-year staggered terms.

TAXPAYER COMPLAINT AND APPEAL PROVISIONS

Assessors in each town and city not governed by special provisions are expected to assess all real property within their jurisdiction (except special franchises) according to its condition and ownership as of May 1.[12] The law requires completion of the tentative assessment roll on or before June 1. A copy must be left with the assessor or the town clerk for public inspection, and notices must be posted in the town and published in a newspaper. At least ten days before grievance day, the assessor must mail notices to those on whose property assessments have been increased.

---

[12] There are differences from the dates named in this section for the special "tax act" counties of Erie, Monroe, Nassau, Suffolk, and Westchester. Tompkins is such a county also, but the dates do not differ except for the city of Ithaca. For most villages, the date of taxable status is January 1; for tentative completion of the village assessment roll, February 1; and for village grievance day, the 3rd Tuesday in February.

Grievance day is held on the third Tuesday in June at the time and place specified in the public notices. Complaining taxpayers may file a statement under oath indicating why the assessment of their property is incorrect. The board of assessment review receives and hears complaints on grievance day, and may adjust up or down the assessments under question. The assessor must attend (in other words, sit with) the tentative assessment roll on at least three days of the public inspection period prior to grievance day. He or she must also attend the review board hearings, and has the right to respond to any complaint. Informal complaints may of course be made to assessors the year-round.

On or before August 1, the assessor completes the assessment roll. The assessor then must file a certified copy of the roll with the town or city clerk where it is open for public inspection. Notices to this effect must be published in a local newspaper, and, in towns, posted at the town clerk's office. The original roll is delivered to the clerk of the county legislative body, and town, special district, and county taxes are entered on it usually late in the fall. It is delivered to the tax collector with a warrant for collection, usually by the first of the year. The taxes must also be entered on the copy of the roll that remains in the town clerk's office as a public record.

If a complaining taxpayer fails to obtain the relief desired at the grievance day proceedings, he or she may carry an appeal to the courts. In presenting the case to a court, the taxpayer must establish the full market value of his or her property and the average level of assessment in the assessing unit. Court appeals, historically an expensive and time-consuming process used by few taxpayers, have been substantially simplified in the last several years by amendments to the law, and more recently by important court decisions. In *Ed Guth Realty v. Gingold*, a case from the City of Syracuse, the Court of Appeals ruled in 1974 that the state equalization rate can be used as the most significant evidence toward satisfying the burden of proof of the average level of assessment in the assessing unit. Shortly thereafter, the ruling was regarded as applicable in another local government in the case of *860 Executive Towers Inc. v. The Board of Assessors of the County of Nassau*. The court (Appellate Division) further concluded that, although the methods used by the State Board of Equalization and Assessment can be improved, they cannot be challenged in a proceeding to review an assessment.[13]

The taxpayer thus has to show in court only that the level of assessment on his or her property is higher than the average level of assessment indicated by the state equalization rate.[14] A customarily long and costly process for the taxpayer of appraising a sample of comparable properties in the jurisdiction is thereby apparently eliminated.

As a result of these decisions, it is said that thousands of similar cases are pending throughout the state.

SOME IMPLICATIONS FOR ASSESSING UNITS

The court decisions in the Guth and Hellerstein cases have helped to open a Pandora's box for assessors, the courts, local governments, state legislative and executive agencies, and perhaps many taxpayers.

Any taxpayer willing to go to the trouble and expense may ask a court to require a revaluation of the assessment rolls at full value in his or her town or city, relying on the Hellerstein case. Any taxpayers who feel that their properties are assessed at a substantially higher ratio than the equalization rate for their towns or cities, may apply to a court for a reduction in assessment, relying on the Guth case rulings.

---

[13] Association of Towns of the State of New York, *Assessors Topics*, October 1976, Albany, New York.

[14] The 1977 State Legislature amended the Real Property Tax Law to qualify in an uncertain way the impact of the Guth decision. See Postscript for further discussion of this change.

An assessing unit can, as many have, anticipate the prospect of a revaluation at full value, and prepare for it. Computer-assisted assessment is one possible line of action already discussed. In practical terms, however, this alternative is probably contingent upon the availability of competent and persistent state support. The prospects for it on the massive scale needed to work with large numbers of local governments and parcels of property are not encouraging in this period of retrenchment. However, one favorable development is 1977 legislation that provides state aid for part of the cost of local revaluation.

The assessing unit, because of the Guth case and for other reasons, also can examine carefully the data used by the State Board of Equalization and Assessment in fixing the equalization rate for that unit. When a Guth-type case arises, it is too late to question the rate in court. The state sampling, appraisals, and other steps and information in the rate-fixing process, can be challenged with solid evidence when found questionable, but this should be done as early in the procedure as possible, and at least by the time the State Board sends notice of the tentative equalization rate.

It is to the advantage of the state as well as local governments and taxpayers that its equalization rates be as accurate as practicable. To improve accuracy, local assessors and governments have customarily been encouraged to contribute information. Among other ways of eliciting information, the State Board has sought through field staff to check its sampling with local officials. The Board has also freely supplied local officials with the data behind its equalization rate, and has acted upon information supplied by them when it is pertinent, substantial, and objective.

In the current period of curtailment and retrenchment, the open relations between state and local governments desired for more accurate equalization rates are in jeopardy. From the local viewpoint, the State Board has reduced local contacts, supplied data less promptly and freely, and given notice of tentative equalization rates so late that studied response is impractical. Efforts toward improving equity in assessment, according to its statutory definition, can be crippled in such a situation. Equalization rates also can gradually deteriorate—as they in fact did earlier in the history of the state[15]—and the state becomes quite remote to a city or town assessor.

COUNTY AND STATE SERVICES FOR LOCAL ASSESSORS

Another major provision of the Assessment Improvement Law of 1970 is that counties and the State Board of Equalization and Assessment provide various forms of technical and professional aid to local assessing units.[16]

County Services. Each county except the two (Nassau and Tompkins) now acting as assessing units has been required to establish a real property tax service agency, and to appoint a director for a six-year term to head it. The law has required the director to meet minimum qualifications set by the State Board, and complete the training courses it prescribes, as with town and city assessors. Appraisers employed by the county agency must meet the same conditions.

In general, the purpose of the agency is to assist towns and cities with assessments and assessing work, and to do work for the county that has been associated with assessing and taxing real property. It must prepare tax maps, keep them up-to-date and provide copies to city,

---

[15] For example, grossly inaccurate rates led to creating in 1949 the present State Board of Equalization and Assessment.

[16] Real Property Tax Law, Article 15-A.

town, and village assessors and others. The initial maps must be completed and State Board approved applied for by October 1, 1979.

At the request of the chief executive or assessor of cities and towns in the county, the agency was to be ready by October 1, 1976, to perform advisory appraisals of "moderately complex properties" requiring engineering skills, or economic analyses of "substantial complexity." The State Board determines the specific types of property included in this provision. It must also review agency appraisals if the town or city assessor thinks them inaccurate or unreasonable and applies for review. The appraisals are not binding upon city or town assessors but must be considered by them.

The county agency must also advise assessors concerning assessment rolls, property record cards, appraisal cards, and other records. It must provide appraisal cards in the form prescribed by the State Board and cooperate in training programs of the Board. It must also provide useful information to the county authorities for fixing town and city equalization rates for county tax purposes, and perform other duties.

State Services. An important responsibility of the State Board not already described is that it was to be prepared by October 1, 1976, to do advisory appraisals of (1) privately owned forest lands in excess of 500 acres, (2) "highly complex properties" requiring highly specialized engineering skills or highly complex economic analyses, and (3) taxable public utility property. These appraisals must be done, as in the case of the county, at the request of the local government's chief executive or assessor.

THE GAP BETWEEN LAW AND PRACTICE

The gap between the legal requirement of full value assessment and local performance is great, and so is the gap between what the state is supposed to do and actually does.

With respect to local deficiencies, many factors contribute to the "appalling randomness" of assessment described by the Governor's Panel. Among them is the deviation of local practice from the idea embodied in the Assessment Improvement Law of 1970 that assessing personnel should be appointed by local governing boards rather than elected, that these individuals should have at least a minimum of prior professional training or experienced or both, and that they should have some assurance of at least a minimum job tenure consistent with conscientious work performance. Approximately half the towns and a few cities apparently continue to elect assessors and each biennial local election results in high turnover, with sometimes cavalier voter disregard for consistent and persistent assessment. Building expertise in functions such as computer-assisted assessments in a locality under these circumstances is probably impossible.

Local boards of assessment review ideally have a quasi-judicial role of correcting injustice, when they hear formal complaints, by referring to the Guth case and related high court decisions and laws. Some local boards can make a shambles of uniform assessment by granting practically any request for reduced valuation. Others can tolerate poor assessment by refusing relief, however, judicially justified it may be.

With respect to counties, considerable variation exists in their capacity to complete and maintain tax maps, perform advisory appraisals, and assist town and city assessing units in other ways prescribed by the Assessment Improvement Law of 1970.

The gap between State Board performance and the requirements of the Real Property Tax Law is substantial. The Board is not providing systematic training for local assessing and appraisal personnel. It has postponed advisory appraisals beyond the legal deadline of October 1, 1976. It lacks the capacity to lend technical assistance and support for widespread local implementation of computer-assisted assessments and other aspects of its Real Property

Information System. It is making more difficult local opportunity for close scrutiny of equalization rates.

Curtailment and retrenchment of State Board activities is inconsistent with the expansion of state responsibilities required by law and recent major judicial decisions. Such reduction is at least partly the result of the more general and severe fiscal pressures upon the state.

The state and local situations do not, and should not, encourage taxpayer belief in early achievement of statewide equity of property assessment according to the statutory definition of equity. It is possible, however, to improve local performance within the present framework in those localities where the will exists and resources are committed to achieve improvement.

CONCLUSION

Inequities in assessing properties are common in New York except in those communities taking vigorous steps to bring assessed value into line with current real estate market values. Reducing inequities by a thorough revaluation or reassessment does not necessarily result in increased taxes for individuals. It will result in a larger share of taxes for those whose properties have been under-assessed compared with their neighbors. A smaller share will be borne by property owners over-assessed theretofore compared with their neighbors.

———